Patrick Francis Moran

Irish Saints in Great Britain

Patrick Francis Moran

Irish Saints in Great Britain

ISBN/EAN: 9783337332150

Printed in Europe, USA, Canada, Australia, Japan

Cover: Foto ©Lupo / pixelio.de

More available books at **www.hansebooks.com**

IRISH SAINTS
IN GREAT BRITAIN.

IRISH SAINTS

IN GREAT BRITAIN.

BY THE

RIGHT REV. PATRICK F. MORAN, D.D.,

Bishop of Ossory.

DUBLIN:
M. H. GILL & SON, 50, UPPER SACKVILLE-STREET;
BROWNE & NOLAN, NASSAU-STREET.
1879.

PRINTED BY BROWNE AND NOLAN, NASSAU-STREET, DUBLIN.

CONTENTS.

CHAPTER I.

FIRST FRUITS OF IRISH PIETY AMONG THE BRITONS, ... 1

Irish Settlements on the British Coasts.—SS. Ursula and Sedulius.—St. Brenach.—Conversion of Brecan of Brecknockshire.—SS. Cynog and Keyna.—St. Germanus.—St. Tathai.—St. Cadoc the Wise.—Irish Saints in Cornwall.—St. Buriana.—St. Livin.—St. Breaca.—St. Finguaire.—St. Hia.—Memorials of Irish Saints along the Western Coast of Britain.—St. Serigi.

CHAPTER II.

IRISH SAINTS IN THE MONASTERIES OF BRITAIN AND ARMORICA, ... 22

Glastonbury of the Irish.—St. David's Monastery at Menevia.—St. Kieran at St. Iltud's Monastery.—Padstow.—Irish Chieftains on the British Coast.—SS. Samson and Iltud.—St. Gildas.—Monastery of Llandeveneck.—St. Joava.—SS. Magloire and Machut.—SS. Kybi and Padarn.—St. Constantine.—Cadwallon and Cadwaladar.

CHAPTER III.

MISSIONARY LABOURS OF ST. COLUMBA AND HIS COMPANIONS IN SCOTLAND, ... 53

Fame of Ireland in the Sixth Century.—Early years of St. Columba.—His Virtues.—Visit to St. Molaise.—The Companions of his Pilgrimage.—Iona.—St. Columba's love of Discipline.—His Visits to Conal, King of Dalriada, and Brude, King of the Picts.—His Labours among the Picts.—The Monastery of Tears.—St. Moluog.—SS. Donnan and his Companions Martyrs.—St. Moljos.—SS. Finnan and Mochouna.—The Four Founders of Monasteries.—Sea Voyages of St. Cormac.—Eilean-na-naoimh.—St. Columba at Druimceatt.—His love of Ireland.—The Monastery of Derry.—St. Columba punishes injustice done to the Poor.—His Visit to St. Kentigern.—His Pilgrimage to Rome.—Inchcolm.—Heavenly favours granted to St. Columba.—His Death.

CHAPTER IV.

THE SUCCESSORS OF ST. COLUMBA IN IONA, ... 103

St. Baethen.—SS. Laisren and Fergna.—St. Cummian's Writings.—St. Adamnan's Visits to King Aldfrid.—The "Lex Innocentium."—Adamnan's Works.—His fame for Sanctity.—Relics which he collected.—The Rule of Life observed in Iona.—The Mass.—Sign of the Cross.—Prayers for the Dead.—The Religious Habit.—Presbyterian Fallacies regarding Iona.—Succession of Abbots.

CHAPTER V.

IRISH SAINTS IN THE KINGDOM OF STRATHCLYDE, ... 127

Early Irish Settlements in Strathclyde.—St. Patrick's Birthplace.—St. Ninian studies in Rome.—The Monastery of Whitherne.—St. Ninian's Cave.—His connection with Ireland.—Irish Saints at Whitherne.—St. Modenna. Her Sanctuary at Maidenkirk.—St. Kentigern under the care of St. Servan.—His Monastery at Glasgow.—Austerities of St. Kentigern.—He visits Wales.—Founds a Monastery at St. Asaph's.—Rederech, King of Strathclyde.—Some Memorials of St. Kentigern.—The Queen's Ring.—St. Servan.—St. Conval.—Revival of Devotion to this Saint.—St. Bea.—Synod of Rome in A.D. 721.

CHAPTER VI.

OTHER IRISH SAINTS IN SCOTLAND, ... 163

Irish Kingdom of Dalriada.—St. Kieran of Ossory.—St. Buite.—St. Modan's Sanctuaries.—St. Bridget's Monastery at Abernethy.—Irish origin of Scottish Sees.—St. Finian of Moville.—St. Coemghen.—St. Moanus.—St. Berchan.—St. Senanus.—St. Finbar.—St. Fechin.—St. Ernan.—SS. Ethernan and Itharnasch.—St. Fintan Munnu.—St. Beccan.—St. Flannan.—St. Dabius.—St. Gervad.—SS. Momhaedog and Tallarican.

CHAPTER VII.

CLOSE UNION OF THE CHURCHES OF SCOTLAND AND IRELAND, ... 186

St. Fiacre.—St. Maelrubha.—St. Fillan.—St. Ronan.—Irish Saints in the Islands off the Scottish Coasts.—They penetrate to Iceland, and probably also to America.—Martyrdom of St. Blaithmac.—St. Cadroe.—St. Dubthach.—St. Malachy.—Legends regarding SS. Regulus and Boniface.—St. Adrian and his Companions Martyrs.—The Culdees.

CONTENTS.   vii.

PAGE

CHAPTER VIII.

FIRST MISSIONS TO THE ANGLO-SAXONS, ... 205

St. Gregory the Great sends the First Missionaries to the Anglo-Saxons.—The Anglo-Saxon Kingdoms.—Conversion of Ethelbert King of Kent, and his People.—The Kingdom of Essex also converted.—Archbishop Laurentius and St. Dagan of Inverdaoile.—Four points of Difference between the Irish and the Continental Churches.—The British Clergy unable to evangelize the Saxons.—Kent and Essex fall away from the Faith.—Conversion and Apostacy of the Northumbrians.—King Oswald's Victory at Heavenfield.—Religion restored in Northumbria.

CHAPTER IX.

ST. AIDAN, FIRST BISHOP OF LINDISFARNE, APOSTLE OF NORTHUMBRIA, ... 222

Early Life of St. Aidan.—Lindisfarne.—Virtues of St. Aidan.—His efforts to train up a Native Clergy.—His Apostolic Labours.—King Oswald interprets his Sermons for the People.—Aidan at the Royal Table.—His care for the Poor.—He adheres to the Irish Customs.—Foundation of Mailros.—Coldingham.—St. Aidan's Hermitage in Farne Island.—Death of Oswald.—Character of this Pious Prince.—The Fortress of Bamborough saved by the prayers of Aidan.—Oswin, King of Deira.—Death of St. Aidan.

CHAPTER X.

THE IMMEDIATE SUCCESSORS OF ST. AIDAN, ... 246

St. Finan, Bishop of Lindisfarne.—Monasteries founded by King Oswy.—The Paschal controversy.—St. Colman, Bishop of Lindisfarne.—Anglo-Saxons flock to the Irish Schools.—SS. Wigbert and Willibrord.—The Conference at Whitby in A.D. 664.—Decision of King Oswy.—Character of the Irish Monks of Lindisfarne.—St. Colman withdraws to Iona.—He founds Monasteries at 'Mayo of the Saxons' and Inisbofin.

CHAPTER XI.

St. Cuthbert, ... 268

SS. Tuda and Eata.—St. Cuthbert born in Ireland.—His early years.—He tends flocks on the Lammermoor.—His life in the monastery of Mailros.—His hermitage at Dull. His austerities.—Succeeds Boisil as Prior. - His charity to pilgrims. - Apostolic zeal.—St. Cuthbert in Lindisfarne.—He retires to Farne Island.—Is appointed Bishop. Death of King Egfrid.—St. Cuthbert's virtues and miracles.—His friendship for Herbert of Derwentwater. He protects the home of his foster-mother.—Visits the monasteries of Coldingham, Whitby, and Tynemouth.— St. Cuthbert's death.—Popular veneration for his memory. —Character of King Aldfrid of Northumbria.

CHAPTER XII.

Irish Missions in the other Anglo-Saxon Kingdoms, 303

Influence of Northumbria on the other Anglo-Saxon Kingdoms.—Conversion of Mid-Angles.—SS. Diuma and Cellach.—St. Chad.—Sigebert, King of the East Saxons, embraces the Faith.—St. Cedd.—Bishop Jaruman.—The East Angles.—Virtues of St. Fursey.—His Monastery at Cnobbersburg.—The Visions of St. Fursey.—His labours among the East Angles.—His life in France.—He visits Rome. - His Death.—His Relics.—The Companions of St. Fursey.—Irish Monks the Pioneers of the Faith in Sussex.—Conversion of the West Saxons.—Agilbert and Mailduff.—St. Aldhelm.—The Irish Missions crowned with success.

IRISH SAINTS IN GREAT BRITAIN.

CHAPTER I.

FIRST FRUITS OF IRISH PIETY AMONG THE BRITONS.

Irish Settlements on the British Coasts:—SS. Ursula and Sedulius:—St. Brenach:—Conversion of Brecan of Brecknockshire:—SS. Cynog and Keyna:—St. Germanus:—St. Tathai:—St. Cadoc the Wise:—Irish Saints in Cornwall:—St. Buriana:—St. Livin:—St. Breaca:—St. Finguaire:—St. Hia:—Memorials of Irish Saints along the Western Coast of Britain:—St. Serigi.

BEFORE the close of the fourth century armed bands of our countrymen had begun to occupy the western coasts of Great Britain. One colony, which settled immediately north of the Clyde, formed, in a short time, an independent principality, and, in the course of centuries, subjected the neighbouring territories to its sway, and placed its chieftain on the throne of Scotland. Other Irish colonists, with varying fortunes, seated themselves in Galloway and Cumberland, and on the banks of the Mersey. All along the Welsh coast, and down to the English channel, they made the whole country, in great part, their own; and such was the terror which they inspired, and so great the influence which they exercised, that they seemed for a time to have within their grasp the sovereignty of the whole island. Indeed, so helpless were the Britons after the withdrawal of the legions of Imperial Rome, that the Irish troops marched in triumph through the very heart of Britain, and it was only in the vicinity of London that they were checked in their victorious career.[1] More than one of our Irish monarchs even assumed the title of King of Alba; and of one of them (Muirchertach Mac Erca, who died in A.D. 533,) it is recorded that, in addition to his Irish titles, he styled himself "King of the Britons, Franks, and Saxons."[2] We learn also from a very ancient Irish record that so extensive were the settlements of our countrymen in Britain, that the Irish territory beyond the channel was equal in extent to Ireland, so that our chieftains "parcelled out the land of Britain, taking each one his share, and they built up strong forts and noble habitations there, and not less did the Gael dwell on the east coasts of the sea than in Erin."[3]

It was among these colonists that the first-fruits of Irish Faith were offered to God on the shores of the sister isle. Some of our countrymen in the north of Britain received the light of faith through the preaching of St. Ninian and his successors, whilst others, towards the south, became devoted children of the cross under the benign influence of the clergy of Wales. When our Apostle St. Patrick accompanied St. Germain of Auxerre to Britain, in the year 428, he met with many of these

---

[1] *Ammianus Marcellinus*, xxviii. 8.
[2] *Irish Nennius*, Public. of I. A. S., p. 180, seqq.
[3] *Sanas Chormaic*, i.e., "Cormac's Glossary," edited by Stokes for I. A. S., in 1868, p. 110. The learned O'Donovan writes that this record, though overlooked by most of our historians, is "one of the most curious and important" preserved to us relating to our early history. *Battle of Magh-Rath*, Public. of I. A. S., p. 339.

Irish colonists in Wales, and being familiar with their language, applied himself, with devoted earnestness, to instruct them in the truths of Religion; and so enamoured was he of the missionary field thus opened to his zeal, that it was his desire to remain permanently amongst them; but, at the summons of St. Celestine, he was compelled to forsake this chosen flock, and to gird himself for the more arduous task of the Apostolate of Ireland.

The children of these Irish colonists continued for a long time to regard themselves as Irish; and, though born by accident on British soil, they centred their affections on Ireland as their home and their motherland. This has given rise to considerable confusion in regard to some bright ornaments of our country at this early period of our history. By Continental writers they are often styled Britons, as born in Britain, and perhaps proceeding to the Continent from the British coast; whilst by Irish writers they are justly claimed as fellow-countrymen, on account of their parentage and their cherished connexion with our island. Thus it is, for instance, with St. Ursula and her heroic companions. Many illustrious writers, even in modern times, have called them Britons; but the more ancient records expressly describe them as Irish, and they are honoured in our Calendars among the first flowers of the martyrs of our Church. Thus, again, in the case of Siadhuil, better known by his Latin name Sedulius, the prince of Christian poets, who holds so prominent a place in the Christian literature of the fifth century. More than one nation has claimed him as its own; but the oldest MSS. styling him "Sedulius Scotigena," fix Ireland as his country.[1] It is probable, however, that he was trained in the higher branches of Latin literature in the great schools of Wales or of the Continent. A like question has arisen regarding Celestius, although the testimony of St. Jerome,[2] his contemporary, should leave no doubt as to his Irish birth. We have not, however, much reason to be proud of his career, for, notwithstanding his brilliant talents and deep research in sacred science, he permitted himself to be led away into heresy by the fanciful theories of Pelagius.

A great number of the devoted men, who associated themselves with our Apostle St. Patrick when he embarked on the holy enterprise of the conversion of our nation, were Britons by birth, and were chosen from the monasteries of Armorica and Wales.[3] Before he closed his earthly career, not only had he gathered our people into the one true fold of Christ, but he had,

[1] It is to be regretted that Professor Stubbs, when treating of Irish matters, has not given proof of that research which characterizes his writings relating to English history. Of Sedulius he writes: "that Sedulius, the Christian poet of the fifth century, was a Scot, rests solely upon his name, and upon a confusion between him and two others of the same name who were undoubtedly Scots, viz., the Bishop Sedulius of the Roman Council of A.D. 721, and the author of the Commentary on St. Paul's Epistles." (Councils, &c., vol. ii., p. 291.) Now besides the old MSS. which style him Scotigena, which may be seen in the Preface to Arevalus's edition of his works, Dicuil, an Irish writer of the ninth century, in his treatise 'De Mensura Orbis,' chap. 5, expressly calls the poet Sedulius—"Sedulius noster." (Edit. Letronne, Paris, p. 19.)

[2] "Habet enim progeniem Scoticae gentis de Britannorum vicinia."—St. Jerome, Prolog. ad. lib. 3, Com. in Jeremiam.—*Lanigan*, Ecc. Hist., i. 16.

[3] In the Catalogue of Irish Saints, published by Usher, it is said of the first class of saints who adorned our country—"Hi omnes Episcopi de Romanis et Francis et Scotis exorti sunt."—See *Irish Eccles. Record*, vii. 213.

moreover, the consolation to see his own true missionary spirit deeply engrafted upon Ireland, whose zealous children, spread over the shores of Britain and Gaul, were soon to repay an hundred-fold the spiritual blessings which she had received.

A holy hermit named Brenach, called by the Welsh writers Brynach, is the first Irish saint[1] whose name has been handed down to us, who chose Wales as the place of his retreat, and made it the theatre of his missionary labours. Even the "Triads," those Welsh records so jealous of the national glory, expressly assign to him the epithet "Brynach Gwyddel," that is, Brenach the Irishman. He flourished before the middle of the fifth century. Though a chieftain by birth, when once he had found the precious gem of faith, he laid aside all worldly pursuits, and led a hermit's life amidst his native hills. He was venerable in mien, was clothed in rough skins, slept on the hard ground, used for his food a little bread and roots, with milk and water, and his whole time was spent in meditation and chanting the praises of God. Filled with the desire of visiting the sanctuaries of Christian piety in other lands, he travelled to Rome, and on his return remained for some years in Brittany, where he soon acquired great fame for sanctity and miracles. Thence he sailed for the British coast, and erected a cell near the confluence of the rivers Cleddau, not far from the present port of Milford. Being disturbed there by predatory bands, he proceeded to the banks of the river

---

[1] His Life, from the Cott. Libr. in Brit. Mus. *Vespasian*, A. xiv., has been published by *Rees* for the Welsh MSS. Society, in "Lives of the Cambro-British Saints," Llandovery, 1853, p. 5, seqq.

Gwain, close to where it now gives name to the town of Abergwain, and having freed that place from unclean spirits, "who hitherto, wandering about every night, and filling the country with horrible cries, had rendered it uninhabitable," he advanced along the valley of Nevern in Pembrokeshire. Finding there the grove of an ancient but long-abandoned church, he chose it for his abode. His life adds, that "as that place appeared well suited for those who desired to lead a life of piety, he and his companions girded themselves for work, and taking hatchets and other tools, for three whole days cut down trees." On rising to their work on the fourth morning, no trace could be found of their preceding labour. This was taken by our saint as a heavenly sign that they should not erect their habitations there; so, advancing farther into the interior, he chose a solitary spot on the banks of the Caman, encompassed by hills, and erecting there a cell and church, served God faithfully till summoned to his eternal reward. The ancient record adds, that "so pleasing was his life to God, that he merited frequently to enjoy the vision and discourse of angels; and the mountain on which they met, at the foot of which a church was built, was called the Mountain of the Angels."[1] This ancient name may still be traced in the modern Carn-Engyli, a mountain which overhangs the Nevern, and at its foot at the present day, as centuries ago, stands the principal church of the district.[2] St. Brenach passed from this world on the 7th of April, and his relics were placed under the eastern wall of his church.

---

[1] *Rees*, "Lives," p. 296. [2] *Fenton*, "Pembrokeshire," p. 543.

It was, however, by the conversion of a Pagan Irish chieftain, named Brecan, from whom Brecknockshire takes its name,[1] that this holy hermit merited, in a special manner, the lasting gratitude of the British Church. Aulach, the father of Brecan, was son of an Irish king named Cormac, and was the leader of an armed band that plundered the Welsh coast towards the close of the fourth century. In one of his predatory excursions, he carried off as a captive, and soon after took to wife, Marchella, daughter of Tewdrig, who was the chief ruler in South Wales. Brecan, the child of this marriage, having come to man's estate, on the death of Tewdrig, about the year 420, claimed that territory as his inheritance, and asserted his claim by the sword. By his valour and prowess he soon became one of the most prominent princes of Britain, and on account of his firm rule and wise administration, merited to be ranked by the Welsh writers, not among the foreign princes, but among their own hereditary chieftains. Through his holy countryman, St. Brenach, he became captive to the mild yoke of the Gospel, and with such true Celtic ardour did he devote himself to every practice of heroic piety, and with such earnestness did he train his numerous family in the paths of Christian perfection, that the Triads reckon the family of Brecan among the "three holy families of Wales;" and they add, that "such was the education of his children and grandchildren, that they were able to teach the Faith of Christ to the nation of the Cymry, wherever it was as yet without the faith."[2] Elsewhere

[1] For the history of this chieftain and his family, see the valuable "Essay on the Welsh Saints," by Professor *Rice Rees.* London, 1836, p. 136, seqq.

[2] Triads, xviii. *Williams*, "Eccles. Antiquities of the Cymry," p. 53.

Brecan and his children are styled "one of the three holy families of the isle of Britain;" and again, "the three holy lineages of Britain are the lineage of Bran, the son of Lyr; the lineage of Cunedda; the lineage of Brecan."[1] Rees also, in his learned "Essay on the Welsh Saints," writes that "the family most distinguished in the Church of Britain, in the middle of the fifth century, was that of Brecan;" and then he enumerates a long list of that chieftain's children and grandchildren, all of whom were eminent for their sanctity and learning, and were honoured in the British Church as saints. Brecan founded a great number of oratories or churches, of fifty-five of which the ruins or the traditions still remain. Twenty-five of these were situate in Brecknockshire; the rest were scattered throughout Caermarthenshire, Pembrokeshire, Denbighshire, and Anglesey, the districts mostly inhabited at that time by the Gwyddyl-Ffichti, or colonists from Ireland.[2]

The eldest of Brecan's sons was St. Cynog, and he merits to be specially named, being one of the few saints whom our early Church has added to the bright array of the martyrs of Christ. Cressy, in his "Church History of Brittany," writes, that "the fame of his sanctity was most eminent among the Silurians." His name is entered in the English Martyrology on the 11th of February, but in Wales his festival was kept on the 7th of October. One ancient authority records that he was martyred by the Pagan Saxons on a mountain called the Van, in Brecknockshire, and a church was erected over his tomb, which, with the parish in which

---

[1] Triads, xlii., first series. "Myvyrian Archæology," vol ii., *Williams*, p. 98.
[2] *Rees*, "Essay," pp. 136 and 158.

it stood, received, through reverence for our saint, the name of Merthyr-Cynog.[1]

Cressy also tells us that St. Cynog's sister, St. Keyna, called by the Welsh writers Ceyn and Ceneu, received, like her brother, the martyr's crown. She consecrated her virginity to God, and for that reason was styled by the Britons "Ceyn-wyryf," or Keyna the Virgin. In search of a solitary place for a hermitage, she crossed the Severn, and finding a densely wooded glen in Somersetshire, she asked a grant of it from the prince of that territory. He replied that he would willingly grant it to her, but that it was so infested with venomous reptiles that neither man nor beast could dwell there. She said she feared them not, for her trust was in the holy name and aid of God. The site was accordingly granted to her, and she erected there her cell, and served God for many years. Through the many pilgrimages to her shrine in after times, a town grew up which still remains, and from her derives its name of Keynsham. St. Cadoc, her nephew, as Cressy writes, "making a pilgrimage to Mount St. Michael, met there the blessed Keyna, and being filled with joy, was desirous of bringing her back to her own country, but the inhabitants would not consent to her departure from them. Some time after, the holy maiden, being admonished by an angel, returned secretly to the place of her nativity, where, on the summit of a small hill, she erected her cell, and at her

---

[1] The resting-place of four members of this family is thus marked in the ancient Welsh tract, called "Bonned y Saint:" the sepulchre of Brecan is in the island which is called from him Inys-Brychan, and is close to the Isle of Man: the sepulchre of Rhun, son of Brecan, is in Llandevaliog: the sepulchre of the martyr Cynog is in Brycheiniog: the sepulchre of Aulach is before the door of the church of Llanspyddyd. *Rees*, "Lives," p. 605.

prayers a spring-fountain flowed from the earth, which still remains, and through her merits affords healing to divers infirmities." She was martyred by the Saxons on the 8th of October, in the year 460, and her remains were reverently interred by St. Cadoc in her own oratory. The Mount St. Michael referred to in this passage is situate near Abergavenny, and still retains its traditional sacred character. At a short distance is the parish of *Llangeneu*, i.e., "St. Keyna's Church," where the saint's well is pointed out, and close to it is the site of her ancient oratory.

When St. Germain of Auxerre visited Britain a second time, in the year 448, he met there an Irish chieftain, whose son, having been instructed in the truths of Faith and regenerated in the waters of Baptism, wished in after life, through love of his Spiritual Master, to bear the name of Garmon or Germanus. He was subsequently consecrated Bishop, and laboured for some years in Ireland under the guidance of St. Patrick, and his name is also met with in the Acts of St. Kieran of Saigher and of other early Irish saints. It was probably this St. Germanus who laboured with devoted zeal in the Isle of Man, and was in after times honoured as its Apostle: but he also evangelized many districts in Wales, and it was at his hands that the great Father of the Welsh Church, St. Dubricius, received the Episcopal consecration. Impelled by the ardour of his zeal, he passed into Gaul, and advancing across the Pyrenees, laboured for some years in winning souls to Christ throughout the Spanish peninsula. He, after some time, returned to Gaul, and on the banks of the Bresle, which, in olden times, was the boundary between Normandy and Picardy, received the martyr's crown. A portion of his relics is still preserved in the Church of St. Germain, at Amiens, which was erected under his invocation, and several churches in Normandy and Picardy still honour him as patron on the 2nd of May.[1]

St. Germanus has this special characteristic: he is the only one of the missionaries that laboured in the early Church of Spain, whom Ireland can with certainty claim as her own. Towards the middle of the sixth century we, indeed, meet with the See of Bretona, in Gallicia, which derived its name from the many fugitives from Wales who took refuge there; and in the year 572 it had a pilgrim Bishop named Mailoc, who was probably of Irish birth, and brother of St. Gildas. It is recorded of him that he upheld the Scotic Tonsure in Spain, but every other tradition which could illustrate his history was, together with his see, very soon absorbed in the Gotho-Spanish Church, which, in its turn, after a lapse of two centuries, was swept away by the Moorish invasion.[2]

St. Tathai[3] was another Irish saint,[4] whose labours

---

[1] *Corbelet*, "Hagiographie du Diocèse d'Amiens." Paris, 1870, tom. ii., p. 508.

[2] See *Haddan's* "Remains," edited by Dr. Forbes, 1877, p. 263; also, "Councils, &c., relating to Great Britain." Oxford, 1873, vol. ii., p. 99.

[3] He is also called Dathi and Tathan. His name is the Irish equivalent for David, but the Welsh writers generally retain the name Tathai to distinguish him from the great St. David, patron of Menevia. It is probable that some of the dedications in Ireland which bear St. David's name may originally have referred to St. Tathai. His Life is printed by *Rees* in "Lives of Cambro-Brit. Saints," p. 580.

[4] Camden applies to St. Tathai the generic designation of a "British Saint." This, however, is well refuted by Usher. The Book of Llandaff calls St. Tathai *an Irishman:* the Life of the Saint in the Cotton MSS., published by Rees, states that he was

before the close of the fifth century produced an abundant harvest in Wales. He was the son of a royal chieftain named Tuathal, and, "like the true metal of gold, was immaculate, pure, and free from the corruption of the world." He applied himself diligently to sacred study, till, "as fruit proceeding from the best blossoms," he was adorned with every virtue. His fame was widespread throughout Ireland, and many persons hastened to receive from him lessons of heavenly wisdom. He was, however, divinely admonished to depart from his own country and to devote himself to labour for God in Britain: "Go to-morrow," said the Angel to him, "and proceed without delay to the sea-harbour, and pass over to Britain, that thou mayest fulfil the designs of God, as I shall direct thee." With joyful heart he set out next day, accompanied by eight companions, for the neighbouring coast; entering a little coracle, without sail or oar, they were carried by prosperous winds to the Severn, and landed in the territory of Gwent, in the modern Glamorganshire. After some time St. Tathai's fame for piety and miracles reached King Caradoc, "who then ruled the two Gwents," and he sent a learned man, accompanied by some soldiers, to invite our saint to settle permanently in his kingdom. St. Tathai gladly accepted the invitation, and founded a church, since called *Llandathan*, that is, "St. Tathai's Church," in

born in Ireland; that his father was an Irish Prince; and gives full details of his life in Ireland before he set out to evangelize Britain. The Life, written by John of Teignmouth, agrees in all these details. So also the Life of St. Cadoc expressly styles St. Tathai an Irishman: Capgrave and all other ancient authorities are agreed on this head. The comparatively modern Welsh genealogies are of no weight in such a matter.

Glamorganshire, "and scholars from all parts flocked to him, to be instructed in all the branches of science." Subsequently Ynyr, the son and successor of Caradoc, having built the Monastery and College of Caerwent, in Monmouthshire, our saint was appointed its first abbot or superior, whilst at the same time he was the guide of Ynyr in all his spiritual works. The most illustrious among his converts was St. Cadoc, who became his disciple, and attained such eminence in sacred learning as to merit the surname of "the Wise." In his old age St. Tathai resigned his charge of the monastery and retired to his former Church of Llandathan. His Life relates, that not far from this place a holy Irish maiden, named Máchuta, tended a flock of sheep committed to her care; it happened that she was put to death by Pagan marauders, and our saint hearing of it proceeded with his clergy to the spot where she had been martyred; and "on that site he founded an oratory, built in honour of the Virgin Machuta;" he would not, however, allow the body of the virgin to remain there, "but, that it might be duly honoured, brought it to the city of Gwent and buried it within the chief church of that city." The Life of St. Tathai ends as follows: "Saint Tathai lived a heaven-seeking virgin, following the Lord to heavenly glory. After his decease he was buried in the floor of the church, and his seven associated disciples attended the burial of their master, whom God elected and predestined to the realms of eternal glory."[1] The Church of Llandathan still retains his name, but it is more generally called Llanvaches, *i.e.*, the Church of

---

[1] *Rees*, "Lives," 591.

the Virgin St. Machuta; and in mediæval records it is presented to us as "Llandathan, *alias* Llanvaches."

St. Cadoc,[1] of whom we have just spoken, having spent twelve years under St. Tathai's care (per duodecim annos), became one of the brightest ornaments of the Church of Wales. He was the founder of Llancarvan; was the intimate friend of St. Dubricius; and a large number of his poems and sacred maxims have been reverentially preserved by popular tradition to our own times.[2] Some of his beautiful aphorisms disclose to us the noble sentiments which pervaded the Irish schools in the golden ages of our country's faith. Thus, in one of them we read—"Without light nothing is good; without light there is no piety; without light there is no religion; without light there is no faith: but without the presence of God there is no light." Again— "No man loves knowledge without loving the light; nor the light, without loving the truth; nor the truth, without loving justice; nor justice, without loving God: he who loves God has perfect happiness." Elsewhere the Disciple asks what is divine love? "Love is Heaven (replies the Master): and what is hate? It is Hell: and what is conscience? It is the eye of God in the soul of man." St. Cadoc was born of an Irish mother, and, having devoted himself to military pursuits, was celebrated before his conversion as one of the bravest of the British knights, and he is styled in the Triads, "one of the three knights of chief discretion in the royal

---

[1] He is sometimes called St. Docus, but he is not to be confounded with St. Docus whose *obit* is given in the Ulster Annals in 473.

[2] They are collected in "Myvyrian Archæology," vol. iii., p. 28.

court of King Arthur." After his conversion he became equally distinguished by his sanctity, and the same Triads again commemorate him as "one of the three blessed youth-teachers of the Isle of Britain;"[1] whilst in the ancient catalogue of Irish Saints, attributed to Tirechan, he is particularly honoured as having, with SS. David and Gildas, introduced some wise reforms in the Liturgy in Ireland.

His Life[2] gives many details of his connexion with Ireland. His first name was Cathmael, but in baptism he received from St. Tathai the name of Cadoc. After building his own monastery, called Kastell-Cadoc—whither the clergy from all parts of Britain came in great numbers to receive his lessons of wisdom—he resolved to proceed to Ireland for the sake of perfecting himself[3] in the spiritual life, under the guidance of its great masters. The brethren, having approved of his design, "he ordered a strong boat, besmeared with pitch, to be prepared in the harbour of the sea, that he might safely sail to Ireland." Many of his disciples wished to accompany him thither, but this he permitted only to a few, desiring the others "to keep faithfully his monastery and town until his return." He remained three years[4] in Ireland, drinking in lessons of heavenly and human science "at the city and monastery of St. Mochuda." This was probably St. Mochuda, senior, who

[1] *Williams*, p. 131.
[2] *Rees*, "Lives," p. 309, seqq.
[3] *Discendi gratia*: *i.e.*, "for the sake of learning." I may remark that the Welsh edition, by a singular mistake, translates it, "for the sake *of teaching*," p. 325. By an oversight, Rev. John O'Hanlon, in "Lives of Irish Saints," vol. i., p. 418, has copied this erroneous translation.
[4] "Per Tres Annos," *Rees*' "Lives," loc. cit.

at this time ruled the great Monastery of Saigher.[1] After three years, Cadoc returned to Wales, and set about erecting a church on the banks of the Neath. "It happened that a certain Irishman, named Linguri, a stranger, but a skilful architect, came at this time, with his family, to the saint," seeking employment. St. Cadoc at once employed him at the work; twelve others were associated with him, but he "excelled them all in skill and ability." The others, envious of his merit, conspired against him, and put him to death. St. Cadoc, being informed of their wickedness, passed the night, with all his clergy, in watching and prayer. The next day he restored the murdered man to life, and asked him to choose, "whether to live again in this mortal state, or to return to eternal life to reign for ever with God." Linguri, with true Irish faith, replied—"I desire that my soul may return to eternal life," and he forthwith expired. The place was called, from his church, Llanlinguri, which is probably the modern Glynleiros, near Neath. St. Cadoc rested in peace about the middle of the sixth century.

During the same period there were several Irish Saints who devoted themselves to the preaching of the Faith or to the practices of religious life in Cornwall.[2] Blight, in his interesting work on the Cornish Churches, thus writes:—"In the latter part of the fifth and beginning of the sixth century, a numerous company of

---

[1] The *Vita*, p. 326, refers it to Lismore, this being the monastery most famous in connection with a St. Mochuda at the time when the life was written. Lismore, however, was not founded till 636.

[2] *Blight*, "Churches in West Cornwall," Oxford, 1865. Cornwall, as its name implies (*i.e.*, Cornu-Walliae), was a part of Wales and continued so till a comparatively late period.

Irish saints, bishops, abbots, and sons and daughters of kings and noblemen (in the words of Leland), 'came into Cornwall, and landed at Pendinas, a peninsula and stony rock, where now the town of St. Iës (St. Ives) standeth.' Hence they diffused themselves over the western part of the country, and at their several stations erected chapels and hermitages. Their object was to advance the Christian Faith. In this they were successful, and so greatly were they reverenced, that whilst the memory of their holy lives still lingered in the minds of the people, churches were built on or near the sites of their chapels and oratories, and dedicated to Almighty God in their honour. Thus have their names been handed down to us." Among these saints was St. Buriana, known in the Irish Calendars as St. Bruinseach. An ancient church erected over her shrine still remains, about five miles from Lands-End, and gives name to the town of St. Burian. When King Athelstan was about to sail on his expedition against the Scilly Isles, he entered her oratory, "and vowed, if God blessed his expedition with success, to erect a college of clergy where the oratory stood, and to endow it with a large income." The historian adds, that having subdued the Scilly Isles, Athelstan on his return founded and endowed the collegiate church as he had vowed, in honour of St. Buriana, on the spot called after her *Eglos-Berrie*. He also gave to the church the privileges of a sanctuary, and the kings of England continued to be its patrons till a very late period. About three miles S.W. from St. Burian is the Church of St. Levan,[1]

---

[1] In some records the name is corrupted to *Silvanus*. Locally his parish is known as *Slevan*. Borlase, "The Age of the Saints, &c." (1878), p. 45.

which takes its name from St. Livin, an Irish Bishop, who subsequently attained the crown of martyrdom in Belgium. The present church was erected on the site of the saint's cell. "It is situated," writes Blight, "in a most romantic spot, in a deep hollow, scarcely a furlong from the Cliffs. The celebrated Logan rock is in the immediate neighbourhood, and the adjoining coast is acknowledged to rank among the finest coast-scenery in England. So abrupt is the hollow, or gulph, as a Cornish historian expresses it, in which the church stands, that the four pinnacles of the tower are all that can be seen of the building for any considerable distance when approaching it from the east or west."[1] The holy well of St. Levan, and an ancient church dedicated to him, stood on the edge of the cliff, a little below the present church.[2]

St. Breaca, a lady of noble birth, and St. Germoe, a royal prince, are also named as belonging to a large company of Irish pilgrims and missionaries, who in the fifth century landed at Riviere, at the mouth of the Hayle. Several of this holy company were slain by a local prince (Tyrannus) of Cornwall; but SS. Breaca and Germoe crossed from Riviere[3] to the Southern coast, where they erected churches and cells. They were

---

[1] *Blight*, p. 10.

[2] *Borlase*, p. 58, informs us that in the last century, over the well, there was a large flat stone, on which a little chapel or cell stood. This structure was only five feet square and seven feet high, with a stone roof. He adds: "A more romantic spot it would be hard to picture."

[3] *Leland*, in his Itinerary (iii. 15), writes that "Ryvier Castle" was situated "at the east part of the mouth of Hayle river," but was now "drowned with sand."

there honoured in after times by the piety of the faithful, and parishes still bear their names.

St. Fingar, or Finguaire (*i.e.*, Guaire the Fair), was another of these pilgrim saints. He was son of Olilt, king of Connaught, and was among the first who welcomed our Apostle St. Patrick on his visit to that kingdom. Being subjected to many persecutions, in consequence of embracing the Christian Faith, he proceeded with some companions to Armorica, and having obtained permission from a petty ruler on the sea-coast to settle there, devoted his time to fishing and the chase. Being one day separated from his companions in a wood, he alighted from his horse, and, entering into himself, began to meditate on the great gifts and mercies which God had bestowed on him. He resolved without delay that thenceforward he would devote himself to God alone; and, penetrating further into the dense wood, chose a sheltered spot near a running stream, and there spent his whole time in prayer. After some days, he was discovered there by his companions, who brought him back to their former abode, but he continued unchanged in his resolve to serve God alone. After some time they returned to Ireland, where he was received with joy; for its hills and valleys were now lit up with the light of God, and it was no longer a matter of reproach to have embraced the Faith of Christ. On the death of his father many wished to choose him for their king, but he declared it to be his only desire to fix his thoughts on heavenly things. To shun the honours that were obtruded on him, he again resolved to set out on pilgrimage, and, accompanied by his sister Piala, who at the hands of St. Patrick had received the virgin's veil, and followed by a large number of his countrymen who wished to share his holy life, he landed in Cornwall, at the mouth of the river Hayle. The next day he, with his sister and many of his companions, received the martyr's crown. This occurred about the year 470. St. Fingar and his companion martyrs are named in the British Martyrology, and he is also honoured at Vannes in Brittany.[1]

St. Iia, or Hia, preceded these martyrs in pilgrimage, and she also landed in Cornwall. She erected her cell near the mouth of the Hayle, and such was the fame of her sanctity, that in the course of time the mariners called the promontory of Pendinas and also the bay of Hayle by her name, and thus to the present day we have St. Ives' promontory, and town, and bay, marking the district which was sanctified fourteen hundred years ago by the vigils and austerities of an humble virgin of Erin. St. Rumon, or Ruan, as Leland informs us, is also styled in the ancient Legenda preserved at Tavistock "an Irish Scot." He made for himself an oratory in a forest in the district now called Meneage, and his relics were enshrined at Tavistock. Three ancient churches bear his name in Cornwall, and the 22nd of May seems to have been kept as his festival.

Such memorials, however, of Irish saints are not confined to Cornwall; they are met with at every step along the western coast of England. St. Warne's Bay in Scilly records the name of St. Warna, an Irish saint, about whom the tradition is handed down amongst the St. Agnes islanders, that he came over from Ireland in

---

[1] *Colgan*, "Acta," p. 387.

a little wicker boat, which was covered on the outside with raw hides, and that he landed at the bay just mentioned.[1] At Bardsey, a small island off the western promontory of Carnarvon, which St. Dubricius chose for his resting-place, and which is called in the book of Llandaff "the Rome of Britain," and by the Welsh Bards "the land of indulgences and pardon, the road to Heaven, and the gate to Paradise,"[2] many pilgrims from Ireland rested in peace, contributing not a few to "the twenty thousand saints who are buried in its sacred ground." St. Dagan, or Degeman, honoured on the 27th of August, passed the river Severn on a hurdle of branches of trees, and withdrew into a mountainous vast solitude covered with shrubs and briars, where he spent his life absorbed in prayer and contemplation; St. Barach, "whose memory is celebrated in the territory of the Silurians and region of Glamorgan (on 29th November), lies buried in the Isle of Barry, which took its name from him;" and the Isle of Man, besides St. German, has Machaldus, Coeman, and Mochonna, all Irish saints, as its chief patrons.[3] One of the most singular, however, of these dedications is that to St. Serigi. When the descendants of the brave Cunedda finally overthrew the Irish settlers, who sought to found in Anglesey and North Wales a kingdom similar to that of Dalriada on the Scotch coast, Serigi was the Irish leader, and was slain fighting at the head of his countrymen. He was, however, so famed for his virtues, that the victors built a chapel over his grave, and honoured

---

[1] *Troutbeck*, "Isles of Scilly," p. 149.
[2] *Williams*, p. 223, and Lib. Landav, p. 142. *Reeves*, "The Culdees," p. 61.
[3] Ir. Ecc. Rec. v. 255.

him as a saint. The church was called "Eglwys y Bedd" and "Llangwyddyl," that is, "the Church of the Grave" and "the Church of the Irishman." It was situated near the present church of Holyhead; and the "History of Anglesey," published in London in 1775, says that a few years before, "its ruins were removed, in order to render the way to the church more commodious. St. Serigi's shrine seems to have been held in exceeding great repute for several very wonderful qualities and cures; but, according to an old Irish chronicle, it was carried off by some Irish rovers, and deposited in the Cathedral of Christ Church in Dublin."[1]

CHAPTER II.

IRISH SAINTS IN THE MONASTERIES OF BRITAIN AND ARMORICA.

Glastonbury of the Irish:—St. David's Monastery at Menevia:— St. Kieran at St. Iltud's Monastery:—Padstow:—Irish Chieftains on the British Coast:—SS. Samson and Iltud:—St. Gildas:— Monastery of Llandeveneck:—St. Joava:—SS. Magloire and Machut:—SS. Kybi and Padarn:—St. Constantine:—Cadwallon and Cadwaladar.

GLASTONBURY was for centuries one of the most famous monasteries in the Western Church; it was the only one[2] which, after holding a prominent place in the early

---

[1] *Rees*, "Essay," p. 166.
[2] "The one famous holy place of the conquered Briton, which had lived through the storm of English conquest."—*Freeman*, "The Norman Conquest," i. 436.

British times, continued to be ranked among the glories of England in the Anglo-Saxon period.

> "O three times famous Isle, where is that place that might
> Be with thyself compared for glory and delight,
> Whilst Glastonbury stood ? exalted to that pride,
> Whose monastery seemed all other to deride." [1]

It was situated in Somersetshire, on an island, called by the Romans Avalonia, *i.e.*, the Isle of Apples, which was once encircled by the waters of the river Brue or Brent, but has long since been joined to the mainland. From the clearness of the stream, it was known to the Britons as Inyswytrin, or "the glassy island," and from the Saxons it received the name Glaestingabyrig, which is supposed by the best modern authorities to mean "the burgh of the Glaestings." The island was covered with fruit-trees and shrubs. Such was its smiling fertility, that it was popularly known as the happy island; and the Laureate merely records the ancient British tradition, when in poetic fancy he transports us to—

> "The island valley of Avilion,
> Where falls not hail, nor rain, nor any snow,
> Nor ever wind blows loudly; but it lies
> Deep-meadowed, happy, fair with orchard lawns,
> And bowery hollows, crowned with summer sea."

It was the tradition of Glastonbury that our Apostle St. Patrick, before coming to Ireland, enrolled himself among the religious brethren of that monastery. It also numbered among its abbots St. Sen-Patrick, who, by St. Ængus, is called "the tutor of our apostle." This holy abbot resigned his charge at Glastonbury,

---

[1] *Drayton*, "Poly Olbion," song 3rd, vol. ii., p. 712.

and came to Ireland with his own great disciple, to labour with him in the conversion of our nation. He was famed for sanctity in our early Church, and is honoured in our ancient Calendars on the 24th of August. At the close of his life he returned to his loved monastery at Glastonbury; and some of his relics were long preserved there, the remainder being enshrined at Armagh. Thus Glastonbury had special attractions for the Irish pilgrims, and in such numbers did they flock thither, that it was commonly known as "Glastonbury of the Irish."[1] Its influence on the

[1] The "Leabhar Breac," the most valuable ecclesiastical repertory that has come down to us from the early ages of our Irish Church, in its glosses on the Feliré of St. Ængus, at 24th of August, feast of St. Sen-Patrick, states that his festival was kept "in Glastonbury of the Irish among the Saxons," and soon after it adds:—"In Glastonbury of the Irish, in the south of Saxon-land, Sen-Patrick is: for, the Irish at first dwelt there in pilgrimage; but his relics are in the shrine of Sen-Patrick in Armagh." Colgan gives us a similar entry from the Martyrology of Marianus O'Gorman: "S. Patricius Senex in Rosdela in regione de Magh-lacha, et Glassiae Hibernorum, quae est urbs in aquilonari regione Saxonum, in qua olim suscepta peregrinatione solebant Hiberni habitare." The Calendar of Cashel has: "Secundum aliquos, et verius, Glastoniae apud Wallo-Hibernos quiescit senior Patricius. Haec enim est civitas in aquilonari regione Saxonum, et Scoti inhabitant eam." Colgan himself adds, that St. Patrick, senior, was buried at Glastonbury, "ubi multi olim erant sancti Hiberni;" and among these saints he mentions SS. Indracht and Benignus (*Trias*, p. 6, n. 22; and p. 10, n. 48). To these proofs may be added the testimony of "Cormac's Glossary," p. 110. St. Indracht was said to have been martyred in the district. A little to the south of Glastonbury, surrounded by a marsh, is a fair green island, still called *Bekerey*, i.e., Little Ireland.

The English writers agree in this with the Irish tradition. Usher cites the Life of St. Dunstan, as asserting that St. Patrick, senior, died at Glastonbury. Camden, also, when treating of Glastonbury, at the time of the conversion of the Anglo-Saxons, writes: "Primis his temporibus, viri sanctissimi hic Deo

Church of Britain was very great. The Welsh Triads record that there were two thousand four hundred religious within its enclosure, of whom "one hundred were engaged alternately every hour, both day and night, in celebrating the praise and service of God, without rest, without intermission."[1] The renowned King Arthur enriched it with many gifts during life, and is supposed to have chosen it as his resting-place in death. St. David, patron of Wales, rebuilt its church, and conferred so many favours on the monastery, that he was considered its second founder. St. Paulinus, Archbishop of York, is also said to have visited this sacred place,

invigilarunt et praecipue Iberni, qui adolescentes pietate artibusque ingenuis instruebant. Solitariam enim vitam amplexi sunt, ut majore cum tranquillitate sacris litteris vacarent et severo vitae genere ad crucem perferendam se exercerent." (*Descrip. Brit.*, p. 158). In another place Camden says, that "for six hundred years the religious of Glastonbury might be said to have reigned over the surrounding territory, such was the influence which they exercised amongst their neighbours" (quasi regnassent, eorum enim nutum vicini omnes spectarunt). I refer to this text for the purpose of calling the reader's attention to the mistranslation of it given by Rev. Mr. Gough, in his edition of Camden (vol. i., p. 81): "The religious," he thus translates it, "*lived like kings, in the utmost affluence.*"

The monastery, which had well-nigh grown to the size of a small city, was levelled with the ground in Henry VIII.'s reign; and its lands, which would be now valued at £70,000 per annum, were granted by Queen Elizabeth to Sir Peter Carew. The last of the abbots, Richard Whiting, proved himself worthy of the long line of saints who had preceded him. Refusing to acknowledge the supremacy of Henry VIII., he was put to death, with two of his monks, by the orders of John, Lord Russell, on the hill called the Torr of St. Michael. The body of the martyred abbot was drawn and quartered, and his head set on the great portals of the confiscated and desecrated sanctuary. The tall green peak of the Torr of St. Michael now looks down on the stately ruins of the great abbey.

[1] *Williams*, p. 212.

and to have covered its church of wreathed osiers with wood and lead. More than once it was threatened with destruction. In the year 577 the exterminating pagan Cawlin approached almost to its very enclosure. At the battle of Deorhamme he had slain three British kings, and advancing northward burned Uriconium, "the white town in the valley," and in the poetic language of the narrative, "the hall of its chieftain was made dark, without fire, without songs, to be tenanted by the eagle who has swallowed fresh drink, the heart's blood of Cynddelen, the beautiful." At this point, however, he was driven back, and Glastonbury was saved. It was not till the reign of Ida, King of the West Saxons, A.D. 721, that the territory in which it stood was wrested from the native Britons, but even then its influence was not diminished. Of this one instance will suffice. St. Dunstan is, perhaps, after Alfred the Great, the most gifted statesman of English birth with whom we meet throughout the whole of the Anglo-Saxon period. It was among the Irish monks of Glastonbury that his genius was developed and his mind perfected in all the learning of that age. His ancient biographer writes, that "numbers of illustrious Irishmen, eminently skilled in sacred and profane learning, came into England, and chose Glastonbury for their place of abode." (*Osbern*, in Vit. S. Dunst.) His latest historian[1] is not less explicit, for he tells us that "Dunstan was fortunate in finding the monastery of Glastonbury a seat of learning. . . . It was at this time occupied by scholars from Ireland, who were deeply read in

---

[1] *Hook*, "Archbishops of Canterbury," vol. i., p. 382, seqq.

profane as well as in sacred literature. They sought to maintain themselves by opening a school to which the young nobility who resided in the neighbourhood repaired for education." The details which have been handed down regarding his studies at Glastonbury give us some idea of the literary course pursued in the Irish monasteries at this period. He was first of all instructed in the Scriptures and the sacred writings of the Fathers of the Church. The ancient poets and historians then engaged his attention; but he showed a special taste for arithmetic, geometry, astronomy, and music. His manual skill was equal to his intellectual power. Bells, which he himself had made for Abingdon, were still preserved there in the thirteenth century. At Glastonbury they showed crosses, censors, and ecclesiastical vestments, the work of his hands. Above all, he loved the Scriptorium, and spent much of his time in writing and illuminating books. His skill in all branches of human science was so great that the only plea his enemies could advance against him was, that "he had been trained to necromancy by his Irish teachers in the island of Avalon."

What shall I say of the monastery of St. David, at Menevia, which was built on the promontory, "thrus out into the sea like an eagle's beak" from the south-eastern corner of Wales, and which was so frequented by Irish pilgrims, that they made it in great part their own? That district of Wales was known in early times as Glen-Rosyn, or "Vallis Rosina,"[1] and was also called by the Britons, Hodnant, or the

[1] *Ricemarch's* "Vita S. Davidis," in *Rees*, "Lives," p. 124 and 406.

"beautiful valley." Jocelyn records the tradition of Wales, that it was from the neighbouring coast St. Patrick sailed for his Irish mission, and it was whilst praying there he was favoured with a heavenly vision, in which all Ireland, with its green hills and smiling valleys, seemed to be stretched out before him, and the angel of God pointing it out to him said, "that is the land marked out as your inheritance for evermore." St. David had at first purposed to found his monastery at a short distance from this place, where a holy relative named Gweslan lived; but whilst making out its enclosure, he was divinely assured that only a few of his disciples would there merit the heavenly rewards: "farther on (the angel added) is the spot chosen by heaven, where few shall suffer the pains of hell provided they do not fall from the faith." St. David, proceeding thither, kindled a fire, the smoke of which seemed to encircle a great part of the surrounding country, and to extend far and wide towards the distant shores of Ireland. The owner of the district was an Irishman named Baya,[1] a pagan and a druid. He was one of those successful rovers who years before had carved out territories for themselves on the Welsh coast, and continued to hold them by the sword. He was filled with terror when he saw the smoke that arose from St. David's fire, and cried out to those that were with him, "The enemy that has lit that fire, shall possess this territory as far as the smoke has spread." They

---

[1] "Baja, vocatus Scotus," *Ibid*. By a curious mistake, *Rees*, in "Lives," p. 406, translates these words "Boya and Scots." Indeed, the whole translation of St. David's Life, published by *Rees*, is most singularly inaccurate.

resolved to slay the intruders, but their attempt was
frustrated by a miracle. Seeing this, Baya made a
grant of the desired site and of the surrounding country
to St. David, whose monastery quickly arose, and its
fame spreading far and wide through Britain and Ireland
and Gaul, merited for its holy founder the title of "the
head of the whole British nation, and honour of his
fatherland."[1] St. David was born of an Irish mother
(*Bolland*, vol. i., Mart., p. 39). It was at the hands of
an Irish Bishop, the great St. Ailbhe of Emly, that he
received the waters of Baptism; and it was in the arms
of a loved Irish disciple that he breathed his soul to
heaven. Most of the great saints of Ireland, in the
sixth and seventh centuries, spent some time at his
monastery, renewing their own fervour within its
hallowed precincts, and maintaining its strict discipline
by the stern severity of their lives. To take a few
instances from the patron saints of the Diocese of
Ossory, we find that St. Senanus was famed there for
his devotedness to manual labour, for the monks were
obliged to work in the forests and to till the land, even
drawing the plough by their own strength.[2] St.
Scothin, of Tescoffin, when crossing the channel to visit
it, was said, in the beautiful poetry of the sacred legend
to pluck wild flowers from the sea, and to entwine
precious wreaths, as though he journeyed through a
rich meadow. St. Brendan went there to rest for

[1] "Omnis Britanniae gentis caput et patriae honor."—*Rees*,
"Lives," p. 140.
[2] "They labour with feet and hands, and put the yoke to their
shoulders; they fix stakes with unwearied arms in the earth; and
in their holy hands carry hatchets and saws for cutting."
Rhyddmarch, Vita, in "Cambro Brit. SS." p. 117.

a while after his seven years' ocean pilgrimage in search of a paradise. St. Modomnoch of Tibrauchny had the care of the bees of the monastery entrusted to him. When, after a long period of labour and virtue, he had taken his farewell of the abbot and the brethren to return home, a swarm of bees came and settled on the bow of the boat, to accompany him. Three times he brought them back to the monastery, but each time they returned in increasing numbers, so that at length, with St. David's blessing, he brought them with him to Ireland, and introduced the culture of bees into the Irish monasteries. The ancient record adds that honey was cultivated in these monasteries not only for the use of the religious, but to procure a more delicate food than their ordinary coarse fare for the poor. St. Aidan, patron of Ferns, was one of those whom St. David chose as his first companions in founding the monastery. He lived there for many years, and governed it for some time as abbot. So cherished was St. Aidan's memory throughout Wales that the Triads adopt him as a native saint, and assign to him a genealogy from one of the most illustrious Welsh princes.[1] We are even told by Giraldus Cambrensis, that after the Anglo-Norman invasion of this country, the religious of Menevia put forward the singular claim of jurisdiction over the clergy of Ferns, on the specious grounds that one of their first abbots

---

[1] *Rees*, "Essay," p. 227, &c. It is seldom that the Welsh writers register the foreign parentage of their saints. There are, however, some exceptions. Thus in the Genealogy of St. Collen, his mother, Melangell, is called the daughter of Ethni the "Irishwoman." St. Melangell was the foundress of Pennant Melangell in Montgomeryshire. Her cell is still pointed out there on a rock near the church. *Rees*, "Lives," pp. 596 and 599.

was the founder, first bishop, and chief patron of that see. Towards the close of the ninth century, another illustrious Irishman held a distinguished place at St. David's. He was styled by his contemporaries "Johannes Erigena;" and having taught geometry and astronomy, and other branches of science, at this monastery, such was his fame, that he was chosen by King Alfred the Great, not, indeed, as some have foolishly advanced, to lay the foundation of Oxford[1]—which was not as yet dreamed of—but to teach the sons of the Saxon nobility in the royal palace. Two centuries later the fame of Ireland was still fresh at Menevia. The famous Sulgen, who held the see about the year 1070, set out to satiate his thirst for knowledge in the Irish schools. He was, however, driven in a storm on the Scottish coast, and was detained there for a long time:—

"With ardent love for learning Sulgen sought
The school in which his fathers had been taught;
To Ireland's sacred isle he bent his way,
Where science beamed with bright and glorious ray.
But sailing towards the country where abode
The people famous in the word of God,
His barque, by adverse winds and tempests tossed,
Was forced to anchor on another coast."

At length, however, he was enabled to continue his journey to Ireland, and having spent ten years in her monasteries and schools, returned to Menevia, to impart to his countrymen his honied store of sacred knowledge:

"Then, having gained a literary fame,
In high repute for learning, home he came,
His gathered store and golden fruit to share."[2]

[1] *Williams*, "Eccl Antiq.," p, 156; see *Giles*, "Life and Times of Alfred the Great," p. 274.
[2] The Latin text may be seen in *Usher's* "Sylloge," praef. p. 5.

In the most ancient extant list of the Abbots of St. Iltud's Monastery, the second name is that of St. Kieran of Saigher, patron of the Diocese of Ossory. The site of the monastery is thus described by the ancient author of St. Iltud's Life :—" Around it there were no mountains or steep inequalities, but an open fertile plain; there was a wood, very thick with various trees growing in it, where many wild beasts inhabited ; a very pleasing river flowed therein, and spring fountains mingled with a rivulet in delightful courses."[1] It was probably about the year 500 that St. Kieran dwelt in this hallowed retreat of piety. Thence he proceeded to a small island situated in the Wye, where he erected a small monastery, and many devout persons flocked thither to receive his lessons of heavenly instruction. St. Kieran, however, soon after proceeded towards the north of Britain and thence returned to Saigher. He had already laboured in the sacred ministry throughout Brittany, where he is still honoured in many places as patron, under the name of St. Sezin. Thence he came to Cornwall, which also retains many memorials of his Apostolate; several churches still bear his name; the most singular being that of Peranzabulo, or " St. Kieran's in the Sands," which, after being embedded in the strand for about 800 years, has been brought to light again in our own days, almost perfect in its rude but solid masonry, and with its sculptured corbels and zig-zag ornaments so complete, that we might almost be tempted to imagine that it was one of our old Irish oratories transplanted to the Cornish shore. St. Kieran is

[1] *Rees*, "Lives," p. 163.

honoured as the special patron of those who are engaged in the tin-mines, and they keep his festival, as in Ireland, on the 5th of March. It is the constant tradition of Cornwall that he was interred there. An arm of the saint was enshrined in Exeter Cathedral, and as late as the 15th century several other relics of this great Irish Bishop were venerated in Cornwall. An inventory, made in the year 1281, mentions a reliquary with St. Kieran's head, a silver plate with his *scutella*, a silver cross containing some small relics of the saint, his pastoral staff adorned with silver and gold and precious stones, a text of the Gospels richly encased, and a small copper bell also belonging to the saint.[1]

Petrocstow, or Padstow, was another monastery closely connected with our Irish schools. Its name was derived from its holy founder, St. Petroc. Before he began his labours there he spent twenty years in the religious houses of Ireland, perfecting his mind in sacred science, and training himself to the practice of heroic virtue. Returning to Britain, he brought with him three Irish monks, remarkable alike for learning and sanctity, St. Croidan, St. Medan, and St. Dagan,[2] and with their aid he laid the foundations of the great monastery which for many years was one of the chief centres of piety and science for all Southern Britain.

As regards Irish chieftains on the British coast, we have seen how important a part in the history of the

[1] See "The Age of the Saints: a Monograph of early Christianity in Cornwall," by *W. C. Borlase*, 1878, p. 49.
[2] *Usher*, p. 564, and Index Chron. ad an. 518; *Colgan*, "Acta," p. 385. See also the learned paper on "Loca Patriciana," by Rev. J. F. Shearman, in Journal of *R. Hist. &c. Association of Kilkenny*, 1876, p. 414.

D

Church of Wales belongs to Prince Brecan and his family. We have also seen how another Irish chieftain, though a pagan, bestowed on St. David the territory around Menevia, on which his great monastery was erected. It is, however, still more strange, perhaps, to find an Irishman ruling a principality of Wales as late as the year 1080. His name, as presented in the Welsh annals, was Gruffyd ap Cynan, or Mac Keenan, and he is there styled King of Gwynedd, in North Wales, having obtained that kingdom, not by force of arms, but by right of inheritance. It is probable we would have been left in ignorance as to the land of his birth were it not for the munificence of his gifts to religion, which were duly recorded by Welsh writers. In the list of pious donations by which he prepared to close his earthly career, comes foremost " a gift of twenty shillings to Dublin, that city being his native place," and this is followed by gifts of a like sum to each of the other principal churches of Ireland.[1]

But we must pass lightly over these and many similar memorials of Irish influence along the western coast of Britain, to fix our attention more particularly on the lives of a few Irish saints, whose virtues shone with special lustre, and whose names stand prominently forth in the Calendars of Wales and Armorica. English writers, indeed, have, as a rule, been content to style them British saints, but the tradition, especially of Armorica, has invariably pointed to Ireland as their country, and modern research has fully justified the accuracy of that venerable tradition.

[3] *Williams*, Ecc. Antiq., p. 162.

In the preceding pages we have already referred to St. Samson. The Book of Llandaff and other early records of Wales inform us that he was brother of St. Tathai.[1] From his tender years he manifested a longing desire for a religious life, and although his father urged him to pursue a worldly career, his mother, with loving earnestness, encouraged him to follow God's holy will. He was in his youth placed under the care of St. Iltud,[2] and this venerable man from the first foretold his future eminence and sanctity. We are also informed that Samson applied himself particularly to the study of the Sacred Scripture, and that his advance in piety and his austerities kept pace with his literary progress. Among his companions were SS. David and Gildas, afterwards so renowned in the Welsh Church. One season, at harvest time, the birds began to pluck the corn of the monastery and to leave the ears almost empty. St. Iltud placed his holy pupils on guard to chase them away. St. Samson, praying fervently to God, blessed the cloud of birds that had settled on the field. They attempted to fly away, but their efforts were in vain; and then, obedient to his voice, they went before him to St. Iltud's cell, and remained gathered around it, till the abbot, rising from prayer, set them at liberty, by his blessing, but with the injunction that they should no longer ravage the fields of the monastery.[3] St. Samson was brought to the holy Bishop Dubricius (grandson of the Irish chieftain Brecan, to whom we have already referred) to be promoted to holy

---

[1] *Rees*, "Lives," p. 591.
[2] The Life of the Saint in *Mabillon*, "Acta SS. Ordinis S. Bened.," vol. i., p. 154, chap. ix., states that he was brought to St. Iltud's school "cum donariis secundum morem."
[3] *Rees*, "Lives," p. 479; *Mabillon*, "Acta Sanctorum," &c., in Life of St. Gildas, i., 130, chap. v.

orders; and when he was ordained deacon, "there appeared to Dubricius and the Abbot Iltud a dove whiter than snow, that rested on the head of the youthful Levite."[1] The great Monastery of St. Iltud, known as *Bangor Iltud*, was situated at the city of Caerworgan, called Bovium by the Romans, and at the time of which we treat was the residence of the Kings of Glamorgan.[2] St. Samson, desirous of greater solitude, with the permission of the holy Abbot, retired to St. Kieran's Monastery, situated in a small island not far distant. He was there welcomed by St. Kieran as an angel from heaven, and when St. Kieran soon after resolved to return to Saigher, St. Samson was chosen his successor in the government of the monastery. The Life adds, that after some time he was there visited by "some most skilful Irish monks,"[3] and these he accompanied to Ireland to perfect himself still more in the paths of holiness. One of the monasteries in which he rested for a time was situated at Rath Airthir (in Arce Aetride),[4] on the sea-coast; and so enraptured were its religious with his zeal and piety, that they solicited him to remain as abbot amongst them. To this Samson would not consent, and returning to Wales, he chose a solitary spot, where he lived in retirement and prayer till the aged Dubricius and the other Bishops of Wales, consulting for the interests of the Faith, "pro Fidei firmitate," obliged him to accept the Episcopal burden. Soon after, being admonished by God that his brethren in Armorica were

[1] *Rees*, "Lives," p. 481; *Mabillon*, "Acta," i., 154, chap. xiii.
[2] *Williams*, "Ecc. Antiq." p. 213.
[3] *Mabillon*, "Loc. Cit.," chap. 37.
[4] *Mabillon*, "Loc. Cit.," chap. 38.

assigned to him as his spiritual charge, he passed the
Severn, and taking with him some chosen religious with
his books, and the chariot " which he had brought with
him from Ireland," set out for the continent. There
he found the whole country a prey to every disorder, in
consequence of the invasion by Childebert,[1] the murder
of their native Prince Jena, and the substitution of the
Frank Conumur in his stead. The labours of St.
Samson throughout Armorica were those of an Apostle.
More than once he visited the palace of Childebert to
remedy the wrongs of his people. The king treated him
with every kindness, and founded for him a monastery
at Pentale, on the banks of the Seine, in the territory of
Rheims. It was, however, at his monastery in the city
of Dôle that St. Samson loved particularly to reside,
and after his death that city continued to be enriched
with his relics till the close of the ninth century, when
they were translated to Orleans. St. Samson was present at the second Council of Paris in the year 557, and
signed its Decrees thus: " I, Samson, a sinner, Bishop,
have approved and signed." His name does not appear
at the Council held in Tours in the year 565, which is a
proof that he had died before that year. He assisted at
the death of St. Dubricius, and entering the saint's
cell, as his Life tells us, " made the sign of Redemption,
as was his custom, on the forehead of the dying
Bishop."[2] He also received the last breath of St. Iltud.
The death-bed scene of this saint is one of the most

---

[1] He reigned from 511 to 560. Gregory of Tours, who was a
contemporary, places the murder of Jena in 546. This fixes the
date of St. Samson's arrival in Gaul.

[2] *Ibid.*, lib. 2, chap. viii.

striking presented in the whole history of the British Church:—

"St. Iltud's death being at hand, he summoned two abbots to his bedside, named Isannus and Atoclius, and when they had come he lovingly embraced them, and giving them his last words of admonition said: The time for my rest in Christ has come, but be comforted, dear brothers, for the day of your own repose is not far distant. It pleases God that this night the angels will bear my soul to bliss, and you my brother Isannus will see it as an eagle with golden plumage soaring swiftly to heaven. In fifteen days brother Atoclius will depart from the flesh, and again Isannus will see that soul as an eagle directing its flight towards heaven; its plumage, however, shall be as lead, and difficult shall be the eagle's flight; for thou, dear brother Atoclius, though pure from thy childhood, hast been much engaged with the world, and hast cherished an avaricious desire of it. And after forty days, brother Isannus will himself depart this life, and his soul shall ascend with the same difficulty to heaven. At midnight, whilst the religious chanted hymns and anthems, and received from their loved Father the kiss of peace, he breathed his soul to God; and, as he had foretold, Isannus saw his soul, as an eagle with golden wings, soaring aloft to heaven. The prophecy regarding Atoclius was also verified; and Isannus seeing the difficulty with which that soul struggled towards heaven, on account of its leaden burden of avarice, caused the prayers of the brethren to be offered up, and many masses to be celebrated for his repose, till he was favoured with another vision, when he saw the soul of Atoclius freed from its leaden burden, and joyously entering into heaven. And when the forty days had passed, Isannus too rested in peace."

Among the chief memorials of St. Samson preserved at Dôle, was his Episcopal Cross, which in his journeys he caused to be carried before him by one of his religious brethren. It was in later times encased in silver and gold, and adorned with precious gems, and was jealously guarded by the piety of the faithful.

St. Gildas was a companion of St. Samson at the monastery of Iltud. He was born in the year 490 at Alcluid, of Irish parents, and hence by many of his biographers is justly called an Irishman. In his thirtieth year, leaving St. Iltud's monastery, he proceeded to Ireland, that he might there perfect himself in the knowledge of Philosophy and the Sacred Sciences, and visiting many schools of learned men, he laid up a honeyed store of spiritual treasure. We next find him evangelizing North Britain, a great part of which was still in the darkness of Paganism, while the rest, owing to the distracted condition of the country, and to the continual irruptions of the Pagan Saxons and Picts, were lost to piety, and immersed in every vice. Having laboured here for some time, he resolved to visit Rome, " to implore the intercession of the holy Apostles SS. Peter and Paul, that through their prayers he might obtain pardon of his sins, constancy in the divine service, and a portion with all the Saints in the heavenly inheritance." At the shrine of the Apostles (in Aula B. Petri) he used to pass the nights in prayers and vigils, and by day he went round to the other sanctuaries of the seven hills (caeterorum oratoria sanctorum Romuleae urbis circumire et suffragia eorum petere), to enlist the suffrages of the countless other saints and martyrs of the eternal city. From Rome he proceeded to Ravenna, to pay the tribute of his devotion at the shrine of St. Apollinaris (gratia orationis B. Apollinaris). Many miracles were performed by him in this pilgrimage, and having satisfied his piety, he turned his steps towards home.

He for a time settled in a little island opposite Ruye, called Houath, situated on the French coast, purporting to lead there an hermitical life. Many persons, however, of the neighbouring territory hastened thither, anxious to receive from him lessons of heavenly wisdom, and to commit their children to his care. The better to provide for those entrusted to him, he proceeded to the mainland, and erected on the ruins of a castle on the hill of Ruye, a monastery, which long continued a source of the greatest blessings for all that country.

Not far from this monastery, he after a time chose for his retreat a solitary spot on the banks of the river *Le Blavet*. Finding there a cave in a high rock extending from west to east, he at the entrance built a wall facing towards the east, and placed in it a small window, which he closed with glass, and this cave he dedicated as an oratory, and made it his constant abode. At his prayer, a spring fountain gushed from the rock. He erected close by a small mill, where he ground the corn with his own hands, and distributed it to the poor and the infirm.

Though all honoured him as their father and abbot, he looked on himself as the last and the least of all. He was at the same time the most meek of men, showing forth his wisdom in action and in word, assiduous in prayer, persevering in vigils, macerating his flesh by fasting, bearing injuries in patience, affable in discourse, abounding in almsgiving, conspicuous by good works of every kind. He taught his disciples to shun heretics, to repair their sins by alms, to love fasting, to be constant in watching and prayer. He was the father of the poor and the orphans, the comforter of those who were in sorrow, the peacemaker among such as were in strife. He reproved sinners without respect of persons, but sought at the same time to bring them to penance, setting before them the promises of God, and the greatness of his mercy towards those who repent. Such is the picture of this saint, presented by his ancient biographer.

Having spent ten years in his missionary labours, St. Gildas retired to the Monastery of Glastonbury, and it was probably there that he composed his famous Epistle on the British Church, which is one of the most remarkable records that have come down to us from this early period. At the invitation of Ainmire, Monarch of Ireland, Gildas quitted his tranquil repose, and hastened once more to awaken the fervour of Christian piety on the shores of Erin, which he had already so learned to love. He seems, however, to have spent but a short time among our people; for it was only in the year 568 that Ainmire ascended the throne, and St. Gildas's death is marked in the Annals of Wales in the year 570. Among the treasures of Kildare, in the ages of Faith, was a small bell worked by St. Gildas, which, in token of spiritual friendship, he had sent to the foundress of that convent, the great St. Bridget.

The Monastery of Llandeveneck was founded by St. Winwaloe[1] about the year 500. This great saint lived

[1] St. Winwaloe was born in 455 and died in 529, "on Saturday, the 3rd of March, in the first week of Lent." These data all agree

with his father near Guic-Sezne, when a fleet of pirates was seen hovering about the harbour. St. Winwaloe gave the alarm, crying out, "I see a thousand sails." Their subsequent defeat was ascribed to his prayers, and in after times a commemorative cross was erected there, which was called "The cross of the thousand sails." He first erected a cell in the island of Sein, off the Point du Raz, but finding it too much exposed to the full swell of the Atlantic, he proceeded to the opposite side of the harbour of Brest, and there founded Llandevenec, which has been well styled *the Glastonbury of Brittany*, "the final resting-place of the monastic exiles, who grew old, but could not die in the wild paradise of their first settlement, and which held fast its Scoto-British customs until the ninth century."[1] Fremenville, in his "Antiquités du Finistère," gives an interesting account of this Monastery of Llandevenech, which he styles the most ancient monument in Finistère, after those of the Druids. Its romantic ruins occupy a little promontory between two rivers. The pillars he especially notices as ornamented with most complicated interlaced work and grotesque figures, precisely after the manner of some of the other oldest works of Irish hands. St. Winwaloe died standing at the altar, after giving the kiss of peace to the religious brethren, on the 3rd of March, 529.

St. Joava is honoured as one of the most distinguished of the Irish monks who lived in this monastery of

with the year assigned to his death. The name of Winwaloe means "He that is fair," and was given to him on account of his great beauty.

[1] *Haddan*, "Remains," p. 264.

Llandevenec.[1] After spending some time in Wales he set out to visit his relative St. Paul, who was afterwards Bishop of Leon, but who at this time governed an island monastery in the Morbihan. A tempest drove our saint on shore near Llandevenec. Being hospitably received by St. Winwaloe, and struck by the fervent piety of the religious, he became a monk there, and subsequently was commissioned by the holy abbot to preach the faith throughout Cornouaille. On one occasion, as his Life records, Joava was engaged in conference with Winwaloe and other holy abbots, and the holy sacrifice was being celebrated by an Irish religious named Taidoc, when they were attacked by an armed party headed by a wicked local prince (Tyrannus) who was enraged at the spread of Christian piety in the district. The priest had just pronounced the words "Nobis quoque peccatoribus," when they rushed in and murdered him at the altar, whilst the other religious sought safety in flight. Divine punishment immediately fell on the wicked chieftain; a noble monastery was erected on the spot where St. Taidoc was martyred, and Joava was chosen its first Abbot. It was known in after times as St. Mary's Monastery of Doulas. St. Paul, or Pol, being chosen Bishop of Leon, summoned Joava to aid him in sanctifying his people, and when a little later, weighed down with infirmities and age, he retired from his see, our saint was appointed his successor. St. Joava died after one year's episcopate in 555, and is still honoured as special patron of two parishes in the ancient see of Leon.

[1] His life may be seen in *Colgan*, "Acta," p. 441. He is expressly styled "natione Hybernus." His Irish name was probably Finnian.

At the time of St. Joava's death another Irish saint stood by his side. This was St. Cianan. Rescued from death in his youth by St. Kieran of Saigher, and for many years disciple of this saint, he resolved, in imitation of his master, to make a pilgrimage to the shrine of St. Martin. Having satisfied his devotion there, he meditated another journey to Rome, and onwards to the Holy Land. Arriving at the Alps, and enraptured with their solitude, he remained there, in imitation of Moyses, in the strictest fast, for forty days. Admonished by an angel that God had accepted his pious will for the remainder of his journey, he turned his steps towards home.

St. Joava detained him for a time at Leon, where he exercised his zeal in leading unbelievers to truth and sinners to repentance. After administering the last sacraments to St. Joava, and assisting him in death, St. Cianan returned to Ireland, and founded in his native district a stone church, in Irish *daimh-leach*, a work of architectural marvel in those days, which gave name to his monastery, and the town that sprung up around the monastery retains the name Duleek to the present day.

St. Magloire and St. Machut belonged to the same holy family as SS. Tathai and Samson. The former succeeded St. Samson as Bishop of Dôle, but in a short time resigned that charge, and founded on the shore of the sea, in the island of Jersey, a monastery, in which sixty-two monks lived with him in the practice of every virtue. The nobleman who owned the island being miraculously freed by the prayers of the saint from a disease which had afflicted him for many years, bestowed half of the island on St. Magloire. All the fertility of the soil and the riches of the sea seemed, however, to forsake the portion which he had reserved to himself, and to be transferred to the portion of St. Magloire. He therefore completed his gift, and made an offering of the whole island to God and to our saint.

St. Maclovius, generally called by the Irish endearing name of Machud or Machutus, was from the years of boyhood trained to piety at the monastery[1] of St. Brendan. That holy abbot loved him as a favourite child, and he was among the religious chosen by St. Brendan for his companions in his wonderful seven years' pilgrimage on the ocean. One fact of his early years is particularly commemorated by his ancient biographer. The monastery of St. Brendan was situated not far from the sea-shore. One day, as the young religious took their recreation on the strand, St. Machut seated himself on a rock, and was soon overcome by sleep. Whilst he slept the returning tide encompassed the rock, and when he awoke he found the waters rising around him on every side. The abbot, hastening to the shore in search of him, saw him standing on the rock, which seemed to rise under his feet as the waves surged around him. To the abbot, who was filled with alarm on the sea-shore, he cried out, with hands uplifted to heaven: "Mirabiles elationes maris, mirabilis in altis Dominus"—wonderful are the ocean's waves, wonderful is the Lord on high; and he added that his only regret was, that he had not with him his Psalter, to chant amidst the waves the praises of God.

[1] The monastery is said to have been situated at *Carvanna* or *Carganna*. This is supposed by some to be Lancarvan, in Wales; but probably it is an attempt to Latinize *Ciarrigi*, where St. Brendan's famous monastery was situated. See the Saint's Life in *Mabillon's* "Acta SS.," vol. i., p, 177.

In after times, when his native territory desired to have him for bishop, he fled to Armorica, and joined the monastery of St. Aaron, which was situated on a tract of land opposite the town of Aleth, and was surrounded by the sea, except at one side, where a mound of sand united it with the mainland. There his only meal was oaten bread with some dry herbs, and water was his only drink. The few Christians who remained in Aleth soon recognised the treasure they possessed in this pilgrim religious, and building an oratory as best they could, prayed him to come amongst them to preach the truths of faith, and offer the holy sacrifice. Moved by their desolate condition, St. Machut undertook their spiritual charge. Many miracles accompanied his preaching, and throughout all Brittany he was soon revered as an apostle of Christ. After the death of St. Aaron, he took charge of that saint's monastery, and around it a large city grew up, which in after time was called St. Malo, from our saint, whom it honoured as its patron. Throughout all his onerous spiritual cares, St. Machut did not omit manual labour. One day, whilst engaged pruning the vines with the religious brethren, as his "Life" relates, he laid aside his mantle, and after the day's labour, when about returning to the monastery, he found that a red-breast (*bitriscus*) had begun to form her nest in his mantle. He would not allow the little bird to be disturbed; and though the mantle was thus left exposed to the rain and wind till the red-breast brought forth her young, yet it was found quite fresh and uninjured, as though it had been the whole time carefully preserved.

Towards the close of his life St. Machut was compelled, by the disorders which prevailed, to abandon his flock. Soon, however, the people felt that they had lost their best friend and father, and they besought him to return to them. Though weighed down by years,[1] the saint joyfully hastened back to comfort them, and with his presence, smiling plenty and every other comfort were restored to them. Knowing, however, that only a little time remained to him of his earthly pilgrimage, and being desirous to end his days in solitude, he once more bade farewell to Brittany, and proceeded southward to the diocese of Saintes, where the holy bishop, St. Leontius, received him with the greatest joy. There he chose the little town of Archambiac for his retreat, and passed his whole time in prayer and penance. Three days before his death a fever set in ; he would not, however, allow any change to be made in his bed of ashes, or in his clothing of sackcloth, nor would he permit his weary frame to be placed in a posture of repose, but with hands and eyes upraised to heaven, and his heart fixed on God, he calmly awaited the summons to his reward. His happy death took place on the 15th of November. The year is uncertain, but as St. Leontius held the see of Saintes about the year 620, the death of St. Machut must be referred to the same period.

Such were the men who, by the heroism of their sanctity, won an undying fame for our country throughout the churches of Britain and North Gaul. In France, at least, their memory is still held in benediction ; and the faithful of Brittany and Normandy have never ceased

---

[1] "Seniles artus ad laborem viae reparat." (Vit. chap. 20).

to cherish a grateful affection for the Green Isle of the West, to whose heroic piety they are indebted for so many patron saints.

But besides the sons of Erin who made Britain and Armorica their home, and scattered there the seeds of Christian piety, it would not be difficult to compile a long calendar of Britons who, though strangers to Ireland by birth, were nevertheless attracted thither by the widespread fame of her monasteries and schools,— devoted men, who, having satiated themselves at her pure fountains, returned to their own countries earnest soldiers of the Cross, and heralds of the glad tidings of Redemption.

Such, for instance, was St. Kybi. A native of Cornwall, he spent four years in the Arann islands, off the coast of Galway, then famous for the virtues and miracles of St. Enda and his disciples. He afterwards preached throughout the greater part of Wales, and churches are still dedicated to him at Caernarvon, Caerleon, and Holyhead. This last town honoured him as a chief patron, and was enriched with his relics. It is strange to find it recorded that as late as the year 1405 some citizens of Dublin planned a raid on that district of Wales, and carried off the treasure of St. Kybi's relics, which they deposited in Christ Church, in their own city.[1]

Such, too, was the great Armorican saint, Padernus or Padarn. He was born in Brittany, but soon after his birth his father, Pedredin, with the consent of his wife, proceeded to Ireland and became a monk there.

---

[1] See "Monasticon Hibernicum," new edition, vol. ii., p. 9.

Though advanced in years this venerable man passed his time "in fasting, prayer, watching, meditation, and bestowing charity on those around him;" he "slept on a rough mat, and prayed to God both by day and night."[1] When the little Padarn asked his mother whether his father was yet alive, she used to reply—"Yes, my child; but he lives to God and not to the world." St. Padarn, having attained the years of manhood, said within himself, "How can a son live better than by imitating a good father?" and accompanied by several others, set out for Ireland. On the way, however, he was detained for a time in Wales, where he erected, in Cardiganshire, the great monastery of Llanbadarn-Fawr. After some time, leaving there his Armorican companions, he continued his journey to Ireland, and living for some years with his father, emulated his piety and austerities, and performed many miracles. He subsequently returned to Wales, and built monasteries and churches throughout the whole region of Ceretica. The Welsh Triads name him as one of the "blessed visitors" of Britain, and they record that he went about the country preaching the faith of Christ, "without pay or reward," to all ranks of people, and spending his life in prayer, fasting, and attendance on the sick.

The President of the Royal Institution of Cornwall, treating of the Cornish Saints of this period, writes, that Ireland "bore fruit in a manner that was truly marvellous. . . . . It became the centre of all the religious and literary life of the north. Thither every

[1] *Rees*, "Lives," p. 104.

peaceful scholar, every philosopher, as the monk of those early days is characteristically called by Sozomen, fled for refuge before the Pagan hordes which, on the withdrawal of the Roman Legions, swooped down into their place. Speaking generally of Cornish antiquities once at Oxford, I have never forgotten the advice given me by my kind friend, Professor Max Müller: 'If you really wish,' he said, ' to go deeply into the antiquities of your country, it is to Ireland you must go to learn about them.' "[1]

Among the Welsh Saints that made Ireland their home I must not omit St. Constantine, that illustrious British prince and saint, who was as reckless in his career of crimes in his early years as he was famed for his penitential austerities and his holiness of life in his old age. He ruled over Damnonia, the territory comprised in the modern Devonshire and Cornwall; and such were his evil deeds, that Gildas classes him among the wicked princes whom he holds up to the execration of posterity. It is in particular recorded of him that, in defiance of his solemn oath, he had slain two royal youths, the sons of Modred, king of the Britons, within the very precincts of the altar. However, a few years after St. Gildas's death, Constantine entered with earnestness on the paths of penance, and proceeding to Ireland, concealed his rank, and enrolled himself among the servants of the monastery of St. Mochuda at Rahen. He chose for himself the humblest offices and the severest manual labour. For seven years he carried the sacks of corn to the convent mill to be ground for the

[1] *Borlase*, " The Age of the Saints," &c., p. 34.

community and the poor. At length his rank being discovered by St. Mochuda, he made rich grants to the monastery, and having attained great fame for virtue, was raised to the dignity of Abbot.[1] The Annalist, Tighernac, marks under the year 588, "Conversio Constantini ad Dominum." The Annals of Ulster have a like entry in 587, and the "Annales Cambriae" in 589. The year of his death is not recorded. He is said to have proceeded from Rahen to Scotland, and to have preached the faith in Centyre and other districts, where he is still commemorated among the patron saints.

Perhaps I should also include in this list Cadwallon, king of Britain, who, together with his family, lived for seven years in Ireland. After his return to Wales, about the year 630, his life was spent in warfare against the ever-increasing tide of the Saxon invaders. He is famed in Welsh history, not for his piety, but for his valour. He is said to have fought no fewer than seventy-four battles in defence of "the most fair Britain," and for this his memory was long held dear by his countrymen—

"As the water flows from the fountain—
Sorrowful will be our lingering day for Cadwallon."[2]

His son, Cadwaladar, supplied abundantly all that was wanting in the father's piety. He was popularly styled "the blessed," and he is commemorated in the Triads as one of the "three kings who conferred blessings" on Britain, and also as one of the "three canonized kings

---

[1] See *Petrie*, "Round Towers," p. 356; and *Forbes*, "Kalendars of Scottish Saints," p. 312.
[2] Elegy by the contemporary, Llywarch Hen, in *Williams'* "Eccles Antiq.," p. 148. It is given in full by *Skene*, "Four Ancient Books of Wales," Edinburgh, 1868, vol. i., p. 433.

of Britain." He was the last of the Cymry who assumed the title of chief sovereign of Britain, and he is said by some of the Welsh chroniclers to have died in Rome.[1]

These instances will suffice to show how fruitful was the faith of Ireland in conferring blessings upon the various British principalities of Wales and Armorica. Holy men from our shores appear in every page of Welsh and Armoric Annals, from the fifth to the eighth century. Their cells and churches and schools and monasteries were spread like a network over the whole country, as so many secure asylums of civilization, science, and religion, and even when the individuals who erected them had passed away, these institutions continued to produce the happiest fruits of social peace and Christian virtue. It is not saying too much to assert that a great deal of the fame enjoyed by the British Church in Armorica and Wales in those golden centuries of its schools and monasteries, was merited for it by the untiring zeal and earnest piety of its Irish saints.

[1] *Williams'* " Eccles. Antiq.," p. 148–9.

CHAPTER III.

MISSIONARY LABOURS OF ST. COLUMBA AND HIS COMPANIONS IN SCOTLAND.

Fame of Ireland in the Sixth Century:—Early years of St. Columba: —His Virtues:—Visit to St. Molaise:—The Companions of his Pilgrimage:—Iona:—St. Columba's love of Discipline:—His Visits to Conal, King of Dalriada, and Brude, King of the Picts:—His Labours among the Picts:—The Monastery of Tears:—St. Moluog—St. Donnan and his Companions Martyrs —St. Molios:—SS. Finnan and Mochonna:—The Four Founders of Monasteries:—Sea Voyages of St. Cormac:— Eilean-na-naoimh:—St. Columba at Drumceatt:—His love of Ireland:—The Monastery of Derry:—St. Columba punishes injustice done to the Poor:—His Visit to St. Kentigern:—His Pilgrimage to Rome:—Inchcolm:—Heavenly favours granted to St. Columba:—His Death.

OUR illustrious countryman, Marianus Scotus, in his chronicle, under the year 589, compendiates in one short sentence the history of Ireland at the close of the sixth century: "Ireland, the island of saints, is, to a sublime degree, full of holy men and innumerable wonders."[1]

The name of St. Columba is, perhaps, the brightest that adorns this brilliant page of our country's history. Venerated at home for his sanctity and wondrous miracles, he has from time immemorial ranked with St. Patrick and St. Bridget amongst the chief patrons of

---

[1] *Marianus*—" Hibernia, insula sanctorum, sanctis et mirabilibus perplurimis sublimiter plena habetur." Pertz, Monumenta Hist. Germ. vii., 544.

Erin, whilst abroad the grateful piety of those whom he evangelized has awarded him the *aureola* of chief Apostle of Caledonia. Many years, indeed, before the mission of our saint others had preached the faith in Dalriada and the southern districts of Alba, but in consequence of the continual wars and predatory incursions, piety had again grown cold, and the light of truth was well nigh spent. Columba revived there the spirit of piety, and renewed the fervour of Christian life. The Northern Picts, however, had never yet received the Gospel, but now that sanguinary and untameable race, which Imperial Rome could not subdue, was conquered by the Irish missionary. Before St. Columba had ended his glorious career, the whole nation was gathered into the one true fold; their glens and forests, their almost inaccessible mountains, and their distant islands were studded with Christian churches and monasteries, and resounded with the praises of the Most High.

St. Columba[1] was born in Gartan, in the County Donegal, on the 7th December, in the year 521, the very day on which the great founder of Monasterboice passed to his reward. An ancient oratory still marks the place of his birth, and in the cemetery, close by, are two old Celtic crosses, with St. Columba's well, whither pilgrims still flock to pay the tributes of their devotion on his festival. By paternal descent he was a scion of

[1] Excellent popular lives of our saint have been published by Montalambert, in his "Monks of the West," and Sister Mary Francis Clare, in Kenmare Series, London, 1877. We are particularly indebted, however, to Dr. Reeves, in his edition of Adamnan's Life of St. Columba, and Mr. Skene, in "Celtic Scotland," vol. ii., Edinburgh, 1877, for the learning and erudition with which they have illustrated the early monuments connected with the saint and his companions.

the royal house of the northern Hy-Niall, and his father, Fedhlimidh, belonged to the tribe of Cinell Conaill, who were connected with the kings of Scottish Dalriada. His mother, Eithne, was of a princely family of Leinster. Before his birth she had a vision in which was foreshadowed the splendour of his future career. An angel appeared to her, bearing in his hand a veil of wonderful beauty, richly variegated with all kinds of flowers. Scarce, however, had she contemplated it for a little time, when he spread it out and allowed it to float away through the air. It gradually expanded as it became more and more distant, till at length mountains, forests, and plains were covered with its shadow. Then the angel said to her—"Thou art about to become the mother of a son who shall blossom for heaven: he shall be reckoned among the prophets of God, and shall lead numberless souls to the heavenly country."

This child of promise was from his infancy placed under the care of a holy priest, as Adamnan informs us. Whilst under his care, an angel came one day to Columba, and asked what special virtues he desired from God. The holy youth replied that he desired above all others virginity and wisdom. The angel then announced to him that God approved his choice, and in token of approval would add the gift of prophecy to these virtues. Soon after, whilst Columba was engaged in prayer, three maidens arrayed in heavenly light stood before him, but Columba heeded them not. "Dost thou not know us?" they asked. "We are three sisters, Virginity, Wisdom, and Prophecy, and we are sent by God to be your inseparable companions during your earthly pilgrimage."

As he grew in years we meet with him in the great schools of Moville, Clonard, and Glasnevin.[1] Whilst he studied at Moville, situated at the head of Strangford Lough, in the County Down, two brilliant lights were seen to illumine the heavens over the monastery, one golden as the sun, the other silvery as the moon. The holy abbot and bishop, Finnian, explaining this vision to his religious, said that Ciaran mac-an-Tsaeor (*i.e.*, the son of the carpenter), who was one of their number, would be as the silvery light by his virtues and good deeds; but Columba would be as the golden sun, and "the fame of his exemplary piety and the brightness of his angelic life, his purity, his wisdom, his knowledge, his word, and his preaching, would extend over all the west of the world."[2]

At Glasnevin, under the care of St. Mobhi, he had again St. Ciaran mac-an-Tsaeor, the future founder of Clonmacnoise, for his companion, and with them were Saints Canice and Comgall. One day as these young saints conversed together, their conversation turned on the new church which the Abbot Mobhi had just completed there. St. Ciaran said he wished that it were full of holy men, who by night and day would sing the praises of God. St. Canice expressed his wish that it were full of sacred manuscripts which would lead many to the knowledge and the service of God. St. Comgall declared it would be his desire that all the pains and afflictions of this world were gathered into it, that he

---

[1] At an early period of his life, on account of his uninterrupted devotion to study and prayer, he was called Columbkille, which may be interpreted Columba of the Church or Columba of the Cell, and in either meaning seems justly applicable to our Saint.

[2] Martyrology of Donegal, p. 161.

might suffer them all for the love of Christ. But Columba said he would wish it were filled with silver and gold, to relieve the poor and to found churches and monasteries. When this was told to the venerable abbot, he prophetically announced that the holy youths would be blessed from heaven in accordance with the pious wishes they had expressed.[1]

The fame of Columba for sanctity and miracles soon became widespread throughout all Ireland. Derry was the first great monastery which he founded, but so untiring were his labours, so ardent his zeal, so generous the munificence of his princely friends, that in a few years innumerable other monasteries and churches sprung up in various parts of the kingdom, all honouring him as their patron and head. But all this did not suffice for Columba's zeal: he sighed for new nations whom he might light up with the fire of God's love, and gather into the fold of Christ; and as he saw a vast missionary field open before him on the neighbouring shores of Alba, he resolved to make that the theatre of his labour, and to devote the remainder of his life to gather in there the harvest of God.

It has been sometimes stated, even by the most conscientious writers, that Columba was in his youth of an angry and vindictive spirit. So, too, it has been said that he more than once stirred up the Irish chieftains to civil strife, in order to avenge some supposed injuries which he had received; and it has been repeatedly asserted that it was in consequence of a penance of perpetual exile imposed on him for the wars he had

---

[1] *Colgan*. Trias, p. 161.

instigated, and for the blood which was shed, that he was obliged to bid farewell to Ireland, and to seek a pilgrim's home on the coast of Alba. For all this, however, there is not a vestige of proof to be found in our earliest and most authentic records. St. Adamnan attributes his journey solely to his boundless love of Christ,[1] and he supposes everywhere throughout his narrative that the saint had no other motive than a desire to carry the Gospel to a Pagan nation, and to win souls to God. The old Irish Life of St. Columba assigns the same reason for his pilgrimage: "His native country was abandoned by the illustrious saint and illustrious sage and son chosen of God, for the love and favour of Christ;" and again it adds that this was "the resolution which he had determined on from the beginning of his life" (Skene, ii. 83, 491): and the Venerable Bede presents the simple record—"there came from Ireland into Britain a famous priest and abbot, a monk by habit and life, whose name was Columba, to preach the Word of God."—(Hist. Ecc. iii., 4). We have further the clearest evidence that the character of Columba was quite free from the asperity and vindictiveness attributed to him. His contemporary, Dallan Forghaill, speaks of him as "a perfect sage, believing in Christ, learned, and chaste, and charitable: he was noble, he was gentle, he was the physician of the heart of every sage: he was a shelter to the naked, a consolation to the poor: there went not from the world one who was more constant in the remembrance of the cross."[2] The ancient gloss on St. Ængus's Feliré, or Metrical Calendar of Saints, also com-

---

[1] *Adamnan*, "pro Christo peregrinari volens," Praef. 2.
[2] *Dallan Forghaill*.—" Amra," edited by Mr. Crowe, 1871.

memorates him as "having given the most intense love to Christ from his youth;" and, not to mention other authorities, Adamnan thus sketches his true charâcter: "From his boyhood he had been brought up under Christian training, in the study of wisdom, and, by the grace of God, he so preserved the integrity of his body and the purity of his soul, that, though dwelling on earth, he appeared to live like the saints in heaven. He was angelic in appearance, graceful in speech, holy in work, with talents of the highest order, and consummate prudence. . . . He never could spend the space even of one hour without study, or prayer, or writing, or some other holy occupation. So incessantly was he engaged night and day in the unwearied exercise of fasting and watching, that the burden of each of these austerities would seem beyond the power of all human endurance. And still in all these he was beloved by all —for a holy joyousness ever beaming on his countenance revealed the joy and gladness with which the Holy Spirit filled his inmost soul."—(*Adamnan*, Praef. 2).

Being connected by birth, as we have seen, with the royal houses of Ulster and Leinster, St. Columba's words and actions may often indeed have been regarded with jealousy by contending chieftains, and may at times have given occasion to quarrels between them; but in such quarrels Columba had no part. Adamnan relates that many venerable seniors, being on one occasion assembled at Taillten, in Meath, they were induced by some such accusations, which had been made against Columba, to cut him off from their communion; but he adds that the accusations thus made were soon found to be groundless and unjust. Whilst the assembly was still sitting, Columba presented himself before them. St. Brendan, of Birr, at once arose from his seat, and, with head bowed down, reverently gave him the kiss of peace: and when called to an account for thus showing respect to one whom they had a little before cut off from their communion, St. Brendan replied: If you had seen what the Lord has vouchsafed to manifest to me regarding him, you would never have passed such an unjust sentence against one whom God has chosen to be the leader of his people to life. He added: "I saw a most brilliant pillar of light preceding this man of God as he approached, and I saw that the holy angels accompanied him whom you would treat with contempt." It needed but few words from Columba to set matters in their true light, and, as the result, the preceding unjust censure was removed, and thenceforth all treated him with the greatest respect and reverence.

Before embarking on his mission, Columba proceeded to Inishmurray, off the coast of Sligo, to enjoy a short interval of spiritual repose, and to take counsel with the holy bishop, St. Molaise, who had chosen that island for his retreat. Thirteen centuries have wrought but little change on the rocky islands off our western coast. The bee-hive cells and oratories and enclosures of Inishmurray, though they betray, indeed, the hoary mark of centuries, yet are in a wonderful state of preservation, and we may safely affirm that they are the very same in which, during his sojourn there, St. Columba dwelt and prayed. St. Molaise exhorted him earnestly to persevere in his generous enterprise, and promised him in God's name, that from the dreary shore of Alba he would lead countless souls to heaven. It was in the year 563 that Columba at length entered his little coracle, or osier boat, and, accompanied by twelve companions,[1] set out on his great missionary enterprise. One of his companions, named Mochonna, was the son of an Ulster chieftain, and Columba represented to him the great good he could effect at home without abandoning his parents and his native land; but the young religious replied: "It is thou who art my father, and the Church is my mother, and my country is wheresoever I can gather the largest harvest for Christ;" and lest further entreaties should be made to him, he added: "I have vowed to follow thee whithersoever thou goest, until thou hast led me to Christ, to whom thou hast consecrated me." This instance shows the devoted spirit which animated the companions of Columba, and made them worthy to share in the glory and the fruits of his Apostolate.

St Columba chose for his new monastic home a small island, now generally called Iona, but which for centuries was known by no other name than Hy-Columbkille, *i.e.*, "Columba's Isle." According to the Irish Life of the Saint, it was on Whitsun eve, which in that year fell on the 12th of May, that he arrived in the island. It was admirably suited for his missionary purposes. Situated midway between the conflicting nations whom he had come to evangelize, his monastery was sufficiently separated from the mainland, whilst at

[1] The following are the names of the twelve companions of St. Columba, as given in a MS. of the British Museum, compared with our ancient Calendars:—"Baithene, who was also called Conin; Cobthach, brother of Baithene; Ernan, Diarmaid, Ruisein and Fiachna, brothers; Scannal, Lugaid, Eochaid, Mochonna, Caornan, and Greallen."

the same time it was easily accessible alike to his kinsmen of Dalriada and to the Picts of North Caledonia.

Those who pay merely a hurried visit to Iona in an excursion steamer with a crowd of tourists, can see little more than a desolate-looking island with a few grey ruins, forming a striking contrast with the fertile soil and the basaltic rocks of the neighbouring islands. And yet Iona has its hidden beauties, " its retired dells, its long reaches of sand or shores, indented with quiet bays, its little coves between bare and striking rocks, and the bolder rock scenery of its north-western and south-western shores, where it opposes wild barren cliffs and high rocky islets to the sweep of the Atlantic."[1] It is about three miles and a half in length, and about a mile and a half in breadth, and it is separated only by a narrow channel from the large island of Mull, whilst an archipelago of small islands is dotted at some distance to the north and south. It has a stream of pure water, and it has also some verdant fertile plains,[2] particularly in the centre of the island, and thence extending along the eastern shore, and sloping gently towards the sea. To the north-west, there is a tract of wilder ground, consisting of small grassy patches, alternating with rocky elevations, which culminate in the highest hill in the island. The north-east has a beach of the purest white sand, and often must Columba have gazed on it with sadness, did he foresee that its

---

[1] *Skene*, " Celtic Scotland," ii. 89.

[2] Innes writing in the beginning of the last century, calls Iona " a pleasant and fertile little island " (page 151); and again he describes it as "fertile of all things which that part of the climate produces " (p. 162).—" Civil and Ecclesiastical History of Scotland," printed by the Spalding Club, Aberdeen, 1853.

snowy whiteness would be empurpled one day with the blood of the religious of Iona, cruelly slaughtered there by the Danes. The ruins which still remain belong to a comparatively modern age, but they probably mark the original sites where stood the oratory, the monastic enclosure, and the cell of Columba.

The holy pilgrims landed towards the south of the island at a little bay still called *Port-a-churich*. An ancient tradition says that they first sailed to the island of Oransay, but as from its hills they could catch a glimpse of the distant shores of Ireland, Columba told them to proceed onward, for he feared too frequent distractions from the lively emotions which the sight of his native land would not fail to excite in his bosom.[1] On landing in Iona Columba proceeded to the top of its highest hill, and as Ireland could no longer be seen, he at once choose it for his monastery. On the summit of that hill, where thus Columba sadly stood for a while stretching his looks towards Ireland, the monks in aftertimes erected a Cairn, and called it Cul-ni-Eri, *i.e.*, 'the farewell to Erin.'

On the eastern coast of this little island Columba and his religious brethren proceeded to erect their monastery and monastic cells, rude wooden structures, formed for the most part of wattles or coarse planks, and covered with reeds or branches of trees. In the centre, on a slight elevation of the ground, was placed

[1] The Duke of Argyll, in his "Iona," after remarking that St. Columba sailed on till he had got out of sight of Ireland, says: "He could not bear to see it and live out of it. The passionate love of an Irish Celt for his native land seemed to have burned in him with all the strength which is part of a powerful character" (p. 78).

the *tuguriolum*, as Adamnan calls it, *i.e.*, the little cell of the abbot. Such were the humble beginnings of the monastery destined to be for centuries the spiritual capital of Caledonia, the fortress of the faith for the Picts and Scots, and the great centre of Christian civilization for all North Britain. Even religious bigotry and national prejudice are constrained to remain silent in the presence of Iona; and although this far-famed monastery, thus founded by an Irish saint, was in after years fed with a never-failing stream of Irish disciples, and derived its chief renown from Irish genius and Irish sanctity, thus blending together national glory and the peaceful triumphs of religion, yet Scottish writers, who have but little sympathy with St. Columba's country or his creed, have been at all times ready to offer it the due meed of praise, and to acknowledge the manifold blessings which it conferred on Scotland.

Who is there that does not know the beautiful words which Johnson wrote when a century ago he visited its historic ruins: "We are now treading that illustrious island which was once the luminary of the Caledonian regions, whence savage clans and roving barbarians derived the benefits of knowledge and the blessings of religion. . . . . . Far from me and from my friends be such frigid philosophy as may conduct us indifferent and unmoved over any ground which has been dignified by wisdom, bravery, or virtue. That man is little to be envied whose patriotism would not gain force upon the plain of Marathon, or whose piety would not grow warmer among the ruins of Iona."

Chambers, in his " Caledonia," writes: "St. Columba came not to destroy, but to save; not to conquer, but to civilize. His name will always be remembered as the disinterested benefactor of Scotland. . . . . Let us not think lightly of the saints of Iona, who were the instructors of our fathers while they were ignorant, and the mollifiers of our progenitors while they were still ferocious. The learning, I was going to say the charity, of those ages centred all in Iona. It received the persons of living kings who retired from unstable thrones, and it equally admitted dead kings from the bloody field. From this seminary went out the teachers of the Caledonian regions. To this school the princes of Northumberland were sent, and acquired the light of the Gospel from the luminaries of Iona."

So, too, the Duke of Argyll, in his work on Iona, published in 1870: "Columba was an agent, and a principal agent, in one of the greatest events the world has ever seen, namely—the conversion of the northern nations. . . . . . . Christianity was not presented to the Picts of Caledonia in alliance with the impressive aspects of Roman civilization. The tramp of Roman legions had never been heard in the Highland glens, nor had their clans ever seen with awe the majesty and power of Roman government. In the days of Columba, whatever tidings may have reached the Picts of Argyll, or of Inverness, must have been tidings of Christian disaster and defeat. All the more must we be ready to believe that the man who at such a time planted Christianity successfully among them, must have been a man of powerful character and of splendid gifts. There is no arguing against that great monument to Columba, which consists in the place he has secured in the memory of mankind."

F

The same grateful sentiments have been gracefully expressed in verse by Mr. Jesse :

"Ye who have sailed among the thousand isles,
Where proud Iona rears its giant piles,
Perchance have lingered at that sacred spot,
To muse on men and ages half forgot,
Though spoiled by time, their mould'ring walls avow
A calm that even the sceptic might allow.
Here where the waves these time-worn caverns beat,
The early Christian fixed his rude retreat ;
Here the first symbol of his creed unfurled,
And spread religion o'er a darkened world."

For two years Columba chiefly applied himself to mould the religious spirit of his new community, and to lay deep the foundations of the great spiritual edifice which he desired to raise. He loved to teach his religious by example as well as by precept. In prayer, and penance, and labour, he was at all times foremost among them. He slept on the hard floor of his little cell. His prolonged prayers excited the admiration and almost the alarm of his disciples. He took part in the out-door work, even as the least of the community, and he added to this the toil of transcription of the Sacred Scriptures. To labour in transcribing the sacred text had been the passion of his youth, and it continued to be his cherished occupation to the last day of his old age. Among the manuscripts which have come down to us from the golden ages of our country's faith, none surpass the Book of Kells, and the other monuments of his piety and skill; and a venerable tradition attests that he transcribed no fewer than three hundred copies of the Gospel. He was at the same time a model of humility. He knelt before the strangers who came to Iona, and before the monks returning from their work, washed their feet, and, after having washed them, respectfully kissed them. His charity made him all to all. He was indifferent to no spiritual or temporal want of those who approached the monastery. Often he was seen to weep over those who in their obduracy would not weep for their own miseries. These tears were at times the most eloquent part of his preaching, and when every other argument had been fruitless, they seldom failed to soften and subdue those savage but simple and earnest souls whom God had entrusted to his care.

No wonder that the fame of such charity and piety would soon attract to Iona not only crowds of Columba's kinsmen from Dalriada, but also countless pilgrims from other parts of Britain and from Ireland, desirous to save their souls and gain heaven under the directions of the man of God. Thus was the seed sown, which, in God's own time, was destined to yield an abundant harvest.

It was one of St. Columba's first cares to visit his cousin, Conal, king of Dalriada, who dwelt at the royal fortress of Cindelgend, in the peninsula of Centyre. He welcomed our saint with every mark of respect and joy, and at his request made him a formal grant of the island of Iona.[1] A venerable Scottish tradition tells us that the curious cave chapel at Cove, on Loch Coalisport, which still bears the name of Columba, was founded by the saint during this his first visit to the mainland : it thus would rival Iona in antiquity, and should justly be

---

[1] The oldest of our Irish chroniclers, Tighernac, in recording the death of Conal in 574, says, that in the 13th year of his reign, "he immolated the island of Hy to Columkille."—See *Skene*, Chron. of Picts and Scots, p. 67, and Celtic Scotland, ii. 86.

styled the earliest church founded by St. Columba in Scotland.

It was not till the year 565, two years after his landing in Iona, that Columba ventured to present himself before Brude, son of Maelochon, the monarch of the Pictish nation. This valiant prince, who is styled by Venerable Bede[1] "a most powerful king," was now in the eighth year of his reign. He had vanquished the Scots or Dalriadians on many a hard-fought battle-field, and triumphed over all his other enemies; and his kingdom being now in peace, he fixed his royal residence at his chief fortress near Inverness. Some writers, with Dr. Reeves, place this fortress at the vitrified fort now called *Craig Patrick*, which crowns the summit of a rocky hill nearly 500 feet high, two miles west of the river Ness. Others have pointed out the gravelly ridge called Torvean, situated a mile south-west of Inverness, part of which is encircled with ditches and ramparts, and which must have been in early times a fort of considerable strength. With two companions Columba entered his little ozier skiff, and traversing Loch Ness and the river that issues from it, presented himself at the doors of the royal mansion. The writers of St. Columba's Acts do not record the names of the two companions chosen by the saint to be with him on this important occasion, so momentous in its results and so fruitful of blessings to the Pictish nation. The Life of St. Comgall, however, supplies this omission. It tells us that his companions on that day were St. Comgall, the illustrious founder of Bangor, and St. Canice, the great patron of

---

[1] *Bede*, Eccles. Hist., iii., 4, " rege potentissimo."

Kilkenny. The king, unwilling to receive the Irish missionaries, ordered the gates to be closed against them; but they had recourse to prayer, and Comgall, having made the sign of the cross on the outer gates, they immediately fell to the ground. Columba made the sign of the cross on the inner door of the enclosure with the same effect. When the strangers stood before the king, he drew his sword, swearing by his false gods that he would avenge the insult offered to him, but St. Canice, making the sign of the cross towards him, his hand was instantly withered, and it so remained till he believed in God, and received baptism from St. Columba.[1]

After such miracles, Columba obtained, without difficulty, permission to preach the Faith throughout the kingdom, and, moreover, the possession of Iona was confirmed to him by the Pictish monarch,[2] so that he now held it under the double protection of the rival kings who shared Caledonia between them. An ancient Irish record registers another incident of this visit: "Mailchu," it says, "the king's son, came with his Druid to contend against Columba and to uphold Paganism, but both perished at the prayer of Columba."[3]

---

[1] Vita Comgalli, cap. 44. See also Skene, ii. 107. Venerable Bede dates the arrival of Columba in Scotland from this visit to the king, which took place in 565.

[2] The 'Liber Hymnorum,' in the preface to the hymn ' Altus Prosator,' states that Brude "immolavit Columbae Hi" (page 204). The Venerable Bede writes that the island "donatione Pictorum, qui illas Britanniae plagas incolunt, jamdudum monachis Scotorum tradita." (Eccles. Hist., iii. 3).

[3] Irish Life of St. Columba, in Advocates' Library. *Skene*, ii. 108.

We have only a few details regarding our saint's labours among the Picts, and yet it is beyond controversy that the thirty-two years which still remained of Columba's life were chiefly devoted to missions throughout the deep glens and hilly straths north of the Grampian range, and in the numerous islands scattered along the Scottish coast which were subject to the Pictish rule. All the ancient writers attest with one accord, that before he closed his missionary career he had gathered all that nation into the fold of Christ. I will briefly put together the few scattered fragments relating to this Pictish mission, though they probably belong to far separate periods of our saint's life.

Adamnan tells us that when "Columba had been tarrying some days in the province of the Picts," he converted a certain family, so that the husband and wife, with their children and domestics, were all baptized. A few days afterwards one of the sons was attacked by a dangerous illness, and was brought to the point of death. Then the Druids began to upbraid the parents, and to extol their own gods as more powerful than the God of the Christians. The sick child died; but Columba, burning with holy zeal to vindicate the glory of God, came to the house of mourning, and, his face bedewed with tears, prayed for a long time: then turning to the deceased he said, "In the name of the Lord Jesus Christ arise:" and taking the child by the hand he raised him up and restored him to his parents. By this miracle their sorrow was changed into joy, and many in the neighbouring districts received the truths of eternal life.

Again we are told that Columba, when staying among

the Picts, heard that there was a fountain among the heathen people where the demon was worshipped as God, and that all who drank of its water, or washed in it, were struck by demoniacal art and suffered excruciating torture. Columba proceeded to the fountain, and having blessed its water, drank of it and washed with it, to let the poor deluded people see that Satan was powerless against God. From that day the waters of the fountain became a source of blessing and wrought innumerable cures.

Broichan, who was the foster-father and chief Druid of King Brude, had used all his arts in vain to prevent Columba from approaching the royal mansion. He announced, however, that destruction awaited the missionary, and that the elements would not allow him to pursue in safety his homeward journey. Scarce had Columba set sail on Loch Ness when the sky was darkened and a tempestuous contrary wind began to blow. Columba armed himself with the sign of the cross, and fearlessly entering his little barque, it sped its way as safely and as swiftly as though it enjoyed a most favourable breeze.

Our saint, in one of his excursions to the north of the Grampian range, said to the disciples who accompanied him : "Let us make haste and meet the angels who have come down from heaven and await us, that they may bring the soul of a dying man to heaven :" this was an old Pictish chief who had led an exemplary life even to extreme old age, and was now on the point of death in the district of Glen-Urquhart. Columba outstripped his companions in the eagerness of his haste ; and the sick man heard from him with joy the Word of

God, and being baptized, rested in peace. His son, with his whole house, received at the same time the sacrament of baptism. Another time St. Columba was staying in the island of Skye, when a boat came into the harbour with a feeble old man seated on the prow. He was the chief of one of the neighbouring Pictish tribes, and it was his only desire that he might become a Christian before death : two young men, taking him from the boat laid him at the feet of the saint. Columba briefly instructed him in the truths of life, and having administered baptism to him, he died on the same spot and was buried there, and his companions raised a cairn of stones to mark his grave.

Through the powerful patronage of King Brude, St. Columba secured the protection of the chieftains who ruled over the neighbouring islands. On one occasion we find him staying at the royal mansion, and in the presence of the chieftain of the Orkney Islands thus addressing the king : " Some of our brethren have set sail, anxious to discover a *desertum*, i.e., a place of spiritual retreat, in the pathless sea. Should they happen, after many wanderings, to come to the Orkneys, be pleased to carefully instruct this prince, whose hostages are in thy hand, that no evil befall them within his territory." Adamnan tells us that St. Columba thus spoke because he prophetically foresaw that in a few weeks some of his religious would visit those islands. The chieftain, on his return, was not unmindful of the commission thus given him, and when the religious visited the Orkneys, he received them with great affection, and granted to them every privilege that they desired.

In the famous poem composed by Dallan Forghaill,

the chief poet of Erin, in praise of St. Columba, special mention is made of the voice of our saint as being strong and sweet and sonorous to a most remarkable degree. Adamnan, indeed, mentions it as a miraculous gift, that whilst to those who recited the divine office with him in the Church, his voice did not seem louder than that of others; yet at a distance of more than a quarter of a mile, it could be distinctly heard by the religious, so much so that they could mark each syllable of the verses which he chanted. In one of his missionary excursions St. Columba, whilst reposing with his companions outside the fortifications of the royal residence, not far from the borders of Lough Ness, chanted the psalms and hymns of vespers. The Druids coming near them did all they could to disturb them in their devotions, and to prevent God's praises being sung so close to the head quarters of their Pagan superstition. Seeing their intent, the holy man began to sing the 44th Psalm, "*Eructavit cor meum verbum bonum : dico ego opera mea regi*," and so wonderfully loud, like pealing thunder, did his voice become, that the Druids fled away, and the king and his attendants were filled with terror.

Although King Brude had renounced the worship of the false gods, nevertheless, the chief Druid, Broichan, who was his foster-father, did not cease to exercise great influence in the royal councils. St. Columba in one of his visits to Lough Ness, found that a poor Irish girl, a Christian, was among the slaves of Broichan. He urgently requested that she might be set free, but his request was rudely refused. St. Columba threatened the Druid with the judgments of God, but in vain. The saint accordingly took his departure, but had not proceeded far when Broichan became dangerously ill, being struck by an angel of God. Two messengers from the king hastened after our saint, informing him that the Irish slave had been released, and praying him to return and restore the Druid to health. Columba returned thanks to God for freeing the poor Christian girl from slavery, and taking up a pebble, blessed it, and gave it to some of his companions, telling them to return with the king's messenger, and to dip this pebble in a little water which they would give to drink to Broichan. The Druid drank of the water and was immediately healed. Adamnan tells us that the pebble thus blessed by Columba was afterwards preserved among the chief treasures of the king.

In the year 584 King Brude died, and Gartnaidh, a Christian chieftain of the Southern Picts, being summoned to succeed him, consolidated the work of St. Columba, and secured the permanent triumph of the Faith among the Picts. He fixed his royal seat at Abernethy, on the southern bank of the Tay, near its junction with the river Earn. Under the guidance of Columba he there erected a noble church, and dedicated it to God, under the invocation of St. Bridget.[1]

[1] St. Bridget's Church at Abernethy has long since disappeared, but a Round Tower, one of those venerable monuments so characteristic of our early Irish ecclesiastical architecture, remains still to mark the site. The tradition of Scotland is, that an earlier foundation had been made here by a Pictish prince, who, when an exile in Ireland in the beginning of the sixth century, had learned to venerate St. Bridget. It is also the tradition that nine holy virgins, nuns of St. Bridget's Community, died there within a few years, and were interred in the northern part of the Church. From the Registry of St. Andrew's it further appears that the Priors of Abernethy continued for many years to be chosen from the ranks of the Irish Clergy.

So untiring was our saint in his missionary toil, that, according to an ancient tradition, he founded no fewer than three hundred churches throughout Caledonia and the adjacent isles. At each of these he left one or more of his religious brethren, who carried out the instructions of their master, and perfected the work which he had begun. Modern research has discovered and registered the traces of at least ninety of these venerable foundations, and many are the holy associates of St. Columba who share with him the honours of the altar in the Scottish Calendars.

Upon the eastern coasts of Scotland, in the district now known as Beecham, various churches trace their origin to an Irish disciple of Columba named Drostan. When our saint, with some devoted disciples, was there announcing the glad tidings of the Gospel, he asked the *Mormaer*, or chief of the territory, to grant them a site on which to erect an oratory. This he indignantly refused, but his son fell dangerously ill, and he at once hastened after the missionaries, offering them the land which they required, and begging them to pray for the dying boy. They prayed, and the child was restored to health. The oratory was soon erected, and Columba, having blessed it, and installed there St. Drostan, proceeded onwards to evangelize other districts. When Drostan saw himself thus about to be separated from his loved master, he could not restrain his tears. But Columba, calling to mind the Gospel words, "He who sows in tears shall reap in joy," said to his disciple: "Let us call this place 'the Monastery of Tears,'" and the great abbey which was erected there, and for a thousand years was so replete with every blessing of earth and of heaven, always retained that name. After the death of St. Columba, the devoted Drostan betook himself to an eremitical life, and built a church at Glenesk, where he was famed for miracles and sanctity. The ancient Breviary of Aberdeen marks his festival on the 15th of December, and adds, that "his relics are preserved in a stone tomb at Aberdour, where many sick persons find relief."

St. Moluog, whose name is sometimes latinized Luanus, was one of the most successful missionary companions of St. Columba. He had been trained in the religious life by St. Comgall at Bangor. St. Bernard, recounting the glories of that great monastery, tells that Comgall was the father of many thousand monks: "Verily," he adds, "the place was holy and fruitful in saints, plentifully rendering a harvest to God, so that one of the sons of that sacred family, Luanus by name, is said himself alone to be the founder of one hundred monasteries. And this I state that from this example the reader may conjecture how great was the multitude of the rest. Finally, their schools so filled both Ireland and Scotland, that these verses of David seem to have predicted those very times:—Visitasti terram, et inebriasti eam : multiplicasti locupletare eam . . . Rivos ejus inebria, multiplica genimina ejus: in stilicidiis ejus laetabitur germinans."—Ps. lxiv. 10. St. Moluog founded the great monastery of Lismore in Scotland, and his church became, in after times, the cathedral of the diocese of Argyll. His bell was held in great veneration there till the time of the Reformation, and his pastoral staff passed into the possession of the Duke of Argyll, in whose collection it is still preserved. St. Ængus in his Feliré, or Metrical Catalogue of Saints, styles him, "Luoc the pure and brilliant, the sun of Lismore in Alba." Marianus O'Gorman also commemorates him as, "Moluoc the hospitable and decorous, from Lismore in Alba."—(Colgan, *Trias*, pag. 481). The Martyrology of Aberdeen declares him to have been "full of the spirit of prophecy," and the ancient Breviary of Aberdeen relates that on the Scottish coast "he preached and built many churches in honour of God and His Mother Mary." He died before St. Columba, on the 25th June, 592.

St. Donnan was already mature in sanctity when he came from Ireland to Iona. After being some time there, he prayed St. Columba to become his *Anmchara, i.e.*, his soul's friend or confessor. St. Columba replied that he was not worthy to become the soul's-friend of one who was chosen to receive the martyr's crown, thus prophetically announcing that Donnan was predestined to glorify God by martyrdom. He erected a monastery in the Island of Eig, and such was its fame for piety and discipline, that many religious came from Ireland to enrol themselves among its members. On Sunday, the 17th April, 617, a body of Picts, instigated by one of the neighbouring chieftains, surrounded the oratory at Eig, whilst St. Donnan, assisted by his fifty-two religious brethren, was solemnly offering up the Holy Sacrifice of the Mass. Only one request was made by the venerable abbot, viz., that, as they were offering sacrifice to God, they would be permitted to finish the sacred rite. This the Picts acceded to, and when the Holy Sacrifice was ended at the altar, the religious joyfully offered themselves a sacrifice to the Most High, and all received the martyr's crown. In after times, this monastery of Irish monks was renewed at Eig, and at least four successors of St. Donnan are named in our Irish Calendars. St. Donnan's Well is still pointed out in the island: other memorials are preserved at Kildonan, on the banks of the Helmsdale river, in the valley called Strath-hill, and his pastoral or abbatial staff was held in great veneration at Husterless, an island parish of Aberdeenshire, but was broken and destroyed by the so-called Reformers.[1]

Popular tradition also reckons St. Moelisa, or Molios, among the illustrious Irish companions of St. Columba. He preached the faith in various parts of Scotland, but chose a cave in the west of Arran, off the Scottish coast, as his chief place of retirement, and there he spent whole days in prayer and penance. The Arran islanders honour him as their patron: his hermitage was for centuries a famous resort of pilgrims from the mainland and the adjoining islands, and the names of

[1] The Martyrology of Tallaght gives the names of the martyred religious of Eig as follows, on the 17th April: Donnani Egha cum sociis ejus LII: hi sunt Aedani: Tarloga bis: Mairie: Congaile: Lonain: Mac Lasre: Johain bis: Ernain: Ernini: Baethini: Rotain: Andrlog: Carillog: Rotain: Fergusain: Rectaire: Connidi: Endae: Mac Loga: Guretii: Juncti: Corani: Baetani: Colmain: Ternlugi: Lugedo: Luctai: Gracind: Cucalini: Cobrain: Conmind: Cummini: Baltiani: Senaig: Demmain: Cummeni: Tarlugi: Finani: Findchain: Findchon: Cronani: Modomma: Cronain: Ciarian: Colmain: Naummi: Demmani: Ernini: Ailchon: Domnani." (From the original vellum MS. now preserved among the St. Isidore's MSS.) The original MS. of the Tallaght Martyrology has further, on the 19th of April, the following entry which is omitted in the printed text: "Communis solemnitas omnium sanctorum et virginum Hiberniae et Brittaniae et totius Europae, et specialiter in honorem sancti Martini Episcopi. Et familiae Ego elivatio." Again, on the 30th April, it has:—"Familiae Ega, ut alii dicunt."

many of these pious votaries of our Saint remain rudely scratched on the sandstone roof. The cave of St. Molios looks out upon the sea, and is scooped in the rock about twenty-five feet above the present sea level. A few yards to the south, a square block of red sandstone is called " his resting-place," whilst a shelf cut in the hard rock in the side of the cave is still called his bed. Near the cave is the saint's well, of purest crystal water, to which the Arran people still have recourse for its healing virtues.

Another disciple of St. Columba was the bishop and confessor St. Finnan, who gives name to the romantic glen of Glenfinnane. On a small green island in the adjacent loch, are the venerable ruins of a monastery founded by him, and its rude bell, said to have been used by the Saint to assemble the religious and faithful to the service of God, is still preserved there. A beautiful new church, under the invocation of our Blessed Lady and St. Finnan, was solemnly dedicated here to the service of God, in the month of August, 1873.

To St. Mochonna, also called St. Machar, of whom we have already spoken, is traced back the first foundation of the church of Aberdeen. He was sent with twelve companions by St. Columba to preach the Gospel on the eastern coast, and he was instructed to erect his monastery and church on the banks of a river, which, in its windings, would resemble the figure of a bishop's crozier. Mochonna found the wished-for site near the mouth of the river Don, and there erected his oratory and cell, which, in after times, became the Cathedral of Aberdeen, dedicated to God under the invocation of our saint. And so the wildest districts of Scotland, and the most remote of its islands, were visited and sanctified by the preaching of the disciples of Columba. We meet with their memorials in the steep and almost inaccessible island of St. Kilda, and their traditions still linger in the Hebrides and even in the far-distant Shetland Islands.

We have already seen how Columba chose SS. Comgall and Canice for his companions when he paid his first memorable visit to King Brude. These saints are said by our ancient writers to have been connected by parentage with the Irish Cruithneach or Picts, and hence it may be supposed they were more familiar than Columba with the dialect of the Caledonian Picts. Adamnan, on another occasion, mentions that when the holy mysteries were celebrated by Columba on the Island of Hinba, there were present the same SS. Comgall and Canice, as also St. Brendan and St. Cormac. These four Irish saints are styled by Adamnan "founders of monasteries," and all four are honoured among the patrons of Scotland.

St. Comgall, who erected his famous monastery at Bangor, in the year 558, was visited there by St. Columba when preparing for his mission to Scotland, and some of the chief companions of our saint seem to have been chosen from that great monastery. Bangor was, indeed, a great seminary of missionary saints, and we find St. Comgall eulogized in the Martyrology of Donegal as one "who fostered and educated very many other saints, and kindled and lighted up an unquenchable love of God in the hearts and minds of men." His chief Scottish foundation was in the Island of Tiree, where he built an oratory in 568. One curious fact in connection with this Scottish settlement is recorded in his Life. While he was working in the fields at Tiree, he put his white hood over his garment. It happened that some heathen plunderers from the Picts came on that day to ravage the island. They seized on everything that was there, whether man or beast, but when about to lay hands on St. Comgall, they feared that the white hood might be his Deity, and, struck with fear, they fled from him. They carried off, however, all the brethren of the monastery, and all their substance. The plunderers, at the prayers of Comgall, were shipwrecked on the coast, and they then humbly came back to the saint, restoring to him their plunder. Soon after, holy men from Ireland came and induced St. Comgall to return to Bangor.

St. Canice's zeal and devoted toil were no less fruitful in Caledonia than in Ossory. He erected an oratory in Tiree island, and the ruins of an ancient church, still called Kill-Chainnech, probably mark its site. He also erected cells in the Island of Ibdon and Eninis (*i.e.*, Island of Birds), and his memory was cherished there in after times. He was honoured even in Iona, where a burial ground still retains the name Kill-Chainnech. On the mainland he built for himself a rude hermitage at the foot of a mountain, in the Drumalban, or Grampian range, and we meet at the present day, fully corresponding to this description, towards the east end of Loch Laggan, the remains of an ancient church, called Laggan-Kenney, *i.e.*, St. Kenney's Church, at Laggan. It is probably to this hermitage that the life of St. Canice refers when it tells us that the saints of Erin, being unwilling to be deprived of the prayers and counsel of St. Canice, sent messengers to him to Alba, praying him to return to his own country. They found him, adds the life, "living as a hermit in Britain, and Canice was then brought from his hermitage against his will." (*Vita*, cap. 19). He founded also a monastery in the east end of the province of Fife, not far from where the River Eden pours its waters into the German Ocean. This place was then called *Rig-Monadh*, or the Royal Mound; and when in after times the noble Cathedral of St. Andrew's was erected on the site thus first hallowed by the Irish saint, we find that it continued for centuries to retain its Celtic name of Kilrimont, by which it is designated in the early charters. The Feliré of St. Ængus contains in its notes on St. Canice's feast at 11th October, a reference to this foundation in Alba: "Achadhbo is his principal church, and he has a Recles, *i.e.*, a monastery at Cill-Rigmonaig in Alba." In many other places St. Canice seems to have erected cells or oratories. Of Maiden castle, in Fife, Boece writes that in his time the remains of the great enclosed monastery, in which the religious brethren of St. Canice had lived for centuries, could easily be traced. Indeed, so many places retain his name and cherish his memory, that Scottish writers have not hesitated to pronounce him, after St. Brigid and St. Columba, "the favourite Irish saint in Scotland "—*Forbes*' Calendars, pag. 297.

St. Brendan, so famed for his seven years' pilgrimage by sea, also laboured for some time in Scotland. He was specially honoured in "the royal Island of Bute"— as the Martyrology of Aberdeen styles it. Eassie, in Forfarshire, was dedicated to him, as was Kilbrandon in the Island of Seil, and also Culbrandon, *i.e.*, St. Brendan's retreat, an island in the Garvelock group, and at least a dozen other places in various districts in Scotland.

St. Cormac was one of those *milites Christi*, or soldiers of Christ, for whom St. Columba secured a friendly welcome at the Orkney Islands, through the authority of King Brude. Three times, as Adamnan relates, St. Cormac betook himself to a long voyage by sea in search of some desert island on which to found a hermitage, that by prayer and penitential exercises, he might there find his paradise. In his third journey he was exposed to special danger. In his frail coracle he was driven northward in a storm, fourteen days' sail, to regions hitherto unexplored, and what increased his peril, the sea was full of a sort of jelly-fish, which he had never before seen. Adamnan calls them "foul little stinging creatures, of the size of frogs," and adds, that they not only clung to the oar blades, but even beat with violence against the sides of the boat in which Cormac and his companions were, and which they expected every moment to be stove in. No wonder that the good monks were filled with alarm, and watered their cheeks with floods of tears, but Columba, far away in his island home at Iona, had a vision of all that they suffered, and summoning together the whole community, bade them pray for their struggling brethren at sea. In response to their prayers a north wind sprung up, which in a few days blew Cormac safe back to Iona, to tempt the waves no more. St. Cormac is one of the chief patrons of the Hebrides, and he is said to have died in Orkney. A short distance from the shore of South Knapdale, in Argyllshire, opposite to the old church of Kilmory, and its wonderful sculptured monuments, is a small island which is still called the "Island of the Great Cormac," and in one of the compartments of its ancient chapel is preserved a recumbent statue of the saint. In our Irish church he was known as "Cormac of the sea, of spotless purity;" he is commemorated on the 21st of June, and is styled Abbot of Durrow, and Bishop and Anchorite. He appears to have been specially beloved by his great master Columba, and it was to him that Columba addressed the remarkable words:

> "Death is better in reproachless Erin
> Than perpetual life in Alba."

The island of Hinba, where Columba and these four saints met, has been of late identified with a small island called Elachnave, a corrupt form of the name "Eileann-na-naoimh," *i.e.*, "the little island of the saints," which is situated to the south of Iona, in the broad channel which separates Mull from the coast of Lorne. No spot could have been better chosen by these great men of God for spiritual conference. M'Culloch has recorded his impressions on visiting it in 1824. On traversing it, he says: "I was surprised at the irregularity and beauty of a spot which seemed at a distance to be a bare hill, and of which, even from the creek where our boat was drawn up, no conjecture could have been formed. Surmounting one ridge after another, a succession of secluded valleys appeared, which, although without other wood than a few scattered bushes, were beautifully dispersed, and were interesting no less by their silence and seclusion than by the intermixture of rock and green pasture. It was impossible to imagine that we were here on a narrow spot surrounded by a wild sea, and far remote from the land: no sound of winds or waves, nor sight of water, interfering with the tranquillity and retirement of scenes which made us forget that the boisterous ocean was breaking all round." —(*Highlands*, &c., ii., 124). Several interesting ruins are clustered together to the south-east of the island, and its beehive cells, which bear a striking resemblance to the primitive cells of the western coast of Ireland, and its oratory constructed of rude masonry, without lime or cement of any kind, betoken an age coeval with St. Columba. At the head of the narrow creek where the landing is usually made, is a little well which bears the name of Columba, and which tradition says he "fashioned and fructified in the living rock." In a sheltered grassy hollow, there is an ancient cemetery; its rude headstones give evidence of a great age, but they have no inscriptions, and only one has a cross incised. On the face of the south slope of this cemetery large stones are piled together like a rude altar, and close by is a square pillar stone, also bearing an incised cross, and locally regarded as marking the tomb of Eithne, mother of St. Columba. How solemn must have been the scene when the great apostle of Caledonia, standing at that rude altar raised by his own hands on the hill side, under the broad canopy of heaven, offered to God the Holy Sacrifice, assisted by such holy men as Canice and Cormac, Brendan and Comgall.

To his own countrymen in the Scottish Kingdom of Dalriada, St. Columba was at the same time apostle, father, and legislator. When Conall, king of Dalriada, died in 574, the succession, according to the law of

Tanistry, would have devolved on Eogan, son of Gabhran. But though he was loved by our saint with special affection, Columba announced to the assembled chieftains that an angel had commanded him in vision to select as sovereign Aidan, a younger brother of Eogan. The angel he said held in his hand "a book of crystal containing the appointment of kings on which the name of Aidan was inscribed," and said: "Know for certain that I am sent to thee by God, that in accordance with the words written in this book thou mayest inaugurate Aidan into the kingdom." Aidan was at once chosen king, and when he hastened to Iona to receive the blessing of the holy abbot, St. Columba, according to the rite shown him by the angel, laid his hands upon his head and consecrated and blessed him and ordained him king. This is the first instance of kingly consecration recorded in authentic history. Some modern writers, with Baring-Gould, in his life of our saint, and Smith, in his "Dictionary of Christian Antiquities," in the article on "*Coronation,*" inform us that Columba, on this occasion, enthroned Aidan on the celebrated stone of destiny, which was taken afterwards from Iona to Dunstaffnage castle, upon the coast of Argyll, and thence to the abbey of Scone, and was finally carried away by Edward the First to Westminster, where it still serves as a pedestal for the throne of the kings of England on the day of their coronation. All this, however, is mere fable, which originated with Hector Boece, and has long since been exploded by the learned Scottish antiquaries.

To place on a permanent footing, and to secure the independence of this Scottish Kingdom of Dalriada, St. Columba soon after set out for Ireland, to assist at the great convention of the Irish clergy and princes which was summoned by Aedh, son of Ainmire, monarch of Ireland, to meet at Drumceatt, in the year 575. This great national convention was held in the county of Londonderry, on the banks of the Roe, about two miles from Newtownlimavady. The precise spot at which the assembly met cannot be fixed for certainty, for whilst some of our antiquaries place Drumceatt at Enagh, on the north side of the river, others mark out its site at Mullagh, in Roe Park on the southern side. It was at all events not far distant from Columba's great monastery at Derry, and as several matters of the deepest interest to our saint were to be deliberated on at the assembly, he resolved to proceed thither with a most imposing retinue. The contemporary chief-poet of Erin, Dallan Forghaill, who himself was present at this convention, tells us that Columba went thither accompanied not only by Aidan, the newly consecrated king of Dalriada, but also by "twenty noble worthy Bishops, forty Priests, fifty Deacons, and thirty Students." When Columba came to the assembly all rose up before him to reverence and welcome him. At his request, the Irish monarch renounced all sovereignty over the Kingdom of Dalriada in Alba, and whilst independence and freedom from tribute were thus guaranteed to the Scoto-Irish colonists, they on their part pledged themselves to a perpetual alliance, maritime expeditions being alone excepted, with their Irish countrymen.

There was another subject to be considered at this convention which also enlisted all the sympathies of Columba. The bards had long been a privileged class in Erin. They were at once the poets and genealogists, the musicians and historians of the nation. They were invested with many special privileges, whilst favours were heaped on them alike by princes and people. One of their privileges, however, called *conmed*, which gave them a right to exact refection from the tribes for themselves and their retinue, gave occasion to many complaints. Their great power, too, and their excessive number, had produced great abuses, and so many accusations had been made against them of insatiable greed and insolence, that the Irish monarch deemed himself sufficiently strong to propose to the assembly at Drumceatt, that the troublesome order should be at length suppressed, and all the bards be banished from the kingdom. Columba, who was himself a poet, undertook their defence, and pleaded their cause with eloquence and success. The king and the whole assembly yielded to his earnest pleadings, the bards were spared, but it was decreed that their number should thenceforth be limited, and that their privileges should be restricted by certain rules, to be drawn up by Columba himself. The bards on their part vowed an undying gratitude to their great patron, and the chief poet composed on this occasion his celebrated *Amhra*, or Eulogy of St. Columbkille; but the saint saying that only the dead should receive praise, imposed silence upon him, and forbade him to repeat this poem so long as he himself should remain in the land of the living.

There was a third matter in which Columba and his friend St. Canice were deeply interested: this was the release of Scannlan-More, king of Ossory, who seems to have been put in bonds for refusing to pay the customary tribute to the monarch. St. Columba failed to procure the immediate liberation of this prince, but he consoled him by the prophecy that he would soon be released, and would then rule for thirty years over his people. As a pledge that this prophecy would not be in vain, he gave to the prisoner the pastoral staff which he had brought with him from Iona, which in aftertimes was preserved as a most precious treasure in the saint's monastery at Durrow.[1]

This visit to Ireland and its assembled clergy and princes, many of whom were so dear to him, awakened the liveliest emotions in Columba's soul, for he had ever loved Erin and its people with the deepest love, and this love of country, instead of growing cold by his voluntary exile in Iona, became rather intensified in a most ardent affection. It was, perhaps, on his return to his island home from Drumceatt that he composed the beautiful poem on Ireland, setting forth the romantic charms of its cliffs and scenery, and expressing the delight which would overflow his soul were it once more given him to visit its beloved shores :—

"What joy to fly upon the white-crested sea, and to watch the waves that break upon the Irish shore! What joy to row the little barque and to land amid the whitening foam upon the Irish coast! Ah! how my boat would fly if its prow were turned to my Irish oak-grove (*i.e.*, to Derry). But the noble sea now carries me only to Alba, the land of ravens. There is a grey eye which ever turns to Erin. From the high prow I look over the sea, and great tears are in my eyes when I turn to Erin,—to Erin where the songs of the birds are so sweet, and where the priests sing like the birds; where the young are so gentle and the old so wise. Noble youth, take my prayer with thee and my blessing, one half for Ireland—sevenfold may she be blessed ; and the other half for Alba. Carry my blessing across the sea, carry it to the west. My heart is broken in my breast; if death comes to me soon, it will be because of the great love which I bear to the Gael."

---

[1] Keating (O'Mahony's Translation), says that this Pastoral Staff of St. Columba was preserved in the church of Durrow in Ossory.

In Columba's dealings with the penitents and pilgrims who flocked to Iona, as detailed by Adamnan, we easily recognise the same passionate love for his native land. The severest penance that he can devise for the guiltiest sinners is—never again to set foot upon Irish soil; but when exhorting others to return home, as if he feared his own emotions should he pronounce the name of Erin, he tells them: you will return to the country that you love. It was on the monastery of Derry, however, that his affections were chiefly centred, and it is probable that after the Convention of Drumceatt he remained there for some time with his loved religious. He beautifully gives expression to his esteem for this monastery in one of his poems :—

> "Were the tribute of all Alba mine,
> From its centre to its border,
> I would prefer the site of one cell
> In the middle of fair Derry.
>
> The reason I love Derry is,
> For its quietness, for its purity;
> And for its crowds of bright angels
> From the one end to the other.
>
> The reason why I love Derry is,
> For its quietness, for its purity;
> Crowded full of heaven's angels
> Is every leaf of the oaks of Derry.
>
> My Derry, my little oak-grove
> My abode and my little cell:
> O eternal God, in heaven above,
> Woe be to him who violates it."

With such an unbounded affection for the land of his birth, and with an unquenchable zeal for the spiritual

welfare of his countrymen, it cannot surprise us that
the Dalriadans were docile to his instructions, and
received his precepts with joy, and welcomed as angels
of heaven the religious whom he sent among them.
At the same time he was not blind to their faults, and
punished them with severity when he found them obdu-
rate in their crimes. One instance will suffice. On the
wild and barren peninsula of Ardnamurchan, a rocky
mass which rises up out of the waves of the Atlantic,
and forms the most western point of the Scottish mainland, there was a poor man, to whom the blessing
of Columba had brought a manifold good fortune.
Through gratitude he had assumed the name of his
benefactor, and his neighbours called him Columbian,
"the friend of Columba." A Scottish petty chieftain
had twice plundered with impunity the home and the
lands of this friend of the Abbot of Iona. A third time
he set out on the same career of pillage, and landing
with his attendants, seized on everything that Columbian possessed. Whilst laden with booty they were
returning to their boat, St. Columba presented himself
before them, and having reproved them for their many
crimes, entreated them to restore their plunder. They
remained silent till they gained the beach and entered
the boat, but then they began to answer the abbot's
prayers by mockeries and insults. The saint, however,
did not cease his entreaties, and following them into the
sea, up to his knees, he warned them not to inflict this
injury on his poor friend; and when the boat moved off
he remained there for a time motionless, bathed in tears,
and with hands uplifted to heaven. Returning to some
of his companions, who were seated on a neighbouring

mound, he said to them: "This miserable man shall never more land upon the shore from which you have seen him depart." Whilst he thus spoke a little cloud appeared on the horizon, and gradually it grew into a tempest, from which the spoilers sought in vain to escape. The storm reached them between the islands of Mull and Colonsay, and their boat perished, with all its crew and all its spoils.

St. Columba frequently visited the King of Dalriada, who was ever anxious to receive his counsel. One day Aidan presented his eldest son to receive the abbot's blessing. Columba, however, was not satisfied with seeing only the eldest. "Have you none younger," he asked, and then added, "Bring them all, that I may fold them in my arms and on my heart." When the younger children were brought, one fair-haired boy, Eochaidh-Buidhe, came forward running, and threw himself upon the knees of the holy abbot. Columba held him long pressed to his heart, then kissed his forehead, and blessed him, prophesying for him a long and prosperous reign, and a happy posterity.

It was towards the close of his missionary career that St. Columba paid a visit to the great apostle of the Strathclyde kingdom, St. Kentigern. This venerable man, famed for his sanctity of life, and for the many trials he had undergone in the sacred cause of the Christian Faith, had at this time erected his church on the banks of the Molendinor Burn, where the cathedral of Glasgow now stands. Thither Columba proceeded, accompanied by several of his religious brethren, and advancing along the banks of the stream they chanted the 84th Psalm—" The saints shall advance from virtue to virtue, until the God of Gods be seen in Sion." St. Kentigern on his part summoned together the clergy and people to welcome the holy visitors, and marshalling a procession in which the children came first, and then the more advanced in years, and last of all the holy bishop himself with his senior clergy, all sang the 138th Psalm—"In the ways of the Lord, how great is the glory of the Lord," with the versicle of Isaiah, "The way of the just is made straight, and the path of the saints is prepared."—(xxvi. 7). Whilst they were yet at a distance, Columba saw a golden crown of heavenly light, set with sparkling gems, descending on the head of St. Kentigern, and he said to those around him: "It is given to me to know that, like Aaron, he is the elect of God, for, clothed with light as with a garment, and bearing a golden crown, he appeareth to me with the sign of sanctity." When they met, the holy men mutually embraced and gave the kiss of peace, and remained for a long time speaking of those things of heaven which were nearest to their own hearts, and taking counsel together regarding the interests of their people. On parting they interchanged their pastoral staffs in pledge and testimony of their mutual love in Christ; and the ancient record adds, that "the staff which St. Columba gave to the holy Bishop Kentigern was preserved for a long time in St. Wilfrid's church at Ripon, and held in great reverence on account of the sanctity of him who gave it and of him who received it."[1]

It was at this time, too, that, as an ancient and venerable tradition attests, Columba made a pilgrimage to

[1] See the Life of Saint Kentigern, in the 'Histories of Scotland, vol. v. p. 109: Edinburgh, 1874.

Rome to visit the illustrious Pontiff St. Gregory the Great, who then sat in the chair of Saint Peter. This tradition is referred to in the Irish life of St. Columba, and is registered in the life of St. Mochonna, and other ancient records: and when I resided some years ago in the Holy City, I found to my surprise that the old guides of the Vatican still preserved the same tradition, and pointed out in the ancient Basilica of St. Peter's, the spot on which the great Pontiff St. Gregory had given the kiss of peace to the venerable Irish pilgrim. Some time after his return from Rome, whilst our holy abbot was alone with Baithene on the island of Iona, seven religious arrived there from the holy city, delegated by St. Gregory to present a collection of Latin Vesper Hymns and other precious gifts to Columba.[1] Among these gifts there was one which in after times was famous as "the great gem of Columbkille." It was shaped in the form of a cross, and, after being held in religious veneration for centuries by the community of Iona, was transferred to the monastery of Tory Island, off the coast of Donegal, where it was still preserved in the sixteenth century.[2] Columba, in return, bestowed many gifts on the Roman visitors, and he prayed them to present to the great Pontiff the hymn "Altus prosator," which he had composed some time before, and which, the ancient record adds, was gratefully received and highly praised by St. Gregory. Thus Columba's fame

---

[1] This fact is recorded in the Preface to the hymn 'Altus,' composed by St. Columba, and preserved in the Leabhar Breac, and in the two ancient MSS. of the 'Liber Hymnorum' in the Library of T.C.D., and in the Saint Isidore's Collection.

[2] *Colgan*, Trias, p. 412; *Reeves*, Adamnan, p. 318.

was spread to distant churches, and Adamnan reckons it among the favours granted to our saint by God, that "though he lived in a small and remote island of the British sea, yet his name is honoured, not only throughout the whole of our own Ireland and in Britain, but even in Spain and Gaul: and the renown of his sanctity hath also penetrated beyond the Alpine range into Italy, and into the city of Rome itself, which is the head of all cities."[1]

It was probably towards the close of his apostolate that St. Columba founded an oratory and monastery in the island of Emona near the northern shores of the Firth of Forth, and within sight of Edinburgh, known in later times as Inchcolm, "St. Columba's island." This monastery was intended to serve as a centre for the various missions extending along the eastern coast of Scotland, and although it never attained the importance or the fame of the parent house of Iona, yet for a thousand years it continued to dispense the manifold blessings of religion to all the surrounding territory. The island is of very small extent, about half a mile in length and 400 feet in width at its broadest part. "The tide of commerce and busy life which ebbs and flows around has left the little Inch in a solitude as profound as if it had gemmed the bosom of some Highland loch, a solitude which impresses itself deeply on the stranger who comes to gaze on its ruined, deserted, and forgotten abbey. Few, even of those who visit the island from the beautiful village of Aberdour, close to it, know anything of its history, and as few out of sight of the island know of its existence at all. But although now little known beyond the shores of the Forth, Inchcolm for-

[1] "Quae caput est omnium civitatum." *Adamnan*, iii. 24.

merly held a high place in the veneration of the Scottish people as the cradle of the religious life of the surrounding districts, and was second only to Iona as a holy isle in whose sacred soil it was the desire of many generations to be buried. It numbered amongst its abbots men of high position and learning. Noble benefactors enriched it with broad lands and rich gifts, and its history and remains, like the strata of some old mountain, bear the marks of every great wave of life which has passed over our country. Picts, Scots, Danes, and English have all been associated with the chequered history of the lonely island, where lie the bones of saints and nobles, monks and soldiers, the patrons, the brethren, and the spoilers of its ancient church, mingled together in this Iona of the east. Apart from the interest arising from such associations, this venerable monastery, notwithstanding that tempest, wars, and ruthless vandalism have laid much of it in ruins, still preserves more of its original plan than any abbey in Scotland, presenting many peculiarities of arrangement to be found in no other building of the kind in Britain. From the position of Inchcolm in the centre of the mediæval as of the modern life of Scotland, it maintained its ancient importance long after many of the famous houses of the primitive Scottish church had fallen into decay, but for the same reason it suffered much from the hostile fleets which made piratical expeditions to the Forth, or were employed in conjunction with an invading force on shore."[1] In the beginning of

---

[1] *Arnold*, 'An Account of St. Columba's Abbey, Inchcolm,' in Transactions of the Society of Antiquaries of Scotland, vol. v., 1874, p. 45.

the twelfth century the abbey buildings were erected here in princely style in fulfilment of a vow by King Alexander the First. Fordun relates that the king when crossing the Ferry "was overtaken by a fierce tempest, blowing from the south, so that the sailors were compelled to make for the island of Aemonia, where there lived a solitary hermit, who devoted himself to the service or rule of St. Columba, living in a cell, and supporting himself on the milk of a cow, and the shell-fish which he collected on the shore. On these things the king and his companions subsisted for three days, during which they were detained by the storm. But when in the greatest peril of the sea and the raging tempest, when fearing and despairing for their lives, the king made a vow to the saint, that if he would bring them safe to that island, he would there found a monastery to his honour, which would become an asylum and refuge for sailors and shipwrecked persons."[1] Beside the ruins of the noble abbey still stands the clochan, or stone-roofed cell, erected by St. Columba. The holy well of the saint, and a fragment of a stone cross with interlaced Celtic ornaments, are the only other memorials of the holy founder that now remain in the island.

So attractive, nay, so charming, is the life of this great apostle of Caledonia, that we are tempted to linger on its most minute details. We must, however, hurry on, and I will merely add a few instances of the special virtues and heavenly favours which marked the close of his blessed life.

Adamnan particularly records that St. Columba was

[1] *Scotichronicon*, lib. v. chap. 37.

favoured with angelic visions. One morning he said to the brethren : " I would be alone to-day in the little plain to the west of the island ; let no one follow me." A brother, more curious than the rest, disobeyed, and following him at a distance, saw him standing on a little mound, erect and motionless, whilst a crowd of angels came down to converse with him. This hillock was known in Adamnan's time as " The Angels' Hill," and it retains the same name at the present day,

As he approached the end of his penitential life, he seemed to redouble his vigils, fasts, and other austerities, thus to make his soul more pure, and to lay up a better store of merits for heaven. On one occasion he went to a neighbouring island to seek greater retirement in prayer. He met there a poor woman gathering wild herbs and nettles, who told him that her poverty forbade her any other food. The holy man at once reproached himself that, though professing a life of penance, he was surpassed in austerities by this poor woman. Thenceforth he would use no other food but wild and bitter herbs, and he severely reproved his attendant Diarmaid, who, out of compassion for his master's old age and infirmities, wished to mix a little condiment with such penitential fare.

The celestial light which was soon to be the eternal reward of his happy soul was granted to him by anticipation during the closing years of his life, and at times it invested him even as a golden and radiant garment, especially when he was engaged in prayer. He had built for himself a solitary cell in the Isle of Hinba, near Iona, and the religious, who stealthily kept watch around it, repeatedly observed that the cell was lighted up with surpassing brilliancy, whilst the saint chanted spiritual canticles or remained entranced by God. One night a religious, who was destined to succeed our saint as fourth abbot of Iona, remained in the church of the monastery whilst the others slept, and there he was privileged to see Columba enter the church, preceded by a golden light, which filled the whole church, even to the heights of the vaulted roof, and to the recesses of the lateral oratory in which he himself lay concealed. Those who passed near the church during the night, while the holy abbot prayed, were dazzled by the brilliancy of this sacred light: but the young religious kept his secret till after the saint's decease.

More than once Columba sighed to be freed from the bonds of the flesh, but it was hard for him to contend against the love of his disciples and their fervent prayers. Whilst two of the brethren assisted him one day, they saw his countenance suddenly change. At first it was filled with a beatific joy, and he raised to heaven a look of the sweetest and tenderest gratitude; but on a sudden this ray of supernatural delight was succeeded by an expression of profound sadness. They prayed him with tears not to conceal from them the revelation which he had received. "Dear children," he at length replied, "know that it is thirty years to-day since I began my pilgrimage in Alba. I have long prayed to God to let my pilgrimage end with this thirtieth year, and to recall me to the heavenly country. When I was filled with joy, it was because I saw the angels coming down to receive my soul. But I was saddened when they stopped in their course, for it pleased God to hear rather the prayers of the brethren, and to direct that I should still dwell in this body for four years."

These years, however, passed quickly on, and now the time was come for our saint to receive his heavenly reward. Towards the end of May, in 597, he wished to visit the western part of the island to take leave of the monks who were working there. Being unable through age to proceed on foot, he was drawn thither in a car by oxen. When the religious brethren had gathered around him he said: "I greatly desired to depart to Christ a month ago on Easter-day, but I feared lest that joyous festival might be changed into a day of mourning and of sadness for you. Now my time is at hand." And when they all wept he addressed words of consolation to them, and turning towards the east he prayed a blessing on the whole island and on those who dwelt in it. The following Sunday, the 2nd of June, he offered up with solemnity the holy sacrifice of the Mass, and as his eyes were raised to heaven, the brethren observed a sudden expression of rapture on his face. When interrogated by them, he told them that he had seen an angel coming from heaven to bring some soul to God, and the angel had looked down upon the brethren as they were assembled around the altar and blessed them. The following Saturday Columba went, leaning on his faithful attendant Diarmaid, to bless the granary of the monastery, and then uttered the prophetic words: "This day is called in the Sacred Scriptures the Sabbath or day of rest, and it shall truly be my resting-day, for in it I shall repose after the fatigue of my labours, and this very night I shall follow in the way of my fathers. Thou weepest, Diarmaid, but console thyself. It is my Lord Jesus Christ who invites me to rejoin him: and He has revealed to me that my summons shall come this night."

As he returned homewards towards the monastery, he seated himself for a little time half-way, where a cross was afterwards erected, which Adamnan writes was still standing in his time at the road side, and, I may add, the spot is still marked by one of the ancient Celtic crosses of Iona. Whilst he sat there the old white horse of the monastery came up, and placing his head on the saint's bosom, by plaintive cries and tears expressed its grief. Diarmaid wished to drive the animal away, but Columba chiding him, said: "let it alone, it is so fond of me it pours out its bitter grief, for it knows that its master is going to leave it." He then ascended the hillock which adjoined the monastery, and standing there for a little time with hands uplifted to heaven, he blessed the whole monastery, and uttered the prophecy thus registered by Adamnan: "Small and low though this place is, yet it shall be held in great and unusual honour, not only by the Irish kings and people, but also by foreign chiefs and barbarous nations; and even the saints of the other churches shall regard it with no common reverence."

After this, descending from the hill, he entered his cell and began to work for the last time. He was then engaged in transcribing the Psalter, and having finished a page with these words of the 33rd Psalm, "*Inquirentes autem Dominum non deficient omni bono,*" "they who seek the Lord shall want nothing that is good," he paused and said: "I must stop here: let Baithen write what follows." Baithen was the saint's successor in the abbacy, and the verse which followed was most appropriate to the father of his spiritual children: "*Venite filii, audite me: timorem Domini docebo vos.*"

"Come, children, hearken to me: I will teach you the fear of the Lord."

Having laid aside the parchment, he entered the church of the monastery to recite the nocturnal vigils of the Lord's day; and when these prayers were said he returned to his cell and lay down on his couch, not so much for repose as to perform his usual penitential exercises for the last time, for his bed was now a bare flag, and a large stone served as his pillow; and whilst he reclined there he commended to his companion his last words: "This, dear children, is my last counsel to you! Let peace and unfeigned charity at all times remain among you: if you thus follow the example of the saints, the Lord, the comforter of the good, will be your helper; and I, dwelling with Him, will intercede for you, that He may bestow not only the temporal blessings which you may stand in need of, but still more, the rewards of eternal life." Having said these words, Columba remained in silence, but as soon as the bell was rung at midnight summoning the religious to prayers, he hastily arose, and running joyfully to the church entered it alone, and knelt down in prayer at the foot of the altar. Diarmaid, who slowly followed, saw at that moment the whole interior of the church filled with heavenly light, which however quickly disappeared; and when he entered the church he cried out in a plaintive voice, "Where art thou, my father?" and feeling his way in the darkness, for the brethren had not as yet entered with the lights, he found the saint lying before the altar, and raising him up a little, and sitting down beside him, he supported his holy head upon his bosom. Meantime the choir of monks came in, and beholding their father dying, whom they so loved, they began to weep. But Columba, once more lifting up his eyes with a wonderful expression of joy and gladness, welcomed the angels who came to receive his soul; and Diarmaid raising his hand, the venerable father made for the last time the sign of the cross over the assembled brethren, and having thus given them his holy benediction, his hand dropped down in death, but his countenance remained sweet and radiant, as if in sleep he enjoyed a vision of heaven.

Thus St. Columba died, on Sunday morning, the 9th of June, 597, after labouring for thirty-four years in his apostolate of North Britain.

CHAPTER IV.

THE SUCCESSORS OF ST. COLUMBA IN IONA.

St. Baethen:—SS. Laisren and Fergna: St. Cummian's Writings:—St. Adamnan's Visits to King Aldfrid:—The "Lex Innocentium:"—Adamnan's Works:—His fame for Sanctity:—Relics which he collected:—The Rule of Life observed in Iona:—The Mass:—Sign of the Cross:—Prayers for the Dead:—The Religious Habit:—Presbyterian Fallacies regarding Iona:—Succession of Abbots.

THE monastery of Iona presents to us the singular spectacle of an Irish missionary community which, though situated at a distance from the mother-land, and subject to a thousand hostile influences, yet, throughout a long period of six hundred years, retained its distinctive character, and preserved an unbroken succession of Irish abbots, who, walking in the footsteps of their founder, proved themselves filled with the spirit of God, and earnestly devoted to the observances of the religious life. The Venerable Bede, speaking of St. Columba, says: "This we know of him for certain, that he left successors distinguished for their great charity, divine love, and strict attention to the rules of discipline; following, indeed, uncertain cycles in their computation of the great festival of Easter, because, far away as they were out of the world, no one had supplied them with the synodal decrees relating to the Paschal observance; yet, withal, diligently observing such works of piety and charity as they could find in the Prophetic, Evangelic, and Apostolic writings."[1] The influence of Iona on the Scottish church did not cease with the death of St. Columba; on the contrary, the missions and monasteries which he had founded throughout Scotland continued to look to his successor in Iona as their head, and as Bede again records: "This monastery for a long time held the pre-eminence over most of those of the northern Scots, and all those of the Picts, and had the direction of their people."

St. Baethen, a near relative of St. Columba, was his immediate successor in the abbacy of Iona. Born in the year 536, he was one of the twelve companions chosen by the saint when setting sail for Britain. A little later he was appointed to preside over the monastery in the island of Tiree; and, at the close of St. Columba's life, we find him receiving the last dictations of the saint. From a narrative preserved in St. Columba's life, we

---

[1] *Bede*, Hist. Ecc. III., 4.

learn the high esteem in which St. Baethen was held by our early saints. We there read that the holy man St. Fintan Munnu, founder of Taghmon, burning with desire to visit Iona, went to an old friend, called in the Scotic tongue Columb Crag, the most prudent and venerable cleric in his country, to get some sound advice. He was counselled by him to cross the sea to St. Columba, but before he could take his departure, two monks of Iona arrived, who, when interrogated, "Is your holy father Columba well?" burst into tears, and answered with sorrow: "Our patron is, indeed, well; for a few days ago he departed to Christ." Hearing this, Fintan and Columb, and all who were there present, fell prostrate on the ground, and wept bitterly. Fintan then asked, "Whom did he leave as his successor?" "Baethen, his disciple," they replied; whereupon all cried out, "It is meet: it is right." And when Columb said to Fintan, "What wilt thou do now, Fintan?" he replied, "With God's permission, I will sail over to Baethan, that wise and holy man, and, if he receive me, I will take him as my abbot."[1] The Martyrology of Donegal numbers Baethen among the saints, and registers two anecdotes relating to him. When he partook of food, before each morsel he was wont to say, '*Deus in adjutorium meum intende.*' When he worked in the fields, gathering in the corn along with the monks, he used to hold up one hand towards heaven, beseeching God, while with the other hand he gathered the corn.

St. Laisren was the next abbot, being translated to

[1] Adamnan, I. 2.

Iona from the monastery of Durrow. He was followed by Fergna, who, though descended from the royal family of Conall Gulban, and closely allied to St. Columba, was surnamed 'the Briton' on account of his having sojourned from his early youth in the sister isle. He was specially beloved by St. Columba, and he was permitted to witness and participate in some of the heavenly visions of his master. He is styled a bishop in some of our ancient kalendars, being probably promoted towards the close of his life to the Episcopal dignity. The Festology of Aengus assigns the second of March to "The festival of Fergna, the fair, of Iona." It was during his abbacy that many of the young and noble Angles of Bernicia, flying from the sword of Aeduin, king of Deira, though yet pagans, took refuge in Iona: they were there instructed in the doctrines of the Faith, and regenerated by the grace of Baptism.[1]

Seghine and Snibhne were his successors, and then we meet with St. Cummian, who was a man of great learning, and is deservedly numbered among the most illustrious saints of Iona. He wrote a life of St. Columba, which has been published by Mabillon, but he is still more renowned for his letter[2] on the paschal controversy, addressed to the abbot Seghine, in which he displays a thorough knowledge of the Sacred Scriptures and the ecclesiastical writers, and an accurate study of the various cycles for the computation of Easter. He adds that he had consulted "the successors of our ancient fathers" in the Irish Church that they might

---

[1] *Bede*, Hist. Ecc., III., 1.
[2] Published by Usher, in " Sylloge," xi.

direct him as to the course he should pursue, and, they having assembled together at Magh-Lena, near Tullamore, "came to the resolution that they ought to adopt without scruple the most worthy and approved practice recommended to them by the successors of the Apostles of the Lord." Not long after, however, dissensions again arose: "wherefore," he writes, "it was determined by our seniors to act in accordance with the Synodical Decree, that if questions of a more weighty character arise they are to be referred to the head of cities; and they sent some whom they knew to be wise and humble to Rome, as children to their mother;" and, having had a prosperous journey by the will of God, they returned in the third year, attesting the discipline of the Holy See, and bearing with them rich treasures of the relics of the Apostles and the Martyrs of Christ. This letter is justly regarded as one of the most authentic and important documents that have been handed down to us from the golden ages of our country's faith, and we could desire no clearer record of the close bonds that united our Fathers with the Mother Church of Rome. In connection with the sacred treasures which the Irish pilgrims bore with them from Rome, St. Cummian writes that many miracles were performed through them: "with our own eyes," he says, "we have seen a girl quite blind, opening her eyes at these relics, and a paralytic walking, and many demons cast out." It is also recorded in the Martyrology of Cathal Maguir that St. Cummian founded a church at Disert-Chuimin, in the neighbourhood of Roscrea, and enriched it with relics of SS. Peter and Paul, which continued to be preserved there till, during the Danish invasion, they were translated to Roscrea.¹ The memory of St. Cummian is preserved in some of the old Scottish sanctuaries. Thus, Fort Augustus is, by the Celtic-speaking population, still called Kilchuimin, and the church of Glenealy is also known as St. Cummian's church.²

The next abbot of Iona was St. Failbhe, who is honoured in our Martyrologies on the 22nd of March; and after him came St. Adamnan, whose name is perhaps the brightest that adorns the long roll of the successors of St. Columba. He was born in Ireland, in the south-west of the county of Donegal, in the year 624. A legend connected with his early years represents him as receiving favour and protection from Finnachta, a chief of the southern Hy Niall, and subsequently monarch of Ireland. When the valiant and hospitable monarch ascended the throne, in the year 675, Adamnan, who had acquired great fame for learning and sanctity, was invited to his court to become his *anmchara* or confessor; and he remained there till summoned to the abbacy of Iona, on the death of Failbhe, in the year 679. Whilst abbot he repaired the monastery, sending twelve vessels to Lorn for oak trees to furnish the necessary timber. In this work, as Boece relates, he was aided by Maelduin, king of Dalriada, whose death is recorded by Tighernac in the year 590. On two occasions Adamnan proceeded to the court of King Aldfrid of Northumbria. This Prince had lived for many years in exile in Ireland, and Adamnan had become acquainted

---

[1] "Cumineus Abbas Hiensis: ipse est qui tulit reliquias sanctorum Petri et Pauli ad Desertum Cumini in districtu Roscreensi," ap. *Colgan*, Acta SS., pag. 411, n. 26.

[2] *Forbes*, Kalendars, pag. 317.

with him at the court of the Irish monarch; some Irish records even add that he was for some time tutor of Aldfrid, and the intimacy which he thus contracted with him proved serviceable to Ireland in after times. One of the Saxon generals, during Ecgfrid's reign, having landed a body of troops on the Irish coast, had plundered the fertile plain of Magh-Bregha as far as Bealach-duin, and carried off a large number of men and women into captivity. When, soon after, Ecgfrid set out on the fatal expedition against the Picts, in the year 685, he is said by our annalists to have met with his death and overthrow in punishment of the cruelty he had shown to the unoffending inhabitants of Erin. Now that Aldfrid was recalled to the throne of Northumbria, Adamnan, in 686, proceeded on his first mission to that court, to solicit the release of the Irish captives. He was welcomed by the Northumbrian prince, and found a ready answer to his petition. "Adamnan's demand was," thus runs the Irish record, "that a complete restoration of the captives should be made to him, and that no Saxon should ever again go upon a predatory excursion to Erin: and Adamnan brought back all the captives." From the details added in the same narrative we learn the road taken by Adamnan on this occasion. He proceeded in his coracle to the Solway Firth, and landed on the southern shore, "where the strand is long and the flood rapid," and thence pursued his way on foot to the royal residence. Two years later Adamnan undertook a second journey to the court of Aldfrid. The object of this visit is not recorded, but "it probably was some matter of international policy which Adamnan was chosen to negociate."[1] It was during

[1] *Skene*, Historians of Scotland, vi., CL. II.

this second visit to Northumbria that Adamnan presented to Aldfrid his invaluable work on the Holy Land, entitled "De Locis Sanctis," a work which Bede can scarcely find words to commend.[1] Adamnan remained for some time in England, and visiting many of its religious homes, became fully acquainted with the correct computation of Easter, of which he soon proved himself a devoted champion. It was on this occasion, too, that he visited the holy abbot Ceolfrid, who, in a letter which is preserved in the Ecclesiastical History of Venerable Bede, took occasion to attest the humility and piety of St. Adamnan, and "the wonderful prudence which he displayed in his actions and words."

Adamnan made frequent visits to his native country, and took a prominent part in the synods and conventions of the clergy and princes which were held at this period. The annalists especially record his journey to Ireland in the year 692. At this time the monarch, Finnachta, had incurred the displeasure of the Hy-Niall race by some concessions which he made to the rival clans of Leinster. He had also incurred the displeasure of the clergy, by refusing to the lands of St. Columbkille the privileges which were granted to those of SS. Patrick and Finnian, and Kieran of Clonmacnoise. Adamnan's mission had for its object to restore peace and to heal the dissensions which had arisen. Finnachta, however, would not yield to his counsel and entreaties, wherefore Adamnan prophesied his speedy overthrow and death, which was verified in 695. In the year 697 he again visited Ireland, and obtained the sanction of the Irish princes that men alone should be subject to military service, for hitherto, writes the annalist, the women and

Bede, Ecc. Hist. v. 15.

the men were alike subject to that law. It is generally supposed that the "Lex Innocentium," with which St. Adamnan's name is linked in all our ancient records, refers to this exemption of women from military service. It seems to me, however, that it further implied that females were not to be subjected to captivity or any of the penalties of warfare. "These are the four chief laws of Erin," writes the Scholiast on St. Aengus in the Laebhar Breac: "Patrick's Law, that the clerics should not be killed; Bridget's Law, that the cattle shall not be killed; Adamnan's Law, that women shall not be killed; and the Law of the Lord's-day, that it be not desecrated." It was in the same year that a great Synod was convened at Tara, at which all the chief ecclesiastics of the Irish Church, with many of the Irish chieftains, took part. St. Adamnan was one of the guiding spirits of this convention, and in connection with it tradition has attached his name to many of the cherished sites which are pointed out on the royal hill of Tara; for instance, 'the Pavilion of Adamnan,' 'Adamnan's Chair,' 'Adamnan's Mound,' and 'Adamnan's Cross.' At this synod, Flann Febhla, archbishop of Armagh, presided, whilst at the head of the laity was Loingsech, monarch of Ireland, and with him were forty-seven chiefs of various territories. The name of Bruide Mac Derili, king of the Picts, is also marked down among the princes present, and it is probable that his friendship for Adamnan led him to take part in this august convention. St. Adamnan's Law was sanctioned on this occasion, and other canons, half civil, half ecclesiastical, which have come down to us bearing the name of St. Adamnan, seem also to have been enacted at this great synod. It was by the order of the clergy and princes thus assembled that the famous collection of canons was made, which is now known as the "Collectio Hibernensis Canonum." The last seven years of St. Adamnan's life were spent in Ireland, and it is affirmed by some that he was at this time consecrated bishop. He died on 23rd of September, 704, in the seventy-seventh year of his age.

It was principally for his great austerities that Adamnan was famed among his countrymen, and, indeed, his penitential exercises, as set down in his Irish Life, can be compared only with those of the great fathers and hermits of the Egyptian deserts. For his literary merit he also holds high place amongst the most illustrious of our mediæval writers. His work ' De Locis Sanctis,' to which I have already referred, was the first after St. Jerome's time which made known to the western world the condition of the holy places, and the sacred traditions of the East regarding them. St. Adamnan had not himself visited Palestine, but a venerable French bishop, named Arculfus, who had spent nine months visiting the holy places, was driven by a storm on the British coast, and being hospitably welcomed in the monastery of Iona, Adamnan carefully noted down the facts narrated by him, and arranging them in due order, composed this most important treatise so valuable for all who desire to become acquainted with the scenes of the Gospel narrative, or who seek to explore the history of the cradle lands of our holy Faith. Adamnan's Life of St. Columba has already been frequently referred to in the preceding pages. As regards the early history of North Britain, it is scarcely second to the great work of

Venerable Bede. Dr. Forbes styles it "the solitary record of a portion of the history of the Church of Scotland" (Kalendars, pag. 265); and Dean Reeves does not hesitate to pronounce it "one of the most important pieces of hagiology in existence."[1] A spirit of piety and filial love for his great patron, St. Columba, may be discerned in every line, and he sketches in it, with the enthusiasm of admiration and the love of a son, an exalted model of spiritual perfection for himself and his beloved brethren, the Irish monks. There is also a very ancient tract in Irish called "The Vision of Adamnan," which under the form of a vision contains a religious discourse on the joys and sufferings which await men in the next world. He mentions as specially condemned to torments those "Airchinnechs who, in the presence of the relics of the saints, administer the gifts and titles of God, but who turn the profits to their own private ends from the strangers and the poor of the Lord." He very explicitly lays down the Catholic doctrine of Purgatory, for he sets before us three classes of those who suffer for a time but "are destined for eternal life, and even in their torments are free from the rule of the demons, whilst those, who are condemned to eternal torments, are subjected to the demons." Having described the joys of Heaven, he adds that "his soul desired to remain in that happy region, but heard from behind him, through the veil, the voice of his guardian angel commanding it to be replaced in the same body from which it had passed, and instructing it to relate in the assemblies and conventions of the laity and clergy

---

[1] *Reeves*, Smith's Dictionary of Christian Biography, I. 49.

the rewards of heaven and the pains of hell, such as the conducting angel had made known to it."

St. Adamnan is named in the Festology of St. Aengus, and in all our martyrologies, on the 23rd of September. He, moreover, receives the highest eulogies in our ancient records. The introduction to the 'Vision,' just referred to, styles him the "high sage of the western world." Venerable Bede says that he was "a good and a wise man, and remarkably learned in the knowledge of the Scriptures."[1] The Abbot Ceolfrid calls him "the abbot and renowned priest of the Columbian order."[2] The Martyrology of Donegal, having entered his feast on the 23rd of September, adds that "He was a vessel of wisdom, and a man full of the grace of God and of the knowledge of the Holy Scriptures, and of every other wisdom ; a burning lamp, which illuminated and enlightened the west of Europe with the light of virtues and good morals, laws and rules, wisdom and knowledge, humility and self-abasement." Alcuin, too, in the verses with which he decorated the church of Tours, mentions St. Adamnan as one of "the renowned fathers and masters of the spiritual life," whose protection he invokes for the faithful. Fordun, in a later age, commemorates him as "adorned with virtues and miracles,"[3] whilst the Four Masters sum up his character thus : "Adamnan was a good man, according to the testimony of Bede ; for he was tearful, penitent, given to prayer, diligent, ascetic, temperate ; he never used to eat except on Sunday

---

[1] *Bede*, Ecc. Hist. v. 15.   [2] Ibid. v. 21.
[3] *Fordun*, " virtutibus pollens et miraculis." 111. 43.

and Thursday; he made a slave of himself to these virtues; and, moreover, he was wise and learned in the clear understanding of the Holy Scriptures of God." St. Adamnan is honoured in Raphoe and many other churches in Ireland. In Scotland he is patron of Furvie on the east coast of Aberdeen, where a venerable ruin still marks the site of his ancient church; it stands in the middle of a small plantation of stunted firs and alder, on a little eminence gently rising from a swampy bottom, with a rivulet half enclosing it on the south side. The church of Forglen, where the sacred banner of St. Columba, called the Breachbannach, was preserved, was also dedicated to him. At Aboyn, on the north side of the Dee, is a large old tree, called 'St. Eunan's Tree,'[1] at the foot of which is 'St. Eunan's Well.' The islands of Inchkeith and Sanda had sanctuaries dedicated to him, and his memory was also cherished in Tannadice, Killeunan, Dalmeny, and Campsie. The ancient records particularly attest that St. Adamnan, emulating the piety of St. Germain of Paris, made it his care to enrich the monastery of Iona with many precious relics of the saints: "Illustrious was this Adamnan; it was by him was gathered the great collection of the relics of the saints into one shrine, and that was the shrine which Cilline Droicthech, son of Dicolla, brought to Erin to make peace and friendship between the Cinel-Conaill and the Cinel-Eoghain."[2] In Lynch's MS. History of

[1] The Celtic name Adhamnan is pronounced Aunan or Eunan, which has given rise to a manifold variety in the form in which the Saint's name appears, as may be seen in the 'Historians of Scotland.' vol. vi. Introduction, pag. clxx.
[2] Ibid., pag. clxv.

Irish Bishops, we are told that Adamnan composed a poem in honour of these relics which he had gathered; and it is added that he caused two rich shrines to be made for the relics, one of which, with its sacred treasure, was preserved at Ardnagelligan in O'Kane's country, the other at Skreen, in the diocese of Killala. This latter spot still retains many memorials of St. Adamnan. The old church is named from him, and a little to the east of it is his well, from which the townland derives its name of Toberawnaun (Tober-Adhamhnain.) Colgan, citing the Life of St. Forannan, tells us that the parish derived its name of Skreen from this famous shrine of Adamnan, "Scrinium Sancti Adamnani;" and that its church was "noble and venerable for its relics of many saints." The list of the relics preserved in this famous shrine may be seen among the Brussels MSS., and in Lynch's MS. History, already referred to. There were in this sacred treasure particles from the bones of St. Patrick and St. Declan; portions of the cincture of St. Paul the Hermit, of the mantle of St. Martin of Tours, and of the habit of St. Bridget: there was also the head of St. Carthage, and other precious relics of Saint Mochemogue, St. Molua, St. Columba-mac-Crimthan, St. Mathan, and other saints. In the same shrine was deposited a MS. copy of the Gospels, as also a collection of Latin and Irish Hymns, the same, probably, as the two MSS. of the 'Liber Hymnorum,' which have fortunately been preserved to our own times.

It is not necessary to dwell on the lives of the later abbots of Iona. They inherited the spirit and walked in the footsteps of their first fathers. We will just now give a complete list of these devoted men who, in a singularly unbroken succession, continued to rule this monastery down to the thirteenth century, but it may not be uninteresting to premit, in a few words, a sketch of the disciplinary observances of this ancient Celtic community, as they are presented in the pages of SS. Cummian and Adamnan.

Those who were enrolled in the monastery of Iona were regarded as soldiers of Christ, whose purpose it was to renounce the world and its cares, and to live and labour for God alone. The monastery was ruled by an abbot, whose ecclesiastical rank, indeed, was that of a priest, but whose jurisdiction nevertheless extended over many bishops. The community lived together as a *Muinter* or family: each one acted towards the rest, and loved them as his brothers, and all obeyed the abbot as their father. Kneeling before the altar, they took the solemn monastic vow, and the tonsure was given them after the Irish fashion, that is to say, the fore part of the head was made bare from ear to ear. Obedience, even unto death, was a fundamental principle of their rule: hence we find them at the whisper of the abbot setting forth, without a moment's delay, to labour and to preach, or again starting on distant and perilous journeys. In Iona, as in the other great Irish monasteries at home and abroad, all things were held in common, and no personal property was allowed. In St. Columba's rule, as in that of St. Columbanus, the monks were directed " to love poverty in imitation of Christ, and in obedience to the Gospel precepts." Humility, too, was commended as a distinctive virtue, which all should cultivate, being the groundwork of all other virtues. Hospitality was enjoined in the outpouring of national generosity, as well as of Christian charity. When a guest arrived, the brethren went forth to meet him, and bid him welcome. He was at once led to the church, and there thanks were returned to God for his safe journey. Thence he was led to the lodging or *hospitium* prepared for him, where water was presented to wash his feet, and food was set before him. Should he happen to arrive on a fast day, the fast was relaxed in his favour.

The brethren were summoned to the church or oratory by the sound of a bell, but except at midnight, and morning and evening, those engaged on the farm in manual work were not required to attend. The Lord's Day and the great feasts of the saints were solemnized by rest from labour and by the celebration of the Holy Sacrifice, and better food was used on these days. Mass was said in some seasons at Prime, in others at Sext, and the brethren received the Blessed Eucharist, which, in their veneration for this great sacrament, was styled "the Sacred Mysteries of the Eucharist," or "the Mysteries of the Sacred Oblation," or "the Oblation of the Body of Christ." Should a bishop be present, he offered the Holy Sacrifice alone in token of his superior dignity; if several priests were there, they united in offering the sacred oblation. The chief festival was the Paschal solemnity; and the whole time from Easter to Whitsunday, called "the Paschal Days," was regarded as a period of special joy and thankfulness.

The fasting discipline was regulated by special rule, and in its observance the holy founder was a model for all the brethren. Every Wednesday and Friday throughout the year, except during "the Paschal days," was a fast day. Lent was strictly observed, and during this season, except on Sunday, the fast was every day prolonged till evening, when a meal of bread and honey, or whitemeats and vegetables, was taken.

Celibacy was enjoined on all the clergy and brethren of the monastery. "There can be no doubt," writes Dr. Reeves, "that celibacy was strictly enjoined on the community of Columba, and that the condition 'virgin in body and virgin in mind,' was held up for imitation."[1]

When a fault was committed, the religious on his knees made public acknowledgment of it before the brethren, and received a proportionate penance from the superior. For the sacrament of Penance each one chose a brother priest, who was styled his *anmchara*, or soul's friend, who was to be his chief guide in all matters appertaining to the spiritual life. No matter what the rank of the penitent might be, the public penance was proportionate to his crimes; sometimes it consisted merely of some short prayers, whilst at others it enjoined a special religious observance for seven years; or, again, the penitent was ordered to spend twelve years in tears and lamentations among the Britons, or to live in perpetual exile from his native land.

The sign of the cross as "a saving sign" was in constant use. The religious armed themselves with it, not only before and after meals, but at every other duty of the day. Adamnan specially mentions that it was

[1] *Reeves'* Adamnan, pag. 344.

customary to make the sign of the cross over the pail before milking, and over the tools before using them. This holy sign was considered efficacious in banishing demons, in preserving from danger, and in obtaining favours from heaven. A large cross was placed at the entrance of the monastery, and it was customary to erect the same sacred standard "vexillum crucis" on the site of every remarkable occurrence. So fully, indeed, was this pious custom carried out in the course of centuries, that Iona became famous for its three hundred and sixty crosses. Even at sea, the cruciform arrangement of the masts with the yards was regarded as boding well for a favourable voyage.

The burial of the dead was regarded as a solemn religious duty, of merit alike to the survivors and to those who had gone to their rest. The lively faith in the resurrection rendered it a consideration of importance to be buried among the honoured members of the society, and, as the day of death was called the natàlis, or birth-day, so the object in the choice of a burial-place was to prepare the place of resurrection. The body of the deceased was laid out in the cell, wrapped in linen cloths; the *exequiae* were then celebrated for his repose, and three days were spent in prayers and chanting the praises of God. The printed rule of St. Columba expressly enjoins that the "Hymns for souls" were to be sung standing, and commands such "fervour in singing the office for the dead as if every faithful dead was a particular friend."[1]

---

[1] *Skene*, "Celtic Scotland," 11, 508.

The three great daily occupations of the community were prayer, reading, and manual labour. "Three labours in the day (thus runs St. Columba's rule) are prayers, work, and reading. The work to be divided into three parts, viz., thine own work and the work of thy place, as regards its real wants ; secondly, thy share of the brethren's work ; lastly, to help the neighbours by instruction, or writing, or sewing garments, or whatever labour they may be in want of, as the Lord says, 'Thou shalt not appear before Me with empty hands.'" The chief study of the seniors was the Sacred Scripture, and one of the duties specially enjoined was to commit to memory the Book of Psalms. The copying of the Inspired Text held a foremost place in manual labour. For St. Columba himself this, as we have already seen, was a labour of love, and his successors seem to have emulated his skill as well as his zeal in this important work. Of St. Baethen, the immediate successor of the holy founder, it is recorded that he was most exact in copying the sacred text, and in one transcript of the Gospels which he had made, the mistake of only one letter could be discovered.

The ordinary garments of the community were two : viz., the *cucula*, or cowl, of coarse texture, made of wool, retaining its natural colour, and the tunic, or under-habit, which was also white. If the weather was particularly severe, an *amphibalus*, or double mantle, was permitted. When engaged at work on the farm, and when travelling, the brethren wore sandals, which were not used within the monastery. Each cell was provided with a bed, which consisted of a straw-pallet, and a pillow also of straw.

The following are among the maxims for the everyday guidance of the religious, as laid down in St. Columba's rule :—

"Let thy mind be at all times prepared for red martyrdom.

"Let thy mind be fortified and steadfast for white martyrdom. Forgiveness from the heart to everyone. Constant prayers for those who trouble thee. Follow almsgiving before all things. Take not of food till thou art hungry. The love of God with all thy love and all thy strength. The love of thy neighbour as thyself. Abide in the Testaments of God throughout all times. Thy measure of prayer shall be until thy tears come. Or let thy measure of labour be till thy tears come. Or let it be the measure of thy work of labour, or of thy genuflections, that thy perspiration should abundantly come, if thy tears are not free."

The question has been asked, how were holy orders conferred in Iona, since the abbot was not himself a bishop? Some Presbyterian writers have fancied that they have in this a proof that ordination was conferred by presbyters. But surely it might be supposed that a neighbouring bishop could, without great difficulty, be called in, even from Ireland, on such an occasion, as we will see was, indeed, done in the consecration of St. Kentigern. At all events, there was no scarcity of bishops within call of the Abbot of Iona. There were bishops subject to his jurisdiction, as is clear from the testimony of Venerable Bede: "That island," he writes, "has always by usage for its ruler an abbot, who is a priest, to whose direction all the province, and even the bishops, contrary to the usual method, are subject."[1] It was, no doubt, a thing not in accordance with the usual discipline of the Church in the sixth

---

[1] *Bede*, Ecc. Hist., 111, 4.

century that bishops should be subject to the jurisdiction of those who were not bishops. It is likewise contrary to our usual discipline at the present day; nevertheless, we know that this usage has been from time immemorial permitted in the monastery of Monte Casino in Italy, and in other great Benedictine monasteries. From the narrative of Adamnan, in St. Columba's life, it is manifest that bishops were invited thither to confer holy orders, and at times, too, were numbered among the brethren of the monastery. Thus, in the case of Aedh Dubh, we find that Findchan, the founder of the monastery of Artchain, in the island of Tiree, called in "a neighbouring bishop" to ordain him priest.[1] On another occasion, when a stranger from the province of Munster, "who," says Adamnan, "through humility did all he could to disguise himself, so that nobody might know he was a bishop," was invited, on the next Lord's Day, by Columba, to join with him in consecrating the Body of Christ, that as two priests they might break the Bread of the Lord together, Columba, on going to the altar, discovered his rank, and thus addressed him: "Christ bless thee, brother; do thou break the bread alone, according to the Episcopal rite, for I know now thou art a bishop. Why hast thou disguised thyself so long, and prevented our giving thee the honour which is due to thee."[2] This narrative contains not only a plain acknowledgment of the distinct order of priest and bishop, but also the holy founder's express declaration of the superior privilege, rank, and honour due to the bishop. Instead of the episcopal

[1] *Adamnan*, 1. 29.   [2] *Ibid.*, 1. 35.

office being ignored, or its proper function being usurped by presbyters in Iona, "a greater respect," remarks Innes, "was in some manner paid to bishops in that monastery, and a greater distinction made betwixt them and priests in the celebration of the sacred mysteries, than in other churches of the West, even in those ages of ours; for, by this relation, it appears that in Ycolmkill, a priest, even the abbot St. Columba himself, looked upon a bishop as so far superior to him that he would not presume, even though invited, to concelebrate or celebrate the holy mysteries jointly with him."[1] We must not omit to add that among the invocations of the Litany of St. Aengus, we find two groups of "the seven bishops of Iona;" and there are grave reasons for supposing that more than one of St. Columba's successors was consecrated bishop whilst holding the office of abbot of the monastery.

We may compendiate the lessons of the disciplinary observances of Iona in the words of Montalembert: "An honest, careful examination," he writes, "of all the monastic peculiarities to be found in the Life of Columba reveals nothing in the way either of observances or of duties, which runs counter to the rules adopted by all the religious communities of the sixth century from the traditions of the Fathers of the desert. But what we see clearly is: first, the necessity of the vow or solemn profession to mark the definite admission of the postulant into the society after a trial of whatever duration; and secondly, the absolute conformity of the religious life followed by Columba and his monks

---

[1] "Historians of Scotland," vi. 263.

with the precepts and rights of the Catholic Church in all ages. Texts, indisputable and undisputed, prove the existence of auricular confessions, of the invocation of saints, the universal trust in their protection, and in their action on temporal affairs, the celebration of the Mass, the Real Presence in the Eucharist, the celibacy of the clergy, fasting and abstinence, prayers for the dead, the sign of the Cross, and a most diligent and profound study of the Scriptures. So fall the fancies of writers who think that in the Celtic Church they discern a primitive Christianity beyond the pale of Catholicism. So once more is the lie given to the absurd but inveterate prejudice which accuses our fathers of having ignored or forbidden the study of the Bible."[1]

It only remains to add the succession of the Abbots of Iona as accurately compiled by Dean Reeves in his edition of Adamnan's Life of St. Columba, which we have so freely used throughout this chapter.

	A.D.	A.D.
COLUMBA	563	597
BAETHEN	597	600
LAISREN	600	605
FERGNA	605	623
SEGHINE	623	652
SUIBHNE	652	657
CUMMIAN	657	669
FAILBHE	669	679
ADAMNAN	679	704
CONAMHAIL	704	710
DUNCHADH	710	717
FAELCHU	717	724
CILLENE FADA	724	726

[1] *Montalembert*, " Monks of the West," 111, 301.

	A.D.	A.D.
CILLINE DROICHTEACH	726 ...	752
SLEBHINE	752 ...	767
SUIBHNE	767 ...	772
BREASAL	772 ...	801
CONNACHTACH	801 ...	802
CELLACH	802 ...	815
DIARMAIT	815 circa	832
INNRECHTACH	circa 832 ...	854
CELLACH	854 ...	865
FERADHACH	865 ...	880
FLANN	880 ...	891
MAELBRIGHDE	891 ...	927
DUBHTHACH	927 ...	938
ROBHARTACH	938 ...	954
DUBHDUIN	954 ...	959
DUBHSCUILE	959 ...	964
MUGHRON	964 ...	980
MAELCIARAIN	980 ...	986
DUNNCHADH	986 ...	989
DUBHDALEITHE	989 ...	998
MUIREDHACH	998 ...	1007
FERDOMNACH	1007 ...	1008
MAELMUIRE	1008 ...	1009
MAELEOIN	1009 ...	1025
MAELMUIRE	1025 ...	1040
ROBARTACH	1040 ...	1057
GIOLLACRIST	1057 ...	1062
DOMHNALL	1062 ...	1098
FERDOMHNACH	1098 ...	1114
MAELBRIGHDE	1114 ...	1117
CONANG	1117 ...	1128
GIOLLA-ADHAMNAIN	1128 ...	1138
MUIREDHACH	1138 ...	1150
FLAITHBERTACH	1150 ...	1175
GIOLLA-MAC-LIAG	1175 ...	1198
GIOLLACRIST	1198 ...	1202

CHAPTER V.

IRISH SAINTS IN THE KINGDOM OF STRATHCLYDE.

Early Irish Settlements in Strathclyde:—St. Patrick's Birthplace:— St. Ninian studies in Rome:—The Monastery of Whitherne:— St. Ninian's Cave:—His connection with Ireland:—Irish Saints at Whitherne:—St. Modenna:—Her Sanctuary at Maidenkirk: —St. Kentigern under the care of St. Servan:—His Monastery at Glasgow:—Austerities of St. Kentigern:—He visits Wales:— Founds a Monastery at St. Asaph's:—Rederech, King of Strathclyde:—Some Memorials of St. Kentigern:—The Queen's Ring: —St. Servan:—St. Conval:—Revival of devotion to this Saint:— St. Bea:—Synod of Rome in A.D. 721.

THE petty kingdom of Strathclyde is not without some features of special interest for the student of the early missions of the Irish Church. Within its territory we must seek for the birthplace of our national Apostle St. Patrick. There, too, very many of our countrymen settled at an early period: several illustrious saints of Irish birth or Irish parentage chose it as the theatre of their missionary toil, and others hastened thither to spend a little time at least in its great monastery of Whitherne, desirous to perfect themselves in the paths of virtue, or to acquire the sublimest knowledge of divine truth.

Under the imperial rule of Rome, the Firths of Clyde and Forth were the northern boundary of Britain. The tides of the opposite seas, flowing far up these estuaries, formed a natural barrier against a sudden irruption of the barbarians of the north, and an earthen rampart, extending from sea to sea, erected in the year A.D. 139, served effectually to isolate the Picts in their wild mountain fastnesses. "This great work," writes Mr. Skene, the latest and most accurate explorer of Scottish antiquities, "consisted of a large rampart of intermingled stone and earth, strengthened by sods of turf, and must have originally measured twenty feet in height, and twenty-four feet in breadth at the base. It was surmounted by a parapet, having a level platform behind it for the protection of its defenders. In front there extended, along its whole course, an immense fosse, averaging about forty feet wide 'and twenty feet deep. To the southward of the whole was a military way, presenting the usual appearance of a Roman causewayed road. This great barrier extended from Bridgeness, near Carriden, on the Firth of Forth, to Chapel-hill, near West or Old Kilpatrick, on the Clyde, having, at intervals of about two miles, square forts or stations, which, judging from those that remain, amounted in all to nineteen in number, and between them were smaller watch-towers."[1] Additional military stations were added by the emperor Severus, and several watch-towers were also erected on the southern banks of the Clyde to guard the province against the incursions by sea of the Scottish rovers, who often infested the coast, from the not far distant shores of Ireland.[2]

The Clyde and this Roman rampart formed also the northern boundary of the kingdom of Strathclyde, which, having the strong city of Alclyde, the modern Dumbarton, for its capital, stretched southwards along

[1] *Skene*, "Celtic Scotland," i. 78.
[2] *Skene*, "Chronicles of the Picts," pag. 224.

the western coast, and gradually absorbed the minor states which, after the abandonment of Britain, had sprung up in the imperial province of Valentia. Its southern boundaries varied with the vicissitudes of war, being at one time limited to the Solway Firth, and at others extending as far as the Derwent or the Mersey. A line running through the centre of Great Britain will serve pretty accurately to mark the extent of Strathclyde towards the east in the days of its greatest prosperity.

The Roman writers of the fourth and fifth centuries inform us that the Picts and Britons found prompt allies in the Scots from Ireland, as well when resisting the attack of the Roman armies as when pursuing the imperial legions in their retreat from Britain. Ammianus Marcellinus makes mention of these Scots for the first time in the year A.D. 360, and he does not hesitate to style them "dangerous enemies of the empire." He, moreover, gives it plainly to be understood that they were even then old offenders, and that in conjunction with the Picts they had made repeated inroads on the territory south of the Clyde, the Roman legions being quite wearied in their pursuit.[1] He also tells us that in the year 364 the Picts and Scots again poured in upon the Roman province, and they were joined by the Attacotts, whom he describes as a warlike people, "bellicosa hominum natio"; and that a third time, increasing in numbers and boldness, they, in the year 368, renewed their attack, and after inflicting more than one defeat on the Roman troops advanced into the very heart of Britain, the Roman General and the Count of the mari-

[1] *Ammianus*, lib. xx., cap. 1., "praeteritarum cladium congerie fessas."

time coast in one of the battles being numbered among the slain. The poet, Claudian, also mentions the Irish Scots among the barbarian confederates who assailed the empire in Britain towards the close of the fourth century: "all Ireland was astir," he writes, "and the sea was covered with her hostile oars":

> ". . . totam cum Scotus Iernen
> "Movit, et infesto spumavit remige Tethys."

And when he subsequently commemorates the triumph of the Emperor Theodosius over the barbarians, he tells us that the distant Thule was soaked with Pictish blood, whilst "wintry Ireland wept over her Scottish slain."

> "Scotorum tumulos flevit glacialis Ierne."

It was in the year 399 that the brave Stilicho vanquished the Picts and Scots for the last time. The interval of peace, however, was but short, for, four years later, their incursions were renewed, and the Roman legions being recalled from the northern province, the whole fair territory of Clydesdale became a scene of ruin and desolation.

These incidental references by classic writers plainly show how close was the union of the Irish Scots with the Picts and Britons at this early period, and they prepare us to receive as strictly accurate the statements of our Irish and Scottish historians, when they of one accord attest that, commencing before the middle of the fourth century, the Irish Scots flocked in great numbers to the shores of Caledonia, many of them settling permanently there, and when they describe this emigration as made on so vast a scale in the district north of the Solway Firth, that the territory became known as the district of the Gallgaedhel, from whom was derived the name of Galloway, which it retains to the present day.

For more than a thousand years it was the uninterrupted tradition of Ireland and of Scotland that our Apostle, St. Patrick, was born in the valley of the Clyde, not far from the city of Alclyde. His father, Calphurnius, held the high Roman dignity of Decurio, and thus, whilst enjoying senatorial rank, discharged the duties of civil magistrate in this perilous outpost of the Empire. The family, however, had come from Celtic Gaul, and thither, too, St. Patrick was sent at an early age to be trained to learning and virtue at the monastery of his relative, St. Martin of Tours. Hence we may, without hesitation, adopt the words of Mr. Cashel Hoey, though entirely differing from him in his opinions regarding St. Patrick's birth-place: "Roman by his education in a province where Roman civilization had long prevailed, where the Latin language was spoken and the privileges of the Empire fully possessed—Roman, too, by the possession of nobility, which he himself declares, and of which his name was a curious commemoration—Roman, in fine, in the connection of his family, which he testifies, with the Roman government and with the Church, St. Patrick was a Celt of Gaul by blood."[1] In his infancy he had been taught to regard as barbarian enemies of the Empire those Irish Scots whose Apostle he was one day to be; but in the ways of Providence this contact with them must have served to make him familiar with their habits and language, a knowledge

[1] *Hoey*, Essay on the birthplace of St. Patrick, in "Essays on Religion and Literature," vol. I., pag. 111.

which was soon to be perfected amid the trials and hardships of his slavery.

I have said that for a thousand years it was the constant tradition of Ireland that we must look to the banks of the Clyde for the birth-place of our Apostle. In the beginning of this century the learned historian, Lanigan, pushed rudely this tradition aside, and with great ability and ingenuity endeavoured to prop up a theory which had already found some favour with Continental writers, that St. Patrick was born in Gaul, in the neighbourhood of Boulogne-sur-mer, and in such esteem have the labours of this ablest of our ecclesiastical historians been held, that since his time most of our popular writers have not hesitated to adopt his opinion. It would be out of place to enter here into the difficulties which this intricate question presents. Suffice it to say that during the past half century many documents have come to light which illustrate the life of our Apostle, and serve to confirm more and more the ancient tradition of our country. We, therefore, in this must part company with Dr. Lanigan, and we gladly accept the more venerable tradition, confirmed as it is by Colgan, and John Lynch, and Usher, and Ware, as set forth in the following words of the Ogygia: "A very great bay of the Irish Western Ocean runs up the British country at a great distance from the west, which formerly divided the Britons from the Picts, and which was appointed as the ulterior Roman limits by Agricola. The celebrated fortress of Dunbriton stands on a very high and craggy clift, and commands a prospect of this bay between Cluide and Lennox. Cluide, called Glotta by Tacitus, is the river that runs through the Archiepiscopal

See of Glasgow, and empties itself in the bay of Dunbriton. From this river Dunbriton was formerly called *Arcluid*, that is, above Cluide; or *Alcluid*, that is, the rock of Cluid: and from the fortress Alcluid, the country or valley of Alcluida, now Cluidesdale, is called: where below Dunbriton is the plain of Taburn, on which the town Nemther stood, which gave birth to the illustrious missionary, St. Patrick; and there he spent part of his youth, as we are assured by the ancient writers of his life."[1] So, too, the learned Innes writes: "It was about this time when the Romans, by the erection of the new province of Valentia, were in possession of all betwixt the walls, from Northumberland to the Firths, that the holy bishop, St. Patrick, Apostle of Ireland, was born upon the confines of the Roman province, at Kilpatrick, near Alcluyd or Dunbriton, in the north of Britain, as the learnedest among the Irish, as well as other foreign writers, do now agree."[2] The memory of St. Patrick was long cherished throughout Scotland, and, to speak only of the banks of Clyde, we find that he was honoured as patron of the city of Dumbarton, and of the two towns east and west Kilpatrick, of Chapel-hill, and of the parish of Dalziel; and in this last-named parish, in Lanarkshire, the holy well of our Apostle was long a favourite place of pilgrimage.

It was among the Gallgaedhels of Galloway that another great ornament of the British Church, St. Ninian, was born about the year A.D. 360. Of his family[3] only

---

[1] *O'Flaherty's* Ogygia, Hely's translation, page 317.

[2] *Innes*, Civil and Eccles. Hist. of Scotland (ed. of Spalding Club), page 34.

[3] However this may be, certain it is that, under the name of Monennio, St. Ninian is honoured in our most ancient Martyrologies.

two traditions have come down to us: one is the tradition of Scotland, that Ninian was nephew of St. Martin of Tours; the other is a tradition of the Irish Church, preserved by Usher, that it was in compliance with a request made to him by his mother, that in his old age he set out to associate himself with St. Palladius in the conversion of Ireland. We might, perhaps, from this fact conjecture that she herself belonged to the Gaelic race. Being arrived at the age of manhood, Ninian proceeded to Rome. Alaric had not as yet knocked at the gates of the devoted city. In the full majesty of imperial sway, it was still at the golden height of its wealth and material splendour; and its palaces, and forums, and public monuments displayed all the profusion of magnificence with which the plunder of the world had enriched the proud mistress of nations. Pope Damasus then ruled the Church of God, and, with the blessings of peace, religion smiled on the seven hills. Silver and gold and precious marbles enriched the Basilicas devoted to Christian worship; the shrines of the martyrs were adorned with the most costly gems; the learning of St. Jerome and St. Ambrose added lustre to its sacred teaching, and Rome was even then not only the source of spiritual authority, but also the great centre of religious life, and of the love and affection of the Christian world. For about twenty years St. Ninian lived in Rome, visiting the sanctuaries, praying at the tombs of the apostles,[1] pursuing every exercise of heroic piety, and

---

[1] St. Jerome, in his Commentary on Ezechiel, gives us the following account of his student life in Rome: "Cum essem Romae puer et liberalibus studiis erudirer, solebam cum caeteris ejusdem aetatis et propositis diebus Dominicis sepulchra Apostolorum et Martyrum circumire, crebroque cryptas ingredi, quae in terrarum profundo defossae, ex utraque parte ingredientium, per parietes

drinking in, day by day, at its salutary fountains the knowledge of divine truth. Being at length consecrated bishop, he set out for his native district of Galloway, to merit by his sanctity and missionary labours the title of its chief apostle.

On his homeward journey he remained for some time at Marmoutiers to enjoy the heavenly lessons of wisdom of its great founder, St. Martin of Tours; and Aelred, in his life of our saint, particularly mentions that he brought with him from that monastery some skilled masons, by whose aid he desired to erect in his native district a church on the model of those which he had seen in Italy and France. He chose for its site a sheltered spot on the southern promontory of Galloway, enclosed on all sides, except to the north, by the sea, and commanding a distant view of the heights of Cumberland and of the Isle of Man. The church was built of chiselled stone, a style of edifice, as Bede informs us, till then unheard of in North Britain, from which circumstance it became known as *Candida Casa*, and in the British language it was called *Whitherne* (that is, "the White House"), or Whithorn, which name the district retains to the present day.[1] We learn from Venerable Bede that, whilst engaged in erecting this church, Ninian received the intelligence of St. Martin's

---

habent corpora sepultorum, et ita obscura sunt omnia, ut propemodum illud propheticum compleatur : Descendunt ad infernum viventes." (*Opp.* tom. v. pag. 433).

[1] In the Papal Bull restoring the Scottish Hierarchy, this diocese is still called *Candida Casa*. To commemorate the restoration of the ancient Episcopal See, the Most Noble the Marquis of Bute has announced his intention of erecting a beautiful new church at Whithorn in honour of St. Ninian.

death, and so convinced was he of the sanctity of that holy man that he at once chose him for his patron in his missionary labours, and dedicated the church to God under his invocation. This fixes the date of the erection of Whithorn in A.D. 402, which seems most probably to have been the year of St. Martin's decease.

Interesting and ornamental remains of the mediæval cathedral of Galloway, supposed to have been erected on the site of the original church, may still be seen at the town of Whithorn. Some antiquarians, however, are of opinion that the Isle of Whithorn, which in former times was probably connected with the mainland, was the site of the first building erected by St. Ninian. It has still the ruins of a very old chapel, but not even a moulding is left to indicate the date of its erection.

I need not dwell on the apostolic labours of St. Ninian. He penetrated into the Pictish territory far beyond the British frontier, and at his preaching, as Bede attests, many of the southern Picts forsook idolatry and became fervent children of God.[1] He was remarkable, like most of the early Celtic saints, for his austerities, and in particular it is recorded of him that, throughout the whole time of Lent, he was accustomed to partake of nothing but the poorest fare, and from sunset on Holy Thursday till after he had offered the Holy Sacrifice on Easter-day, he wholly abstained from all corporal refection. Like St. Martin, he loved to withdraw himself from time to time from the busy world in which he laboured, to renew his spirit by meditation on heavenly things. The cave is still pointed out on the seashore of

[1] *Bede*, Hist. Eccl. iii. 4.

Wigtownshire, in Galloway, whither he was wont to retire. It is placed high up in a white lofty precipitous range of rocks, against which the impetuous waves of the stormy Irish Sea unceasingly spend their fury. The cave is open to the winds and spray, but runs inward about twenty feet. At the mouth it is twelve feet high, and about as many in width, and it is only accessible by climbing from rock to rock.

St. Ninian's preaching was attended with many miracles. Among others, a pagan chieftain of Galloway, named Tuduvallus, which corresponds to the Celtic name Tuathal, was struck with blindness for his resistance to the faith, but upon his repentance was restored to his sight by the prayers of the holy man. St. Ninian's death is marked by Scottish writers in the year A.D. 432; his remains were interred in St. Martin's Church, and so many were the miracles performed there through the intercession of our saint, so sweet was his memory among his spiritual children, and so great their veneration for him as their own apostle, that throughout all Scotland the church and monastery became known only by St. Ninian's name.

The saint is honoured in our Irish Calendars on the 16th of September, under the name Monennio, and it is a very ancient tradition, preserved in the Festology of St. Ængus and other authentic records, that a few years before his death he came to Ireland to aid in the missionary enterprise of Palladius, and erected at Cluain Conaire, now Cloncurry, in the north of the present County Kildare, an oratory and religious institution, which reproduced in miniature the great church and monastery of Whitherne. Bishop Forbes gives a list of more than sixty churches dedicated to him throughout Scotland; and Chalmers, in his Caledonia, writes that "the name of St. Ninian was venerated in every district in Scotland, and in the Northern and Western Isles."

Such was the fame of Candida Casa for the piety and learning of its holy inmates, that for centuries it was popularly known in Ireland as "Magnum Monasterium," the great monastery. Innumerable pilgrims from our shores visited it, and many of our early saints made it, for a time at least, their home. Thus St. Finian, of Moville, lived there for some years, desirous of acquiring an accurate knowledge of the Sacred Scriptures, and of the rules of the monastic life.[1] St. Enda, so famed for his island sanctuary and school at Arann, by the advice of his sister, St. Fanchea, became also an humble religious within its walls. St. Tighernach, of Clones, St. Eoghan, Bishop of Ardstraw, St. Rioch, who is numbered among the relatives of St. Patrick, and St. Talmach, all spent a portion of their lives in the fervent practice of penance and piety within its hallowed enclosure. St. Manchan, patron of Limerick, was at first a student there, and subsequently became one of its brightest ornaments and most learned teachers; and there also St. Mugint composed his beautiful penitential prayer, which was much used in the early Irish church, and is preserved in the Book of Hymns.[2]

The memory of some of these saints was long cherished in Galloway, and Dr. Forbes writes that "the

[1] "In ejus sede quæ Magnum vocabatur Monasterium regulas et institutiones monasticæ vitae aliquot annis probus monachus didicit, atque in Sanctarum Scripturarum paginis non parum proficiens insudavit," &c. *Colgan*, Acta SS. pag. 438.

[2] *Todd*, Lib. Hym., part I., pag. 94.

christianizing influence of Ireland was strongly felt throughout the whole of that territory."[1]

St. Modenna, also called Moninna, was an Irish virgin saint for whom the early Scottish Church cherished a special devotion. She flourished towards the close of the fourth century and the beginning of the fifth, for her death is marked in the Annals of Ulster in the year 516, on the 6th of July, on which day her name is entered in all our Martyrologies. St. Ængus thus commemorates her in his Feliré :

> " Moninde of Slieve-Cuillin,
> A beautiful pillar ;
> A bright pure victory she gained,
> The sister of Muire-Mary."

She was born in the district of Conaille, and had the privilege of receiving the virgin-habit from St. Patrick. She lived for some time near Carlingford, and then proceeding to a solitary island off the western coast of Ireland, placed herself under the spiritual guidance of St. Ibar. With St. Bridget she was united in the closest bonds of spiritual friendship, and she received from her the gift of a silver shrine, which was long held in great veneration. Returning to her native province, she erected a cell at the hill of Faughart, and a little later retired to a desert place at the foot of Slieve-Cuillin (now Slieve-Gullion), where, at Killeevy, three miles from Newry, the venerable ruins of her oratory may still be seen.[2] The cyclopean door-ways of massive

---

[1] *Forbes*, Historians of Scotland, vol. v., page XLII.
[2] The name of this place was originally Kill-Sleibhe-Cuillin, from which in common use it became known as *Kill-Sleibhe*, pronounced *Killeevy*.

construction which still remain, and the round tower which, till the last century, stood at the south side, incorporated with the wall of the oratory, sufficiently mark the early period to which these hallowed ruins must be referred. Her life by Conchubran, to which Usher attaches great weight, relates that she proceeded to Scotland, and lived there for many years. The greatest of her religious foundations in North Britain was at Chilnecase, in Galloway, where for centuries a flourishing community of nuns perpetuated her virtues and lived faithfully in the service of God. Six other Scottish churches are also known to have been founded by her, three of which—viz., at Dundevenal, and Dumbarton, and Dunpeleder—were situate in the kingdom of Strathclyde, the others being at the castle of Strivelin, and in Edinburg, and at Longforgan, near Dundee, where Scottish tradition supposes her to have rested in peace. Capgrave writes that in North Britain, as in Ireland, she led a most penitential life, and that, clothed in rough garments, and with her feet bare, she made a pilgrimage to the shrines of the Apostles in Rome. The learned antiquarians of Scotland at the present day have not failed to recognise the merits of this great saint and to illustrate her history. Mr. Skene has successfully identified her with St. Edana, or Medana,[1] who is named in the Breviary of Aberdeen, on the 19th of November, as a virgin saint and a native of Ireland, and this identification has led him to an important discovery. Edinburg is commonly supposed to have been so called from a fort erected there

---

[1] The name Medana is formed from Mo-Edana, by contraction, of which we have many instances in the lives of our early saints. Thus St. Ita's name becomes Mida, &c.

by King Edwin, but long before that monarch's time St.
Edana's sanctuary there was a place of pilgrimage, and
it is, in truth, from this virgin saint of Ireland that the
modern names of Maiden Castle and Edinburgh are
derived. In the Aberdeen Breviary we read an interesting legend relating to our saint. One day, being pursued by a rude soldier, she climbed into a tree, and,
being told that it was her beauty which attracted him,
she plucked out her eyes and cast them to him. The
soldier was at once filled with remorse, and repented of
his wicked course, and the pious virgin, descending
from the tree, washed her wounds in a neighbouring
fountain, and her sight was miraculously restored.

One of the most interesting of the hallowed places
that now remain connected with this saint is her cave
chapel, situated close to the Mull of Galloway, the
most southern point of Scotland, in the parish which
from her derives its name, Kirkmaiden or Maidenkirk,
which I find thus described by a Scottish writer:—
"Descending a high and steep rock of the shore, you
find the cave-chapel secludedly shelved in the face of the
rock, and looking down upon huge, jagged rocks, lying
huddled in heaps at the foot of the crag, and running
out in long pointed ridges a good bit into the bay. To
its situation its escape from total destruction must be
attributed. Nevertheless, it is now sadly dilapidated.
The roof, probably rudely arched, has long since
disappeared. The artificially-builded portions consist
only of the wall fronting the sea, and that which is laid
up behind against the face of the cliff, the side ones
being naturally supplied by great jutting slabs of whin,
or whatever it is. The area of the cell is nearly a

square of very small size, the builded portion of great thickness, and rudely made up of uncemented stones of all sizes and shapes. The wall facing the sea contains traces of a door-way, and an inwardly-splayed window, the clear of which is not more than nine inches wide. In the other wall the door-way is happily entire, forty-four inches in height, with slightly-sloping jambs, and long narrow stones roughly set over its massive lintel, in form of an arch. The cave to which this aperture gave entrance is of very irregular form, small and low in the roof. Of what height the roof of the cell or chapel was it is impossible to say; but, as in a building so diminutive, it could not have been great; it is puzzling to find the inner, or cliff wall, reaching as much as twenty feet up from the ground. If by this we are led to believe that another apartment—an upper sanctuary, or dormitory, or refugium, whilst the wild Picts were down on the shore—rose above the cell, what would we not now-a-days give to have it entire?"[1]

There is yet another saint of Strathclyde, to whom we must devote more than a passing notice. St. Kentigern—popularly known by the name of St. Mungo—is justly reckoned among the chief patron saints of Scotland. He was born about the year 514. His mother was Irish, and in the saint's life her name is presented to us under the form of Thenew or Thenog. As yet a pagan, she had, by intercourse with Christian friends, become acquainted with the truths of faith, and had learned to honour with special reverence, and to invoke with earnest devotion, the holy Mother of God.

[1] *Muir's* "Lighthouse," pp. 65–68.

Being accused of a grievous crime, she was sentenced to be cast down from a high rock called Kep-duff in the Lammermoor. In this terrible trial she had recourse to the Blessed Virgin, and by her protecting aid was miraculously saved from death. This, however, did not secure her pardon. By order of the chieftain of the district, she was placed in a little coracle[1] at the mouth of the river Aberlassig (now Aberlady), and being conducted into the open sea, beyond the Isle of May, was there abandoned to her fate. "If she be worthy of life," he said, "the God whom she invokes will free her, if He wills, from the perils of the sea." Here again the powerful aid of the Blessed Virgin did not forsake her. Without sail or oar the little boat drifted to a sandy beach at Culenross (the modern Culross) in Fifeshire, not far from the hermitage where St. Servan, called by the Scots St. Serf, led a life of prayer and penitential exercises. She found shelter in a cave close to the beach, and there she gave birth to Kentigern. The shepherds from the adjoining hills ministered food and clothing to the mother and child, and after a time brought her to St. Servan's cell. On learning her miraculous preservation, he took both mother and son under his protection, and, administering Baptism to them, declared that henceforth he would be a father to them. To the child he gave the name of Kentigern (*i.e.*, *Ceann*, head or chief, and *Tighearn*, lord or master), prophetically announcing that he would one day be the great leader and spiritual guide of the people

---

[1] "Parvissimo lembo de corio juxta morem Scottorum confecto." *Vita.* cap. 3.

of all Strathclyde. As the child advanced in years such was his amiability, and so endeared was he to everyone by the sweetness of his virtues, that his holy master was accustomed to call him by the name *Munghu* (which in Celtic means an amiable and beloved one), and by this endearing name he continued to be generally known in after years.

As for Thenog, she made great proficiency in the paths of heaven under the guidance of St. Servan, and becoming famed for sanctity, merited in after times a place in the Scottish kalendars. A chapel was built upon the spot where she had given birth to Kentigern, and the ruins of a mediæval church may still be traced there. At an early period a church was also dedicated to her in Glasgow, but it was demolished at the Reformation period. St. Enoch's Square now marks its site, and seldom do the thrifty Scotchmen of the present day advert that it is from St. Thenog, our Irish saint, their busy mart is named, and that thus in some little way at least they unconsciously pay a tribute of honour to her memory.

St. Kentigern, as the writer of the life informs us, made rapid strides in virtue and learning at St. Servan's school, for "there were bestowed upon him by the Father of Light, from whom is every good and perfect gift, an apt intelligence and a docile heart." The armorial bearings of the city of Glasgow perpetuate the memory of one of the miracles performed at this time by St. Kentigern. On a shield argent is a robin-redbreast. This little bird was wont to perch itself and sing upon St. Servan's shoulder, but one of St. Kentigern's ccmpanions pulled off its head, and, envying the special affection shown to Kentigern by their master, threw it into his lap. When St. Servan approached, the holy youth made the sign of the cross upon the bird and breathed a fervent prayer, and in vindication of his sanctity the little red-breast gathered together its limbs, flapped its wings, and resting on St. Servan's shoulder, began to sing once more.

Having attained the years of manhood, the saint took his departure from St. Servan, and crossing the estuary of the Forth, pursued his way to "Cathures," which is now called Glasgow. As he journeyed on, he found at a place called Carnock, an old man, who, having led a long life of holy conversation, had received the promise from heaven that he would not die till he was visited by a servant of God. As the saint now entered the dwelling, the old man intoned the *Nunc Dimittis*, and "making his confession, and being anointed with the oil of forgiveness, and strengthened by the vivifying sacrament of the Lord's Body and Blood,"[1] he joyfully closed his eyes in peace. At Cathures, Kentigern built for himself a cell on the banks of the Mellendonor, close by a cemetery which had been blessed by St. Ninian, and there he lived in great holiness of life. It is specially recorded that he planted the cemetery with trees, and as late as the year 1500 we find "the trees of St. Kentigern" used as a landmark in the deeds of the city of Glasgow. Disciples soon gathered around him, and he erected for them a rude monastery, with an earthen rath and wattled church. This chosen spot, thus blessed by SS. Ninian and Kentigern, and hallowed a

[1] *Vita*, cap. ix.

few years later by the presence of St. Columbkille, was marked out for special blessings from God, and we cannot wonder that it should be styled in after times "the bright and lovely spot," for such is the meaning of the name—*Glasgow*. As the city and canton of St. Gall's, in Switzerland, had their origin in the cell of the Irish missionary, Saint Gall, and Armagh grew up around the church blessed by St. Patrick, and Wurzburg around St. Killian's tomb, so from the humble beginnings of St. Kentigern's monastery has sprung up the queenly city which adorns the banks of the Clyde, and with its 600,000 inhabitants now ranks as second city of the Empire.

Owing to the distracted state of Strathclyde, arising in part from the invasion of the Saxons, and in part from the perpetual intestine wars among the petty princes of the British race, irreligion and iniquity had undone in great measure the holy work of St. Ninian, and paganism—once more in the ascendant—seemed to rule supreme throughout a considerable part of the kingdom. Now, however, the king and people were moved by the example and the lessons of Kentigern, and with one accord asked him to become the shepherd and pastor of their souls. Kentigern for a while was unwilling to assume this charge, and pleaded his inexperience, for he had not as yet attained his thirtieth year. But they overruled all his difficulties, and, as the Life takes care to add, "sending for a bishop to Ireland," Kentigern was duly consecrated, and was solemnly enthroned as their bishop. We are not told the name of the Irish bishop thus chosen to impose hands on Kentigern, and to cement thus early that spiritual union of Glasgow with the Irish Church which has continued to the present day; for Glasgow is even now quickened by Celtic faith in the renewed splendour of the hierarchy of the Scottish Church. The city is still one of the greatest centres of Irish piety, and the Archiepiscopal See numbers almost as many Catholics as are found in all the rest of Scotland.

The consecration of St. Kentigern is generally assigned to the year 540. There were many holy bishops at that time in Ireland. The first order of the saints of our country, who were for the most part bishops, did not close till the year 544, and not to mention others of less note, there were St. Ailbhe, of Emly; St. Fedhlemidh, of Kilmore; St. Lugadh, of Connor; and St. Nathy, of Achonry, still living and watching over their spiritual flocks, and it is not improbable that it was one of those that consecrated St. Kentigern. For a while peace and sunshine smiled on the labours of our saint, many of the pagan inhabitants were brought to the paths of Christian life, and many, too, who had been deceived by heretical teaching[1] were reconciled to the one true church. Some of the details of St. Kentigern's life at this period, as set forth by his biographer, are full of the deepest interest. He made the visitations of his vast diocese on foot, and from Loch Lomond and Stirling to Windermere and beyond Appleby, he went about with his disciples, everywhere preaching the faith of Christ. From his episcopal consecration till his death, his food was bread, milk, fruits, herbs, and water, breaking his fast only once in three or four days, and abstaining from flesh-meat and wine. For his dress he wore, besides a hair shirt, a long garment of goat-skin, with a narrow hood

[1] *Vita*, cap. xix.

like that of a fisherman, and over it an alb and stole. He carried in one hand a pastoral staff of simple wood bent backwards, and in the other his ritual or the scriptures, ever ready to exercise his sacred ministry. His couch was more like a sepulchre than a bed, and was of rock, with a stone for his pillow. He rose in the night and chanted psalms and hymns till the second cock-crowing. He then plunged into a cold stream, and with his thoughts fixed on heaven finished the recital of the psalter. During Lent he retired to desert places, and how he was fed there was a mystery to his disciples. In one of his instructions, however, he instanced that a certain person whom he knew had lived sometimes on roots, and sometimes had been so sustained by the power of God as to live without any food; and the Life adds, none doubted that he spoke of himself. He returned to his episcopal duties on Holy Thursday, spent the two following days in meditation on the Passion of our Blessed Lord, and celebrated Easter Day with great solemnity and joy. Leading such a life of self-denial and holiness, we cannot be surprised that many miracles accompanied his preaching. Thus, on one occasion, when Morcant, the ruler of the district, had said to him in mockery before his attendants: "If, trusting in thy God, thou canst transfer to thy dwelling all the corn that is in my barns and granaries, I will gladly be obedient to thee, and will for the future grant all thy requests." Soon after the waters of the Clyde overflowing their banks, surrounded the barns of the king, and drawing them into its own channel, carried them along, and deposited them upon the banks not far from the Mellendonor, where our saint dwelt.

St. Kentigern had much to suffer for a time from this wicked prince, so much so that the death of Morcant was attributed to Divine vengeance for the insults offered to our saint. After the death of this chieftain, Satan stirred up new commotions against our saint, and plots were laid against his life, wherefore he deemed it prudent to withdraw for a time from Strathclyde, and to seek an asylum in the monasteries of Wales. As he journeyed thither he turned aside at Carlisle, for he heard that "there were many in that mountainous district given to idolatry, or ignorant of the divine law." Carlisle was, from the time of the Romans, an important city. From them it received the name of Luguvallium (contracted to *Luel* by the Angles, and subsequently, when fortified, called *Caer-Luel*), and even in the time of Bede retained the traces of its former splendour; and its walls and ornamental structures betokened the munificence of its imperial masters. St. Kentigern remained here till he brought the erring inhabitants to the light of truth. Not far distant, at a place thickly planted with trees, he erected a cross, whence it took the name of Crossfield (now Crosthwaite), and in later times a noble basilica was erected there "to the name of blessed Kentigern." From thence he directed his steps along the seashore, scattering everywhere the seeds of the Faith, and gathering a rich harvest to God. Eight churches in Cumberland still bear the saint's name; and at Bromfield, close by the church, there is a spring of pure water called St. Mungo's Well.

St. David's was at this time at the head of all the monasteries of Wales, and Kentigern was welcomed by its holy founder, not as a disciple, but as a father and master. Caswallawn, king of Wales, and his son, Maelgwyn, soon offered to the pilgrim bishop a site wheresoever he would choose for a new monastery. He went around the land, says his biographer, and finally selected a spot on the banks of a river, and there disciples flocked around him. The work of erecting the new monastery was distributed amongst them. Some levelled the ground and cleared the forest, others dug the foundations of the church and fitted the planks of the trees together, for Kentigern directed them to erect the church of wood " after the fashion of the Britons, seeing they could not yet build of stone, nor were they so wont to do."[1] Thus was founded the great monastery of Llanelwy, called in after times St. Asaph's. The stream on whose banks it stood was called the Elwy, and the valley was named the Valley of the Clyde, now Clewd, probably from some fancied resemblance to the river and valley where he had before fixed his original seat. The piety of Kentigern was not less fruitful in Wales than it had been in Strathclyde. "There flocked to his monastery old and young, rich and poor, to take upon themselves the easy yoke and light burden of the Lord. Nobles and men of the middle class brought to the saint their children to be trained and educated. He divided his disciples into three classes of religious observances. Three hundred, who were unlettered, he appointed to the duty of agriculture, the care of the cattle, and the other necessary duties outside the monastery; to another three hundred he assigned the duties of manual work within the enclosure; and the remaining monks who

---

[1] *Vita*, cap. xxiv.

were lettered, he appointed to the service of the altar by day and by night, and seldom were they allowed to depart from the sanctuary, abiding there as in the holy place of God. But those who were more advanced in wisdom and holiness, and who were fitted to teach others, he was accustomed to take with him when he went forth to perform the duties of his episcopal office."[1] Such is the picture of this Celtic monastery of St. Kentigern, which his Life presents to us, and we cannot be surprised that it was soon reckoned among the chief centres of piety in North Wales. When the saint at length took his departure from Wales, he chose a monk of the monastery named Asaph to take his place, and the fame of this pious man for learning and sanctity in after years justified the choice. The Cathedral Church was dedicated to God under the invocation of this saint, and many places in the adjoining territory still bear his name, as Lan-Asa (St. Asaph's Church), Ffynnon-Asa (St. Asaph's Well), Pantasa (St. Asaph's Hollow), &c.[2] His memory is also cherished in the island of Skye, and among the springs with which that island abounds there is one considered superior to all the rest, and is called *Tober-Asheg, i.e.*, the miraculous well of St. Asaph.

In the meantime great changes had taken place in Strathclyde. Providence had raised up an illustrious prince—Rederech—to restore peace in that distracted territory. He was surnamed *Hael* or *Hial, i.e.*, ' The Bountiful,'[3] and it seems to be now unquestioned that

[1] *Vita*, cap. xxv.
[2] *Thomas*' ' History of the Diocese of St. Asaph.' page 55.
[3] Geoffrey of Monmouth latinizes his name *Rodarchus Largus;* and he is honoured in the Welsh Triads as one of the "three liberal princes of Britain." *Triad* xxx., Myvyr. Archæol., ii., p. 63.

he was of Irish parentage, for his father's name was Tuathal, and his mother Eithne, in the genealogies of the saints, is expressly styled *Gwyddles*, i.e., 'The Irishwoman.' Aided by Aedan, king of Scottish Dalaradia, and by Maelgwyn of Wales, he defeated the pagan king Gwendoleu at the great battle of Ardderyd, in the year 573, and by his wisdom and valour soon moulded all the contending tribes of Strathclyde into one powerful kingdom.

Rederech was a Christian. He had been instructed in the divine truths by the disciples of St. Patrick in Ireland, as St. Kentigern's Life expressly records, and being baptized there had been solidly grounded in the Faith.[1] It was one of his first cares to invite St. Kentigern to return to his kingdom. The saint set out with joy, and Rederech, hearing of his approach, went forth accompanied by a numerous retinue to welcome him on his return. They met at a place called Holdelm, now Hoddan, in Dumfries-shire, and as an immense multitude soon assembled, St. Kentigern embraced the opportunity to address them; and from his discourse as registered in his Life, we may gather what were the main features of the paganism into which the inhabitants had fallen. Three things he specially dwelt on: 1st, they should not adore the elements, for these were not self-originated, but owed their existence to the one true God who made all material things for the use and service of man. 2nd, the idols should not be worshipped; they were the work of their own hands, fitter far to be burned than to receive religious worship. 3rd.

---

[1] *Vita*, "A discipulis Sancti Patricii in Hibernia baptisatus fide Christianissima," cap. xxix.

Woden, whose worship the Angles had introduced, was no deity, but a mere mortal man, the father and leader of one of their tribes, consigned to the grave like other men. We are also told that the saint when beginning his discourse pronounced the solemn words: "Let all who obstruct the salvation of this people, depart hence," whereupon a number of frightful spectres fled away in the sight of all the people, who were filled with astonishment and holy fear.

Holdelm, the place where Kentigern had thus met his royal patron, was chosen by him as his residence for a time, and thence he made missionary excursions among the Picts, and in the eastern districts of Scotland, north of the Firth of Forth, where he erected many churches. After some time he returned to his original seat at Glasgow, and continued there to guide his spiritual children. Several ancient churches still bear his name in various parts of Scotland. They are particularly found in Aberdeenshire and Lothian, and in the districts evangelized by his master, St. Servan. St. Kentigern used to erect crosses wherever he preached. Two of these were still extant in the twelfth century—one in the cemetery of the Church of the Holy Trinity, the other at Lotherwerd. Seven times he made the pilgrimage to Rome, and on the occasion of his last visit enjoyed a long conference with the holy Pontiff, St. Gregory the Great, who bestowed upon him copies of the sacred scriptures and relics of the saints, and many ornaments for the altar, and other rich gifts.

In extreme old age—knowing that his hour was at hand—he summoned his disciples around him, and exhorted them to the observance of their rule, mutual charity, hospitality to the poor, and study; and he left to them, as his last bequest, that they should shun the communion of heretics, and be ever united with the Roman See. Then he blessed each one in turn, consigning them to the tutelage of the Blessed Trinity, and to the protection of the holy Mother of God. He then gathered himself upon his stone couch, and arming himself with the sign of the cross, soon after rested in peace on Sunday, the 13th of January, in the year 603.[1] The well of our saint still exists in the Cathedral, and his body is supposed to lie buried in the crypt. St. Kentigern's bell, which is said to have been brought by himself from Rome, was preserved till after the period of the Reformation, but cannot now be traced.[2] For centuries it was tolled through the city at the close of day, to warn the citizens to pray for the repose of the faithful departed souls.

Several relics of the saint are mentioned in the ancient Inventories of the Cathedral of Glasgow, but they are supposed to have been destroyed by the vandalism of John Knox and his followers in the sixteenth century.

Among the legends connected with St. Kentigern, that of the ring is one of the most beautiful. It has also been perpetuated in popular tradition, and has left its record on the Arms of the City of Glasgow. It is as follows:—
The Queen, in token of affection, bestowed on a young courtier a valuable ring, which was a marriage gift of

---

[1] This seems the most probable date of St. Kentigern's death. Chalmers, in his "Caledonia," writes: "St. Kentigern died on the 13th January, 601, after performing for the improvement of the people all that zeal could suggest, or perseverance could execute." However, the 13th of January, in 601, did not fall on Sunday.

[2] Reg. Ep. Glas., vol. ii., page 334.

the king. This was pointed out to the king, and one day as the courtier slept, fatigued by the chase, the king drew the ring off his finger and threw it into the Clyde. Returning home enraged, he demanded of the queen where was the ring which he had given her in token of conjugal affection. She replied that she would search for it and bring it to him. She soon learned from the courtier all that had occurred, and going to Kentigern, made known her misery to him. Commiserating her weakness, and full of compassion for her in her affliction, the saint desired her to send to the Clyde, and to bring to him the first fish that would be caught. When the fish was brought, the ring was found in it, and to the great joy of all, the queen thenceforward proved herself most faithful and affectionate to her royal husband.

The name of St. Servan has been repeatedly mentioned in the preceding pages in connection with St. Kentigern. He was a disciple of St. Patrick, and sailed for Scotland, where he erected a monastery on the winding shores of the Forth, near the town of Culross, and trained many fervent souls in the paths of perfection. He cherished Kentigern, as we have seen, with special affection, and when that saint departed from Culross, he went after him, crying out: "Alas, my dearest son! light of mine eyes! staff of my old age! wherefore dost thou desert me? Call to mind the days that are past, and remember the years that are gone by; how I took thee up when thou camest forth from thy mother's womb, nourished thee, taught thee, trained thee, even unto this hour. Do not despise me, nor neglect my grey hairs, but return, that in no long time thou mayest close mine eyes."[1] And when St. Kentigern nevertheless continued his course, Servan again cried aloud, asking to be permitted to accompany him, and to be reckoned among his disciples; but Kentigern replied: "I go whither God calls me, but do thou return, I pray thee, my father, to thine own disciples, that in thy holy presence they may be trained in sacred doctrine, guided by thy example, and restrained by thy discipline."[2] Wherefore, Servan, returning to his monastery, awaited the day of his repose, and soon after was gathered to his fathers. He is honoured in the Scottish Calendars on the 1st of July. By our Irish writers he is called St. Serb, whilst in some parts of Scotland his name has been corrupted to *Sair* and *Sare*.[3] At Culross, till a late period, an annual procession was held in his honour. "Early on the morning of the feast (thus runs the official account) all the inhabitants—men and women, young and old—assembled and carried green branches through the town, decking the public places with flowers, and spent the rest of the day in festivity."[4]

One of the most illustrious of St. Kentigern's disciples was St. Conval, who inherited in an eminent degree the zeal and sanctity of his great master. He was the son of an Irish chieftain,[5] and forsaking his country and friends, through the desire of winning souls to God, sailed to the banks of the Clyde,[6] and enrolling himself

---

[1] *Vita S. Kentig.*, cap. viii. [2] *Vita*, ibid.
[3] See Forbes's Kalendars, page 447.
[4] *Old Stat. Account*, vol. xviii., page 649.
[5] Forbes's Kalendars, page 315.
[6] "Ad clodum flumen, cujus ager propter omnia fructuum genera, aliasque amoenitates, Scotiæ paradisus habetur." *Bollandists*, Acta SS. Maii, tom. iv., page 182.

among the clergy of St. Kentigern, soon proved himself
a devoted missioner, and became a bright ornament of the
Scottish Church. In many of the mediæval records he
is styled Archdeacon of Glasgow, and by his untiring
labours he merited to be honoured as a second apostle
of that great city. Each memorial of the saint was long
cherished by the faithful to whom he ministered. The
rock on which he landed on the sea-shore, and on which
in after years he was wont to pray, was held in the
greatest veneration, and several churches erected under
his invocation attested the reverence and fond affection
in which his hallowed memory was held.[1] It is recorded
that he visited his countryman, King Aidan, of Dalriada,
and was welcomed by that prince with the highest
honours. The purport of St. Conval's visit was probably
to secure the aid of King Aidan for the religious works
in which he was engaged south of the Clyde; and we
are further told that, at that pious monarch's request,
St. Conval passed into the Pictish territory, and there
gained many souls to God. He also visited St. Columba,
and seems for a time to have been associated with that
great saint in his missionary labours.

He is venerated as patron at Inchinnan, in Renfrewshire, on the Clyde, about seven miles below Glasgow,
and Boece writes that the saint's relics were still preserved there in his time.[2] Near the ancient fort of

[1] The ancient Martyrology of Aberdeen gives us the following
eulogy of St. Conval:—" In Scocia apud Inchenan Sancti Convalli confessoris cujus prædicatio præclaram sanctitatis suæ
excellentiam signorum choruscatione posteris morum præbet
incrementum."

[2] *Boetius* Hist. Scot.: " Convalli divi Kentigerni discipuli Reli-
quiæ celebri monumento in Inchennan haud procul a Glascuensi

Inchinnan there stood, till a comparatively late period, an ancient Celtic cross, erected in honour of St. Conval. Now its base alone remains.[1] He was also venerated at Cumnock and at Ochiltree. The parish of Pollokshaws had also our St. Conval for its patron, although his feast was there kept in the month of May. "Its ancient church," thus writes the learned Cosmo Innes, "probably stood beside the castle upon the bank of the Cart. It was dedicated to St. Convallus, the pupil of St. Kentigern, whose feast was celebrated on the 18th of May." A church bearing St. Conval's name existed at Eastwood down to a comparatively late period. The burial ground attached to it is still used, and a portion of it near the still-flowing fountain that supplied the monks with water is set apart for the exclusive interment of Catholics, but no trace of the ancient church or monastery now remains. Near the burial ground there was a ruin known as the "Auld House," which, with its enclosure, was called "St. Conval's Dowry." His memory—after having been forgotten for three hundred years—has been revived in our days by the erection of a beautiful church at Pollokshaws, dedicated to God under the invocation of the Blessed Virgin and St. Conval. The site is a truly noble one; and the traditions of the district in which it stands point to many events of Catholic interest. "The new church," writes the present zealous pastor, "stands on the top of a hill, within a gunshot of, and looking over upon the fatal battlefield of Langside, where three hundred years

civitate, a Christiano populo hactenus in magna habentur veneratione:" lib. ix.

[1] *Stuart:* Sculptured Stones, &c., ii., 38.

ago, the death-knell of Catholicity in this country was said to have been sounded, on the occasion of the final defeat of its Catholic Queen, Mary. This defeat left Calvinism in the ascendant, by whose infatuated followers the old parish church was razed to the ground, and almost every local vestige of the ancient worship obliterated." The new church on the top of the hill is a sufficient proof that Catholicity has arisen from the tomb, and that the light of divine truth shines once more upon the children of St. Conval.

Contemporary with St. Conval was the royal Irish virgin, St. Bees. At an early age she sailed for the Northumbrian coast, and having received the religious veil at the hands of the illustrious Bishop, St. Aidan, she chose a desert island for her retreat, where a flourishing monastery soon grew up around her, which was celebrated for its piety throughout the whole kingdom of Northumbria. After some time she prayed to be relieved from the charge of this monastery, and to have St. Hilda appointed abbess in her stead, and this request being granted her, she proceeded to the kingdom of Strathclyde, and on the east coast of Cumberland, in the year 646, founded another monastery which gave name to the town and promontory of St. Bees, and for nine hundred years preserved the fragrance of the piety of its holy foundress. Rich grants were made to it in the course of centuries, not the least remarkable being "the grant of the island of Nendrum, with its appurtenances," off the coast of Ulster, made by John de Courcy, in the year 1178.[1] St. Bees died there in the

---

[6] *Reeves*, Eccles. Antiq., page 163.

odour of sanctity about the year 650, and her feast was kept throughout Britain and Scotland on the 31st of October. Many miracles were performed at her shrine, and around her monastery the pretty town of St. Bees sprung up, but not a trace of the original foundation can now be seen.

The legend of this saint, as given by Montalembert, merits to be cited at full length. "In the county which we now call Cumberland, upon a promontory bathed by the waves of the Irish Sea, and from which in clear weather the southern shore of Scotland and the distant peaks of the Isle of Man may be seen, a religious edifice still bears the name and preserves the recollection of St. Bees. She was the daughter of an Irish king, the most beautiful woman in the country, and already asked in marriage by the son of the king of Norway. But she had vowed herself, from her tenderest infancy, to the Spouse of virgins, and had received from an angel, as a seal of her celestial betrothal, a bracelet marked with the sign of the cross. On the night before her wedding-day, while the guards of the king, her father, instead of keeping watch with sabres at their sides and axes on their shoulders, were, like their guests, deep in the revel, she escaped alone, with nothing but the bracelet which the angel had given her, threw herself into a skiff, and landed on the opposite shore, in Northumbria, where she lived long in a cell in the midst of the wood, uniting the care of the sick poor around with her prayers. Fear of the pirates who infested these coasts led her, after a while, farther inland. . . . She was celebrated during her lifetime for her austerity, her fervour, and an anxiety for the poor, which led her, during the building of her monastery, to prepare with her own hands the food of the masons, and to wait upon them in their workshops, hastening from place to place like a bee laden with honey. She remained down to the middle ages the patroness of the laborious and often oppressed population of the district, in which tradition presents her to us as arriving alone and fearless on a foreign shore, flying from her royal bridegroom. In the twelfth century the famous bracelet which the angel had given her was regarded with tender veneration: the pious confidence of the faithful turned it into a relic, upon which usurpers, prevaricators, and oppressors, against whom there existed no defence, were made to swear, with the certainty that a perjury committed on so dear and sacred a pledge would not pass unpunished. It was also to St. Bees and her bracelet that the cultivators of the soil had recourse against the new and unjust taxes with which their lords burdened them. In vain the Scottish rievers, or the prepotents of the country, treading down under their horses' feet the harvests of the Cumbrians, made light of the complaints and threats of the votaries of the saint. 'What is the good old woman to me, and what harm can she do me?' said one. 'Let your saint come,' said another; 'let her come and do what she likes; she cannot make our horses cast their shoes.' Sooner or later Divine vengeance struck these culprits; and the fame of the chastisements sent upon them confirmed the faith of the people in the powerful intercession of her who, six hundred years after her death, still gave a protection so effectual and energetic against feudal rudeness, to the captive and to the oppressed, to the chastity of women, and the rights of the lowly, upon the western shore of Northumbria, as did St. Cuthbert throughout the rest of that privileged district." (Vol. v., p. 249).

During the five following centuries the religious history of Strathclyde is little more than a mere blank. Throughout all this period one authentic entry alone is found in the history of the councils, which modern Scottish antiquaries assign to this church, and it presents to us an Irish bishop holding the crozier of St. Kentigern, and ruling this British see. In the year 721 Pope Gregory the Second held a Synod in Rome, in which the Iconoclast Emperor, Leo, was condemned, and the people of Italy were declared free from all allegiance to him. Among the signatures to its decrees we find the following :—

"Sedulius, Brittaniæ Episcopus, de genere Scotorum.
Fergustus, Episcopus Scotiæ, Pictus."[1]

The name Sedulius corresponds to the Irish Siadhuil, or Shiel, and many bishops of that name appear in our annals. No Anglo-Saxon bishop would at that period have assumed the title of "Brittaniæ Episcopus." The sees of Wales were already closely defined, and in Dalriada or Pictland far different would be the episcopal designation. Wherefore, as Dr. Forbes justly concludes, his see must have been among the Strathclyde Britons. The other bishop was probably "St. Fergus, the Pict," whose name appears in our Martyrologies on the 8th September, and who, as we read in the Lessons of the Aberdeen Breviary, lived for many years in Ireland, and was there raised to the episcopal rank, but towards the

[1] *Mansi*, Concilia, viii., 109.

close of his life returned to Scotland, and preached the faith along the confines of Strogeth, and throughout Caithness and Buchan. He was probably as yet bishop in Ireland at the time of the Roman Council. A noble basilica was erected over his tomb at Lungley, and his head was enshrined in a silver case in the Abbey of Scone.

CHAPTER VI.

OTHER IRISH SAINTS IN SCOTLAND.

Irish Kingdom of Dalriada:—St. Kieran of Ossory:—St. Buite:— St. Modan's Sanctuaries: —St. Bridget's Monastery at Abernethy:—Irish origin of Scottish Sees:—St. Finian of Moville:— St. Coemghen:—St. Moanus:—St. Berchan:—St. Senanus:— St. Finbar:—St. Fechin:—St. Ernan:—SS. Ethernan and Itharnasch:—St. Fintan Munnu:—St. Beccan:—St. Flannan: —St. Dabius:—St. Gervad:—SS. Momhaedog and Tallarican.

THE Irish annals assign to the close of the fifth century[1] the first Christian settlement, which landed from Ireland on the Scottish coast, immediately north of the Firth of Clyde, and gave the name of Dalriada to that portion of the Pictish territory. Many of our pagan countrymen, indeed, had already preceded them, and by their predatory incursions had made the name of the

---

[1] The Irish chronicler, Flann, of Monasterboice, marks the date of this colony as follows :—" Twenty years from the Battle of Ocha to the arrival of the sons of Erc in Britain." The Battle of Ocha is generally assigned to the year 478. The Annals of Tighernac place the death of Fergus Mor in the year A.D. 501.

Scots a byword of terror and reproach throughout all Britain. Now, however, the three leaders of the colony were brave and Christian men—Fergus Mor, and Lorn, and Angus, the sons of Erc, chieftain of Dalriada—and though the territory which they occupied was little more than the present county of Argyll, yet such was their bravery and prowess in arms, and such, too, the wisdom of their rule, that the neighbouring districts very soon acknowledged their superior sway, and for a period of sixty years the rulers of Scottish Dalriada are honoured by our annalists with the title of Kings of Alba. About the year 560 they met with a momentary humiliation at the hands of Brude, the Pictish monarch; still they did not cease to assert their independence, and for two centuries their power and influence continued to be felt throughout north Britain. Their chief fortress was called Dunadd or Dunmonadh, from the River Add, on the banks of which it stood, and from the bog or marshy ground which stretched around it: "In the centre of the possessions of the Cinel Gabhran (writes Mr. Skene), at the head of the well-sheltered Loch of Crinan, lies the great Moss of Crinan, with the river Add running through it. In the centre of the Moss, and on the side of the river, rises an isolated rocky hill, called Dunadd, the top of which is strongly fortified. This was the capital of Dalriada, and many a stone obelisk in the Moss around it bears silent testimony to the contests of which it was the centre."[1]

About the middle of the eighth century this Scottish kingdom of Dalriada was well nigh destroyed by the

---

[1] *Skene*, Chronicles of the Scots and Picts, page cxiii.

Picts, but soon again its independence was restored, and its heroic chieftain, Cenneth Mac Alpine, being reinforced by fresh bands of his Irish fellow-countrymen, completely vanquished the Picts, and uniting all north Britain into one powerful kingdom, gave to it his royal dynasty, together with the name of Scotia. From Scottish writers he receives the title of "Primus Rex Scotorum," first king of the Scots: whilst the Irish chronicler briefly relates that "it was he who gave the kingdom of Scone to the Gael;" and Giraldus Cambrensis, an English writer of the twelfth century, treating of this period, adds his testimony that "the Scots having occupied the whole of north Britain, from sea to sea, gave to it their name, and continue to rule over it to the present day."[1]

It will not surprise us to find that Irish bishops and Irish priests soon followed in the track of the brave colonists of Dalriada. Their zeal, however, was not confined within the limits of that territory. They penetrated far beyond its frontiers, even to the wildest and remotest parts of north Britain, and there are few districts of modern Scotland in which these Irish missionaries may not be traced by the popular veneration in which their memory is held, or by the lonely and melancholy ruins of the oratories which bear their names, and of the cells and monasteries in which they dwelt. "All over Scotland," writes Dr. Forbes, "we note the close connection of this country with Ireland,

---

[1] *Giraldus Cambrensis*, De Instruct. Princ. "totam a mari usque ad mare terram illam, quam a suo nomine Scotiam dixerunt, usque in hodiernum obtinuerunt." See *Skene*, loc. cit., pag. 165.

although naturally it is in Argyllshire that we find the strongest evidence of the connection of the Dalriada Scots with their brethren of Erin; and through this province, above all, does our country claim a share in that wonderful Christian civilization and culture which is the glory of Ireland."[1] At times, indeed, we are only able to glean some vague and imperfect traditions relating to these pilgrim saints, who in those early ages shed such lustre upon our country; even these traditions, however, should be guarded with zealous care, for, like the remnants of their monasteries, they serve to mark the course of their missionary labours, and to remind us of that beauty of Christian life which the ruthless fanaticism of the sixteenth century sought for ever to obliterate in the fairest districts of Scotland.

St. Kieran, patron saint of Ossory, was among the first of the missionary bishops who hastened to minister to the spiritual wants of his countrymen in Scottish Dalriada. We have already seen how he laboured in Wales and along the southern coast of Britain, and with what reverence his memory is still cherished there. He is not less honoured, however, to the present day at Campbeltown, and all along the Mull of Cantyre, where the Scottish mainland approaches nearest to Ireland. The oldest church of Campbeltown still bears his name, and other churches were dedicated to him in Carrick, and Islay, and Lismore. His feast was kept throughout Argyll and Ayrshire, as it is in Ossory, on the 5th of March. His hermitage, near Campbeltown, and his cave, deep hidden in the rocks, whither he used to retire

---

[1] *Forbes*, Kalendars, pref. pag. xlviii.

for prayer and solitude, and his holy well, are visited by pilgrims; and year by year on each recurring festival, pious crowds may be seen wending their way for about a quarter of a mile along the path of pilgrimage, from the venerable oratory of the saint down to the seashore, to St. Kieran's rock, which bears the impress of his knees, for there he was wont to kneel, and oftentimes, thence looking towards Erin, he prayed a blessing upon his native land.[1]

St. Buite, founder of the great monastery of Monasterboice, was a contemporary of St. Kieran, and preached in Scotland for a little while towards the close of the fifth or the beginning of the sixth century. By our early writers he was likened for his virtues and manner of life to the Venerable Bede, and his death is marked with great precision in our annals on the 7th of December, in the year 521. The following particulars are taken from the MS. Life of the Saint,[2] which is pre-

---

[1] The Island of Sanda, situated off the southern coast of Cantyre, has two Celtic crosses and the ruins of a chapel, called Kilmashenaghan, but no tradition is now preserved in the island in regard to the Saint Shenaghan, from whom it takes its name. However, the island was visited two centuries ago by F. Edmund MacCana, and, in a short record of his visit, which has fortunately been preserved, he relates that there was a small chapel in the island dedicated to St. Ninian, and united to it the burial-place of the fourteen sons of the most holy Irishman, St. Senchan, all of whom were famed for their sanctity, and are named in our calendars on the 23rd of June. Their tombs were marked by seven large and polished stones, and the enclosure was regarded as an inviolable sanctuary. F. MacCana adds that the arm of St. Ultan, preserved in a silver reliquary, was found in this island, and was then in the possession of one of the noble clan of the MacDonells. See the original Latin text of F. MacCana's interesting record in the Proceedings of the R.I.A., vol. viii., pag. 134.

[2] Bodleian MSS., Rawlinson, 505, fol. 154.

served in the Bodleian Library at Oxford. He was a native of the county of Londonderry, and from his infancy was endowed with the gift of miracles; he was even said to have been instructed by the angels in the knowledge of the sacred Scriptures. To perfect himself in divine truth, and in the practices of piety, he proceeded to Italy, and, entering a monastery there, lived for several years unknown to the world, but endeared to the religious brethren by his meekness and other virtues. Being divinely admonished, he resolved at length to direct his steps towards home,[1] and receiving many precious gifts of copies of the sacred Scriptures, and vestments for the altar, and relics of the saints, he set out from Rome, accompanied by a venerable senior, whose special duty it was to check his ardour while assailing the enemies of truth. On their homeward journey they were joined by a religious company from Germany of sixty men and ten virgins, all of whom desired to put themselves under the guidance of our saint, and to become pilgrims with him for God. Sailing from Gaul, they landed in the Pictish territory in north Britain, and found the people in the greatest grief and commotion in consequence of the death of their king, Nectan, who had just then departed this life. At the prayers of our saint, the monarch was restored to life, to the indescribable joy of his subjects, and to the great glory of God. St. Buite was in consequence permitted to preach the faith, and received in token of gratitude a gift of the royal fort in which the miracle

---

[1] The MS. says that he left the monastery, "trigesimo peregrinationis suae anno." This may mean the thirtieth year of his age, or the thirtieth year of his monastic life.

took place. He tarried there for some time, and erected an oratory, and many of the inhabitants were led to the saving knowledge of divine truth. Leaving some of his companions to continue the work of the mission which he had so successfully begun, he proceeded to the sea coast, and sailed for Ireland. Such is the concise narrative of St. Buite's labours in Scotland, which his life presents to us, and the ablest Scottish antiquaries in our own day have not been able to question its accuracy. The religious company from Germany, who sought a secure asylum under the guidance of our saint, were probably driven from their monasteries beyond the Rhine by the sword of the victorious pagan Franks, pretty much as the religious of our own times have been obliged to fly from the same territories by the persecuting laws of triumphant infidelity. Scottish writers point out at Dunnichen the site of the great fortress of King Nectan, and not far from it are the ruins of an ancient fort, still known by the name Carbuddo, which is supposed to be a corruption of Caer-Buido, that is to say, "St. Buite's Fort."

St. Modan, whose spiritual labours may be traced all along the west coast of Scotland, was also an Irish saint. In the Kalendar of Adam King his death is marked in the year 507, but other Scottish writers generally assign it to A.D. 522. He was the son of an Irish chieftain, and devoted his life to minister to the spiritual wants of his countrymen in Scottish Dalriada. Several places still bear his name, though in too many of them his teaching and his virtues are now forgotten. The picturesque glen and ruins of Balmodhan, that is, "St. Modan's Town," situate at a short distance from the site of the ancient priory of Ardchattan, on the shores of Loch Etive, mark the spot on which he erected his first oratory. A few paces from the ruins we meet St. Modan's well, a clear, refreshing spring, at which pilgrimages were made within the memory of persons still living. An interesting sketch of Balmodhan, and the other sanctuaries of St. Modan, has been lately published by Rev. Mr. Story, from which I take the following extracts: "The ruins of Balmodhan," he writes, "crown a grassy knoll, which overhangs the glen, and is divided from the upper slopes of the hill by a deep green hollow. The masonry is strong and rough, but little more than the gables and the outline of two broken walls remain, overshadowed by the ash trees that have planted themselves among the stones, the existing trees growing out of the remains of roots, all gnarled and weather-worn, of immensely greater age. In every crevice thorn, rowan, ivy, and fern have fastened themselves, softening and concealing the sanctuary's decay. When you turn to the west you realise the full nobleness of the site chosen for St. Modan's chapel. Your eye passes quickly over the waving woods that stretch along the nearer braes, and over the narrow entrance to the loch, to rest on the broader and more distant waters of the mighty Sound, bounded on the right by the green meadows of Lismore; while, filling all the rest of the horizon, stretches the grand and towering range of Mull, now shadowing with mist, now purple in sunshine, always vast, lonely, solemn. Descending from the ruin to the glen, a few paces bring you to the Well of Modan, which sends a tiny rivulet, pure and cold, to join its tinkle to the murmur of the burn that hastens downwards betwixt banks rich in fern and fox-glove. Above the well the young branches of an aged yew-tree have been trained with their dark arms to form a circling bower."[1] Near the shores of another loch, on the verge of the Western Highlands, in Dumbartonshire, stands the church of Rosneath, which also honours St. Modan as patron. It was formerly known as *Rossneveth*, *i.e.*, the Promontory of the Sanctuary, and sometimes it was called simply *Neveth*, the Sanctuary.[2] The promontory is formed by the Gairloch, and Loch Long, and here, too, a glen was the saint's abode, not unlike that which surmounts the priory of Ardchattan. It is called the " Clochan Glen," probably from the saint's cell or oratory, and tradition says that a miraculous well was formerly here resorted to by pious pilgrims. Now the ancient burial-ground and adjacent kirk alone retain the name of St. Modan. The site was admirably selected by the saint. "In the morning he could watch the sun striking the grim summit of Alcluyd, the stronghold of the Britons, and in the evening see it tinge with gold and purple the rugged screen of Highland hills, on which the race of Diarmaid had not yet laid their tenacious grasp, and behind whose wild barriers lay the broad waters of the west." (Story, pag. 42). The Canons Regular came hither in later times to carry on the work of religion and civilization begun by St. Modan. Their cloister stood on the fertile plain beneath the sanctuary, or "heavenly ground," hallowed by the saint; now not a stone upon a stone remains to mark its site. Under the wild ranges of

---

[1] "Saint Modan," by R. H. Story, D.D., 1878, pag. 13.
[2] Origin., Paroch. I., 28.

Ardgour stood another church, dedicated to St. Modan, a few ruins of which may still be seen beside the ancient churchyard. In the mediæval charters, by a corruption of the name, it is called Killevaodin and Kilbodane. In at least one other place in Argyllshire, St. Modan's name is still preserved, for we meet with the parish of Kilmodan, above Loch Riddan, on the Kyles of Bute. The modern kirk stands on the site of the ancient church, close by the flat sandy shore of the loch, where the Ruel, which gives its name to Glendaruel, discharges its shallow waters. St. Modan's work of evangelization extended as far east as Falkirk, for the old church of that town, called *Eglais Breac*, was dedicated to him, and the High Church of Stirling also honoured him as patron. Till a few years ago a large flat stone was preserved near Balmhaodan, known as *Suide-Mhaodain*, or St. Modan's seat, but some ruthless Presbyterian split it into lintels for doors and windows. Some curious traditions regarding the " Yellow Bell" of the saint, and its wonderful cures, are also jealously preserved on the shores of Loch Etive.

The Lessons in the ancient Breviary of Aberdeen for the saint's festival, on the 4th of February, give some details regarding his life. From his early years he lived under the monastic rule, and as a faithful soldier and servant of Christ continually warred against his spiritual enemies. His food was of the austerest kind, and he never used wine or other delicacies. By his preaching "the whole Scotic race, which dwelt on the west side of the Forth and at Falkirk," became instructed in divine truths. Finding that his end approached, " he retired to a lonely place near the ocean of Scotia, not far from Dumbarton and Lochgarloch," where the church of Rosneth now stands, and there rested in peace : "his most sacred relics repose in a certain chapel of the cemetery of the same church, and are held in the highest veneration." Devotion to St. Modan continued popular till a late period. Sir Walter Scott introduces it into the Sixth Canto of the Lay of the Last Minstrel :—

"Then each to each his troubled breast,
To some blest saint his prayers addressed—
Some to Saint Modan made their vows,
Some to Saint Mary of the Lowes."

In the north-east of Scotland, throughout Buchan, we find another Irish Saint Modan honoured on the 14th of November. The parish of Fintray was specially dedicated to him. The minister of St. Giles' Kirk there has in his possession (writes Dr. Forbes in 1872) a silver cup belonging to the parish, bearing the date of 1632, said by tradition to have been formed of the shrine which encased the relics of Saint Modan, and which in Catholic times was wont to be carried in procession through that parish, to awaken the piety of the people and to obtain the mercy of God at times of calamity and distress.

St. Bridget, chief patroness of Ireland, was also venerated in many churches of Scotland. The Scottish antiquarians teach us that in the beginning of the sixth century she proceeded thither, accompanied by nine saintly virgins, and settled at Abernethy. There she erected a church, under the invocation of the Blessed Virgin, which in the course of time became enriched with many royal gifts.[1] St. Darlughdach was chosen

[1] *Skene*, Chronicles of the Scots and Picts, pag. 6.

first abbess of the new community, and it is recorded in the Pictish Chronicle that Nectan Mor, in the fourth year of his reign "offered Abernethy to God and to Bridget, in the presence of St. Darlughdach, who chanted Alleluja over his pious gift."[1] It is added that this gift of Nectan extended from the termon of Apurfort to the termon of Lethfoss, and thence northwards to Athan. The same ancient record assigns the cause of Nectan's munificence to St. Bridget. He had been forced into exile in early life through the violence of his brother, Drust, and had sought a place of refuge in Ireland. Hearing of the sanctity and miracles of St. Bridget, he proceeded to Kildare, and besought her to be mindful of him in her prayers. St. Bridget comforted him by the prophetic announcement that he would return to his country, that God would have mercy on him, and that at no distant day he would possess the kingdom of the Picts in peace. The ancient Scottish dedications to St. Bridget were very numerous, especially along the western coast. Thus we find St. Bridget's convent in the parish of Kilmore in Bute, and her churches at Kilbride, seven miles from Glasgow, and at Rothesay, and Arran, and Uist, and in several other places. Again, there is St. Bridget's Well at Dunsyre, in Lanarkshire, and we meet with her chapel and burn at Kilbarchan, in Renfrewshire, and her chapel and holy well at Beath in Ayrshire. Her dedications are also found in the Lewes at Borve, and in Stronsay and Papa in the Orkneys. Her church, in the province of Athol, was famous for miracles, and a

---

[1] "Immolavit Nectonius Aburnethige Deo et Sanctæ Brigidæ, praesente Darlugdach quae cantavit Alleluja super istam hostiam." *Skene*, ibid.

portion of her relics was kept with great veneration in the monastery of Regular Canons at Abernethy. St. Bridget was the patroness of the great family of Douglas, and the church of Douglas still bears her name.[1]

It was from a portion of the religious territory of Abernethy that in later times was formed the Diocese of Brechin. The town of Brechin, too, had St. Bridget for its patron, and it is strange to find that the only two Round Towers on the mainland of Scotland must be sought for at the churches of Abernethy and Brechin. Of Brechin Diocese, Skene writes that "it emanated from the Irish Church, and was assimilated in its character to the Irish monasteries, and to this we may, no doubt, attribute the well-known Round Tower of Brechin."[2] Another portion of the religious territory of Abernethy was erected into the Bishopric of Dunblane. The origin of this church is assigned to the seventh century, when it was formed as an offshoot from Kingarth, and it had the Irishman, St. Blane, for its founder. The old church of Dunblane was situate in the vale of the river Allan, not far from its junction with the Forth, but during the reign of Kenneth MacAlpine it was burned by the neighbouring Britons of Strathclyde. St. Blane succeeded his countryman, St. Cathan, as bishop of Kingarth; he is named in the Festology of Ængus as "Blann, the mild, of Kingarth," and the gloss adds: "he was bishop of Kingarth: Dunblann is his principal city, and he is also of Kingarth among the Gallgael."

[1] *Forbes*, Kalendars, pag. 290. *Barbour's* Bruce, lib. iv., pag. 118. Spalding Club.
[2] *Skene*, Celtic Scotland, II., 400.

Thus it was that new sees sprung up in the Scottish Church through the fruitful labours of Irish saints. Brechin and Dunblane, however, are not the only dioceses in Scotland that must look to holy Irishmen for their origin. We have already seen how the first foundations of the great city and see of Aberdeen were traced by an illustrious disciple of St. Columba.[1] So, too, it was from the religious institutions built up by Irish piety that the primatial see of St. Andrew's sprung. Nor was this all. When Kenneth MacAlpine assumed the sovereignty of Scotland, Dunkeld[2] was for a time declared the chief see of Scotland, and it, too, had the Irishman Tuathal for its first bishop. After an interval, under the rule of king Constantine, St. Andrew's was once more restored to its place of privilege and honour, and again the name of the Irish bishop Cellach appears first on its primatial roll.[3] And it is to this illustrious bishop that the Scottish nation is indebted for the first great charter of its rights and liberties; for it was on the mount of faith at Scone, the Runnymede of Scotland, that the pious prince Constantine, and all the chieftains of the Scots assembled around Cellach, the bishop, and vowed "that the laws and disciplines of faith, and the rites of the churches, and of the Gospels likewise, should be observed."[4]

---

[1] See pag. 79.

[2] As late as the end of the 12th century, we find a bishop of Dunkeld, named John the Scot, petitioning the Holy See to have Argyll, which hitherto formed portion of his diocese, erected into a separate see, assigning as his reason that "the people thereof did only speak Irish," so that they could not understand him, nor he them. See Spottiswood's History of the Church of Scotland, ed. of 1847, vol. i., pag. 194.

[3] *Skene*, Chronicles, &c., clxii.   [4] *Forbes*, Kalendars, xlvii.

Before we part with St. Bridget, we must make mention of St. Finian, the illustrious founder of Moville. He was one of the greatest saints who adorned our country in the sixth century: he is honoured in Italy as the chief patron of the city of Lucca, and he is named with eulogy by the holy Pontiff, St. Gregory the Great. It is only, however, the Scottish traditions that record his spiritual labours on the mission in Scotland. The Breviary of Aberdeen relates that, whilst he preached the faith in Alba, he made with his own hands a stone cross of marvellous workmanship, and erected it in honour of St. Bridget.[1] St. Finian was long honoured at Kilwinning, as also at Holywood in Dumfries-shire, and at both places his holy well is still pointed out. He seems also to have preached at Dalry, where there is an ancient enclosure called Caer-Winning, or St. Finian's Fort.

And now a long list of Irish saints presents itself, pious anchorites or zealous missionaries, who evangelized Picts and Scots alike, that they might gain all to Christ, and the names of many of them shine brightly on the honour-roll as well of Ireland as of Scotland. I will do little more than mention the names of a few of them. St. Coemghen, the fair saint, who for his strict discipline and manner of life, is compared by our ancient writers with St. Paul, the first hermit, founded about the year A.D. 550 the famous monastery of Glendaloch, in which the angel's prediction was fully verified: "it shall be holy and honoured, and the kings and great ones of Ireland shall show it reverence for the sake of God and St. Coemghen." A little later he proceeded to Scotland,

[1] *Forbes*, Kalendars, pag. 290 and 463.

and seeking out some solitary glens, lived there for a time, emulating the austerities of the fathers of the East, and of the hermits of the Egyptian deserts. Down to the Reformation period his memory was cherished at Machririoch, in Argyllshire, and he was also venerated at Kilchevin and Kilchowan.

St. Moanus seems also to have led a life of heremitical austerity in Fife. He was the patron of Portmoak, and it is a tradition that it was at his invitation St. Brendan visited the islands to the north of the Scottish coast, and preached there the doctrines of heavenly life.

St. Berchan of Cluainsosta, in Offaly, spent half of his missionary career in Alba and half in Erin. In our Martyrologies he is styled "a Bishop and Apostle of God," and together with St. Columbkill, St. Moling, the perfect, and St. Brendan of Birr, he is numbered among the great prophets of our early church. Scottish writers tell us that he was bishop in the Orkney islands, and that he was venerated for his sanctity in the province of Stirling. He was also patron of Inchmahome, in the lake of Menteith, and of Kilbarchan in Renfrew. From Stuart's 'Sculptured Stones of Scotland' we learn that in the parish of Houston, in the barony of Barochan, there is a fine ancient Celtic cross dedicated to this saint.[1]

St. Senanus, patron of Iniscattery island, is honoured in Scotland under the name of Kessog and Moshenoc. At Eives, in Eskdale, he is joint patron with St. Cuthbert, and he was venerated at Achdashenaigh and Killenach in Mull, and at Kilmahunah in Cantyre. Robert Bruce

[1] *Stuart*, I., 35.

in 1318 granted to the church of Luss a sanctuary-territory of three miles, "Deo et sancto Kessogo," in a charter which is preserved at Buchanan. The bell of the saint "Sancta campana sancti Kessogii" was preserved in the Lennox in the seventeenth century. He was also patron of Callander, where his fair, called *Fel machessaig*, was kept on the 21st of March; there is also a curious artificial mound, where the old church stood, called by the people "Machessaig's mound."

St. Finbar, patron of Cork, was renowned for sanctity throughout Leinster and Munster. The first school which he established in the south was at an island in Lough Eirce, now known as Gougane-Barra. Colgan tells us that thither "as to the abode of wisdom, and the sacred storehouse of all Christian virtues, so many came through zeal of leading a holy life, that it changed a desert into a great city, from the number of its cells and of the holy men inhabiting them."[1] A later writer, speaking of this island, says that St. Finbar "wishing to lead a life of pious retirement, found a situation there, beyond all others, suitable to his desire; a retreat as impenetrable as the imagination could well conceive, and seemingly designed by nature for the abode of some sequestered anchorite, where, in undisturbed solitude, he might pour out his soul in prayer." Following the example of his fathers, St. Finbar made a pilgrimage to the shrines of the Apostles,[2] and subsequently laboured for a long time in North Britain. Dr. Forbes writes that "the cultus of this saint was very prevalent in Scotland."[3] It is strange to find that

[1] *Colgan*, Acta SS. ad diem 14th, Martin.
[2] *Usher*, Works, vol. vi., p. 521.   [3] *Forbes*, Kalendars, p. 275.

even as at home in Lough Eirce, so in Scotland it is in solitary islands that we are to seek for his chief sanctuaries. Martin, in his Western Islands, writes that Finbar is "the patron of Dornoch and of the island of Barra, which takes its name from him" (page 92). In the parish of Kilberran we find that the island now called Davar was known in former times as St. Barre's Island:[1] and again in the island of Barray, at Shilbar, which is a manifest corruption of his name, a statue of the saint was held in great veneration. In the 'Origines Parochiales Scotiæ,' we read that at Eddlestone his yearly festival was kept on the 25th of September, and it adds that "he obtained special reverence in Caithness" (vol. i., page 211).

St. Fechin, too, receives a high place in the Scottish Kalendars. A native of Leyney, in Connaught, his first spiritual work was at Easdara, now Ballysadare; and subsequently he founded a monastery at Fore, in Westmeath, where his community consisted of 300 monks. He received from king Guaire a gift of Omey island, off the coast of Connemara, the natives of which had hitherto led a pagan life, but were now converted by his preaching. He was also honoured at Inis-iarthair, or Ardoilen, which is described in his life as an almost inaccessible island. This saint would seem to have combined a strong national spirit with his piety. Before his death, in 664, he requested his disciples that no one from Cambria should ever inherit his abbacy. One characteristic miracle is also mentioned in his life. After the Anglo-Norman invasion there was an English friar in the monastery of Fore who hated the Irish, and

[1] Origin. Paroch. II., 12.

made no secret of the contempt with which he regarded their Irish patron, St. Fechin. One day, whilst he knelt before the altar, the saint appeared to him, and struck him with his pastoral staff; and, such was the violence of the blow, that in three days the unhappy man expired. In Scotland St. Fechin appears under the name Vigean and Viganach. His name occurs in the Dunkeld Litany. His chief sanctuary was at Grange, close to the ancient abbey of Arbroath, where, till the last century, a fair was held in his honour on the 20th of January. He was also honoured as patron at Ecclefechan, which, in mediæval charters, appears as "Ecclesia Sancti Fechani."

St. Ernan, or Mernog, who, though a poor neglected boy, when he touched the cowl of St. Columbkille at Clonmacnoise, yet merited to hear from the lips of that great saint the prophetic words that he would one day be an ornament of God's Church, appears in Scotland under the name Marnan and Marnock. The Breviary of Aberdeen states that he died at Aberkerdoure, "where to this day, through his intercession, the sick are restored to health." In the ancient Registry of of Aberbrothock mention is made of a portion of his relics held in veneration there, and also of the bier on which his relics used to be borne through the parish of Marnock. He was patron of the Innes family. About three miles south of Kilfinnan, and not far from the seashore, is to be seen the foundation and a small part of the wall of a chapel, surrounded by a churchyard, on a field called Ard-Marnoc ; and about three hundred yards above this chapel, on an eminence, there is a cell in which, according to the tradition of the country, the saint lived in the exercises of prayer and of a penitential life. There were other dedications to him at Inchmarnock, an island off the coast of Bute, and in several districts of the mainland.

There are two other saints who, on account of similarity of name, have sometimes been confounded by Scottish writers with St. Ernan, but who, nevertheless, have each a distinct place in the Irish Kalendars. These are St. Ethernan, who built a religious house in the Isle of May, and whose death is marked in the Annals of Ulster in the year 669; and St. Itharnasch, "the silent," one of the chief patrons of Clane, in the county Kildare, who was venerated at Lathrisk in Fife. In the Breviary of Aberdeen the following special prayer is assigned for his festival on the 22nd of December: "O God, who didst will that the soul of blessed Ithernasc, thy confessor, should penetrate to the stars of heaven, vouchsafe that, as we celebrate his venerable feast, we may, in thy mercy, through his intercessions and merits, be found worthy to ascend to the joys of his blessed life, through our Lord," &c.

St. Fintan Munnu, whose festival was observed as well in Ireland as in Scotland, on the 21st of October, was, from his youth, remarkable for sanctity. He is famed among the Irish saints for his austerities; his life was, indeed, a continuous martyrdom, and he looked on it as the greatest privation to be healed of the infirmities from which he suffered. The Feliré of St. Ængus commemorates him as

> "The torch with the ascending flame,
> Fintain, pure tested gold,
> The powerful abstemious son of Tulchan,
> A warrior religious and crucified."

His chief monastery in Ireland was Teach-Mun, now

Taghmon, and it is specially related that it was he that administered the holy viaticum to St. Canice. In Argyll he chose for his retreat an island in Loch Leven, which in after years was called by his name, and is still known as Eileanmunde. His chief Scottish foundation, however, was at Kilmun, on the north side of the Firth of Clyde, in Argyllshire, which to the present day honours his memory, and a picturesque old burial ground still marks the site of the ancient monastery. It is beautifully situated in a cluster of trees in a recess among the hills which branch off from the Firth of Clyde. A high hill rises behind it, and glens of the wildest kind abound on every side, and make it one of the most picturesque spots in the Western Highlands. In front of the burial place is a small sheet of water, still called the Holy Loch. There is a curious tradition relating to the origin of this name. A shipload of earth, it says, was conveyed from the Holy Land to be placed in the foundations of the old church of Glasgow, but the ship being wrecked in this small loch, the blessed clay was thrown overboard, and hence the whole sheet of water was reputed holy. It seems more probable, however, that the sanctity of the place was derived from the monastery on its shore and from the virtues of the holy men who dwelt there. There is still preserved a charter of the fifteenth century by which the ancestor of the Argyll family engages to found a collegiate church at Kilmun " in honorem sancti Mundi abbatis " for the repose of the souls of some deceased members of the donor's family. This charter was confirmed at Perth by James the Second of Scotland, on the 12th of May, 1450. The mediæval records also make mention of the saint's pastoral staff, which was held in the greatest veneration throughout Argyllshire, but of which no trace can now be found.

St. Beccan, from his love of serving God in solitude, was surnamed 'The Solitary.' He was of the race of the chieftains of Tyrconnel; leaving Ireland, he spent some time in a solitary cell at Iona, whilst his uncle Seghine was abbot there. Seeking a more desert place, he retired to the island of Rum, in the western isles, and there, erecting his hermitage, led a long life of prayer and penitence, resting in peace, as Tighernach records, in the year 677.[1]

St. Flannan, patron of Killaloe, is named in the Scottish Kalendars on the 18th of December. To the west of the island of Lewis, in the Atlantic, about twenty miles from the shore, are the Eileanan Flannain, or 'the little islands of St. Flannan,' and on the largest of the group stands the *Teampull Beannachadh*, that is, the blessed chapel of our saint. Martin, in his 'Western Isles,' page 17, states that such is the traditional veneration with which the fowlers from the Lewis regard these islands, that they never approach them but with prayers and ceremonies.

Of St. Dabius, Alban Butler[2] writes, that he was an Irish priest who preached with great success in his own country and in Alba. He is patron of Donach-Cloney, in the county of Down, and of Kippen, in Scotland, where a church is dedicated to him by the name of Movean. In the parish of Weem his holy well is pointed out; and tradition relates that he had a chapel on the shelf of the rock, still called *Crag-na-t'Scheapail*, or the Chapel Rock. Here also was a burial ground called Cill-Daidh. Other churches dedicated to him are

[1] *Skene*, Celtic Scot., II., 249. [2] *Butler*, Lives, at 22 July.

found in the north of the parish of Kilninian, in Mull, and in the parish of Kilblane, in Bute.

In the Breviary of Aberdeen, at the 8th of November, St. Gervad is thus commemorated: "Gervad, an Irishman, left his home, and coming to Scotland, in the province of Moray, associated with himself some followers of Christ at Kenedor, where he built a cell. In that place he had a stone bed." The saint's cave, not far from Elgin, was long a favourite resort of pilgrims. In the Elgin charters it is denominated Holyman Head. It was about twelve feet square, and commanded a long but solitary prospect of the eastern coast. In later times it was ornamented with a Gothic doorway and window, but these were ruthlessly demolished some years ago. A spring in the rock, above this cave or hermitage, was called St. Gervad's Well.

The Feliré of St. Ængus styles St. Momhaedog, who is patron of Fiddown in Ireland, "the gem of Alba." The Scottish Kalendars, however, give us no particulars regarding his missionary career. On the other hand St. Tallarican, or Tarraglen, though omitted by the Irish Martyrologies, is one of the few whom the Breviary of Aberdeen expressly commemorates as an Irish saint. "Tallarican," it says, "an Irishman, who was raised to the episcopal dignity by Pope Gregory, is noted as having daily offered the Holy Sacrifice. His manner of life was conformable to this devotion; and he submitted himself to stern self-discipline. He laboured in the north of Scotland, and various churches in his honour, in the dioceses of Aberdeen, Moray, and Ross, witness to his labours."[1]

[1] *Brev. Aberdon.* pars aest., fol. CXXXIV. b.

CHAPTER VII.

CLOSE UNION OF THE CHURCHES OF SCOTLAND AND IRELAND.

St. Fiacre:—St. Maelrubha:—St. Fillan:—St. Ronan:—Irish Saints in the Islands off the Scottish Coasts:—They penetrate to Iceland, and probably also to America:—Martyrdom of St. Blaithmac:—St. Cadroe:—St. Dubthach:—St. Malachy:—Legends regarding SS. Regulus and Boniface:—St. Adrian and his Companions Martyrs:—The Culdees.

To the Irish missionary saints of the seventh century, enumerated in our last chapter, we must add St. Fiacre. Born in the west of Ireland about the year 590, he, at an early age, devoted himself to the service of God. His hermitage and his holy well, on the banks of the Nore, a few miles south of Kilkenny, still retain his name, and till the beginning of the present century were a favourite resort of pious pilgrims. He closed his days at Brie, in the neighbourhood of Meaux, in France, where many miracles attested his sanctity, whilst his shrine became one of the richest and most famous of all that Catholic land. It was probably when pursuing his pilgrimage to France that he dwelt for some time in Scotland, and reaped there a rich spiritual harvest. In the parish of Nigg, on the opposite side of the river Dee from Aberdeen, he is honoured as patron, and the church is still called 'St. Fiacre's church.' The old burial-ground also retains his name. Close by is his holy well, and the adjoining bay is corruptly called 'St. Ficker's Bay.' His name appears in the ancient Dunkeld

Litany of the Saints, and several churches throughout Scotland were placed under his special patronage.

We must not attempt, however, to name all the Irish Saints, who, during the sixth and following centuries, laboured to promote the practice of piety in the Scottish Church. Interesting as such a task should be, it would lead us far beyond the limits of this little book. We must therefore rest content to mention only a few of those saints whose piety was conspicuous in handing on from age to age the sacred traditions of divine faith, and whose zeal was instrumental in cementing those spiritual bonds of union which so long and so happily subsisted between the Celtic churches of Alba and Erin.

" Next to St. Columbkille, there is no ecclesiastic of the ancient Scottish church whose commemorations are more numerous in the west of Scotland, or whose history is marked with greater exactness in the main particulars of his life."[1] He was an Irishman of princely birth, being of the race of Niall of the Nine Hostages, and he was born on the 3rd of January, 642, as is recorded in the annals of Tighernach. On his mother's side he was akin to St. Comgall, founder of Bangor, in the county of Down, and he embraced the religious life at an early age in that famous monastery. In the year 671 he withdrew from his native country to Ross-shire, on the north-west coast of Scotland, and two years later founded there the church and monastery of Aporcrossan—now Applecross— where he continued for fifty years to exercise the abbatial office with such a reputation for sanctity and miracles that, throughout all that territory, he was in after times

---

[1] *Reeves*, ' St. Maelrubha and his Churches,' pag. 3.

regarded as the patron saint. The Scottish legend makes him a martyr; and it relates that, being wounded by some pagan pirates from the Norwegian coasts, and left for dead, he was for three days consoled by the angels of God. A bright light made known to a neighbouring priest the place where he lay, at whose hands he received the body of the Immaculate Lamb, and he then tranquilly yielded his soul to God. In the Festology of St. Ængus he is commemorated on the 21st of April:

> "In Alba, in purity,
> After forsaking all comforts,
> Hath gone from us, with his mother,
> Our brother, Maelrubha."

The Lessons in the Aberdeen Breviary narrate that on the spot where he first expired a wooden chapel was at first constructed, which was subsequently superseded by the parish church of Urquhart. His body, however, was removed to Applecross, where it was solemnly interred, and, in reverence to his sanctity, the lands of Applecross, within a radius of six miles from the saint's church, enjoyed the rights and privileges of sanctuary. When the Danes were engaged in their work of plunder along the Scottish coast, they invaded this district, pillaged the monastery, despoiled the clergy, and carried off the booty to their ships; but the vengeance of God overtook them, and they perished within sight of land in the tranquil sea. Applecross still retains many memorials of its great patron. The little stream which there falls into the bay is called *Amhain Marea, i.e.*, "Maelrubha's river." The cemetery also bears his name. A little to the south is a mound, called *Cloadh Maree*, which is supposed to mark the founder's grave. Then there is the *Suidhe Maree*, or " Maelrubha's seat," and again, *Loch Maree*, "Maelrubha's lake," on the shores of which stand a rude monolith, eight feet in height, showing traces of a cross on the west face, and supposed to have been erected by St. Maelrubha. He is honoured also as patron of the parish of Loughcarron in Ross-shire, which is sometimes designated *Comaraigh Mulruy*, i.e., "Maelrutha's sanctuary," and which still retains the *Clochan Mulruy*, or the "stone cell of Maelrubha." In the parish of Gairloch, to the north of Applecross, there is a long narrow lake called after our saint; its principal island is *Inis Maree*, or "Maelrubha's island," where may still be seen the ruins of the saint's oratory. Pennant, in his 'Tour in Scotland,' calls this island "the favoured isle of the saint, the patron of all the coast from Applecross to Loch Broom. In the midst is a circular dike of stones, with a regular narrow entrance; the inner part has been used for ages as a burial-place, and is still in use. A stump of a tree is shown as an altar, probably the memorial of one of stone; but the curiosity of the place is the well of the saint, of power unspeakable in cases of lunacy. . . . This is the most beautiful of the isles."[1] At Contin there is an old cemetery called *Praes Marea*, or "Maelrubha's bush," and, indeed, all through Ross-shire we meet with frequent memorials of our saint. The connection of Applecross with Ireland did not cease with the death of St. Maelrubha. The annals of Tighernach, at the year 737, as also the Annals of Ulster and the Four Masters, record the death of Failbhe, son of Guaire, abbot of

---

[1] *Pennant*, Tour, p. 330.

Aporcrossan, "comharb of Maelrubha," who, with twenty-two of his religious, perished at sea. Again, in the year 801, the Annals of Ulster have the entry, "Mac Oigi of Aporcrossan, abbot of Bangor, happily ended his life in peace."

St. Faolan, called in Scotland St. Fillan, is named in the Irish and Scottish Kalendars on the 9th of January. He was born in the county of Wexford in the beginning of the eighth century, and was trained to piety in the monasteries founded by St. Ibar and St. Fintan-Munnu. At Taghmon, that he might more easily devote himself to divine contemplation, he secretly constructed a cell, not far from the cloister, where he spent his whole time in prayer. Being chosen abbot, he, "by his virtues and good example, ruled wisely, and instructed and informed his brethren in all holiness, chastity, and humility." (Brev. Aberdeen). Following the summons of heaven, he forsook his native country, and betook himself to Lochalsh in Northern Argyll (the ancient name for Ross-shire), whither his uncle, St. Congan, had preceded him : at the present day two ancient churches, Kilkoan and Killellan, preserve there the names of these two holy Irishmen. At Pittenween, St. Fillan's cave is shown, and the neighbouring parish of Forgan, in Fife, was in ancient documents sometimes called St. Fillan's parish. Strathfillan also takes its name from him, and the ruins of his ancient church and his holy well still frequented by pilgrims, and his bell, which was long venerated there as a holy relic, but is now preserved in the Museum of the Antiquarian Society in Edinburgh,[1]

---

[1] These particulars have been taken from an interesting paper on "The Ancient Bell of St. Fillan," by Dr. Forbes, in the 8th volume of Proc. of Scot. Antiq. : Edinburgh, 1870.

sufficiently attest the veneration in which he was held. It was near Strathfillan that the famous battle of Bannockburn was fought. Robert de Bruce, as we are told by Boece, passed the night before the battle in prayer "to God and St. Fillan," and caused the arm of St. Fillan, set in a silver case, to be brought to his camp. This is said to have been effected by miracle; whereupon the next morning the abbot of Inch-affray (*i.e.*, Insula Missarum), having offered the holy sacrifice and ministered the Blessed Eucharist, the king addressed his soldiers, and told them that "the miracle of St. Fillan was a presage of certain victory." The Bachul, or pastoral staff of St. Fillan still exists, and has been described in the Proceedings of the Society of Antiquaries of Scotland, vol. iii., pag. 233. We learn from Dr. Forbes that this saint was also honoured as patron in the parish of Killallan (a corruption of Kill-Fillan) in Renfrew; close to the church is "St. Fillan's seat," and at a short distance from it "St. Fillan's well."[1]

The Ulster Annals, in the year 737, mark the demise of Ronan, abbot of Cinngarad in Scotland. He is commemorated by Ængus on the 9th of February, and is styled "Ronan, the kingly." More than one of his churches bears the name Kilmaronock. He is also patron of a little island called Ronay, of Raasay, and of another island called Rona, sixty miles to the northeast of the Lewes, where there is a very ancient Irish oratory, and some venerable Celtic crosses. There is also an islet on the west coast of the mainland, in Zetland, called St. Ronan's Isle. "Very far south in

---

[1] *Forbes*, Kalendars, at pag. 468.

the bay of Scalloway, lies the peninsulated eminence of St. Ronan's, joined to the mainland by a low sandbank, which in high tides or gales is occasionally overflowed: the foundations appear of an old chapel."[1]

The fact of these desert islands being chosen by some of the greatest saints of our early church, as silent retreats for their exercises of prayer and penance, has elicited the warm admiration of Scottish writers, who, nevertheless, have but little in common with the promptings of Irish piety: "The same aspect of religion" (it is thus Dr. Forbes writes,) "which peopled the deserts of Egypt with the followers of St. Anthony and St. Paul, filled the storm-beaten islets of the Atlantic and German oceans with solitaries who, amid the roaring of the waves, and the screams of the sea-birds, sang praises to God, and practised austerities which this age can hardly realize. They were said, as it were technically, *quærere eremum in oceano*, to seek a desert spot in the ocean. From Eilan Rona, which stands sixty miles to the north-west of the Butt of Lewes, past the Flannan Islands and St. Kilda, down to Ailsa Crag and Sanda, the traces of hermitages and oratories are found throughout the great insular range of the Hebrides; and, although the east cost, by the comparative absence of islands, did not afford the same facilities, yet wherever they existed, they were used for this purpose."[2] The Irish anchorites, however, penetrated even far beyond the Hebrides; for we learn from one of our ancient writers named Dicuil,[3] who flourished in the ninth

---

[1] *Hibbert*, 'Shetland,' pag. 456.   [2] *Forbes*, Kalendars, pag. 273.
[3] Dicuil's work is entitled "De Mensura Orbis terrae." There are two MS. copies in the National Library, Paris, and one in the British Museum. It was published by Walckenaer in 1807, but

century, and whose work, as appears from intrinsic data, was written in A.D. 825, that the Feroe Islands, which are situate about two hundred miles farther than the Hebrides from the mainland, and which hitherto had been uninhabited and even unknown to the civilized world, were peopled for a time by holy men from Ireland. Having treated of the Hebrides, and the other islands off the British coast, Dicuil thus continues: "There are many islands in the North ocean of Britain which by sailing in a direct course, with full sails and favourable winds, may be reached in two days and nights from the islands off the north coast of Britain. A certain religious, by name Probus, narrated to me, that being on sea for two summer days and the intervening night, in a little boat with two sets of oars, he reached one of these islands. Some of these islands are but small. Most of them are in a group, separated only by narrow straits, and for almost a hundred years hermits who sailed from our Erin inhabited them. But as from the beginning of the world to that time they had been uninhabited, so now, on account of the northern marauders, the anchorites have abandoned them, but they are full of innumerable sheep, and of very many different species of sea-fowl. We have not in any author found mention of these islands."[1] It was in the year 725 that the

far more correctly by Letronne, in Paris, in 1814. Dicuil leaves no doubt as to his country. In cap. 6, he speaks of his teacher, Suibhne, and of the *clerici et laici ex Hibernia* who visited Jerusalem. In cap. 7 he writes: "Circum nostram insulam Hiberniam, sunt insulæ, sed aliæ parvæ, atque aliæ minimæ."

[1] As this work of Dicuil is very rare, I here add the original text of this important passage: "Sunt aliae insulae multae in septentrionali Britanniae oceano, quae a septentrionalibus Britanniae insulis duorum dierum ac noctium recta navigatione, plenis velis,

Scandinavians seized upon these islands; and it strangely corroborates Dicuil's statement that they gave them the name of *Foereyar*, precisely on account of the sea-fowl abounding there. It was probably from the Feroe Islands that the Irish hermits pushed on to Iceland, for we learn from the Scandinavian records that the first northern rovers who proceeded to Iceland in the year 860 pursued the same course. Dicuil incidentally makes mention of some religious who, in the year 795, remained in Iceland from the 1st of February to the 1st of August, and the famous *Landnamabok*, compiled from Icelandic traditions in the twelfth century, expressly attests that: " Before Iceland was inhabited by Nordmen, there were men living there who were called Papæ, who professed the Christian religion, and are supposed to have come thither by sea westwards, because Irish books (*Baekor 'Irskar*), bells, and croziers and other things belonging to them, which were found there, indicated that they were Westmen. These things were found in Papeya, on the east coast, and at Papyli in the interior."[1]

But to return to our Irish missionaries in Scotland, we have seen in a former paper how Ireland added a long list to the roll of the Martyr Saints who shed their

assiduo feliciter vento, adiri queunt. Aliquis Probus, religiosus, mihi retulit, quod in duobus aestivis diebus et una intercedente nocte navigans in duorum navicula transtrorum, in unam illarum introivit. Illae insulae sunt aliae parvulae. Fere cunctae simul angustis distantes fretis, in quibus, in centum fere annis, eremitae ex nostra Scotia navigantes habitaverunt. Sed sicut a principio mundi desertae semper fuerunt; ita nunc, causa latronum Nortmannorum vacuae anachoretis, plenae innumerabilibus ovibus, ac diversis generibus multis nimis marinarum avium. Nunquam eas insulas in libris auctorum memoratas invenimus." Edit. Letronne, pag. 39.

[1] *Johnstone*, Antiqut. Celto-Scandinav., pag. 14.

blood for the faith in North Britain.[1] We are indebted to Walafridus Strabo, an illustrious Benedictine abbot of the monastery of Reichenau in the ninth century, for an account of the martyrdom of another of our countrymen, St. Blaithmac, who, on the shores of Iona, most probably in the year 825,[2] sealed with his blood his reverence for the relics of St. Columba, and his devotion to holy Faith. St. Blaithmac, whose name, derived from *Blaith*, "a flower," has been latinized Florentius, was of princely birth, but, renouncing in his youth the attraction of the world, embraced a religious life. By his fervour and his many virtues he was a model to all the brethren, and, being chosen abbot, displayed a heavenly wisdom in the government of the monastery. From his early years, however, his soul had yearned for the martyr's crown, and more than once he had solicited permission to set out for distant lands to preach to pagan nations, in the hope of winning that coveted prize. It was in Iona, however, that he was to receive the palm of martyrdom. Since the pagan Danes had begun to ravage the British coast, the monastery of Iona had become a perilous post, and it was only after repeated requests that Blaithmac was permitted to leave his own monastery, and to enrol himself there among the religious of St. Columba. One day, during the absence of the abbot, he announced to the community, in a spirit of prophecy, that an irruption of pagan marauders was at hand, and he exhorted them to make

[1] See part II., pag. 185.
[2] The year 825 is that adopted by Dr. Reeves in his *Adamnan*, pag. 389. O'Donovan places this martyrdom in the year 823. *Four Masters*, i., 436. Mabillon and other Continental writers assign it to A.D. 789. *Annales ord. S. Benedicti*, iii., lib. 26, 27.

their choice: "If you wish to endure martyrdom for the sake of Christ," he said, "and fear it not, remain with me, and arm yourselves with becoming courage ; but if you wish to avoid impending danger seek at once for safety in flight." The shrine of St. Columba's relics was then carefully concealed, and some of the religious took refuge on the mainland. The next morning, whilst Blaithmac was as yet at the altar, after offering up the Holy Sacrifice, and the other religious were kneeling around, a band of pagan Danes rushed in and put the religious to the sword. They offered to spare Blaithmac if he would make known to them where the rich treasure of St. Columba's shrine was preserved; but when he refused to betray the secret, they hewed him into pieces still standing at the altar of God. When the marauders took their departure, the religious returned to Iona, and interred the remains of St. Blaithmac in that place, where his glorious crown of martyrdom had been obtained, and his biographer adds that many miracles were afterwards wrought in favour of several persons through the merits and intercession of this great soldier of Christ.[1]

Among the Irish missionaries of the tenth century I may name St. Cadroe. Scottish writers at the present day are generally, indeed, agreed in reckoning him among their sainted countrymen. However, Colgan seems to me to have satisfactorily defended the Irish parentage of the saint. At all events, as well the Scot-

---

[1] The Life of St. Blaithmac, by Strabo, in Latin hexameter verse, is inserted by Messingham in his "Florilegium Insulae Sanctorum," pag. 399, and has been often reprinted. See the Patrologia of Migne, vol. cxiii., pag. 1043.

tish as the Irish writers attest that St. Cadroe pursued his studies in Armagh, and led a religious life there for many years. In his life the special branches of study which he pursued beneath the shadow of St. Patrick's primatial See are set forth in detail; besides Theology and the Sacred Scriptures, Philosophy is mentioned, and Oratory, and Astronomy, and Natural Science; and in all of them he is said to have acquired a profound knowledge. From Armagh he proceeded to Scotland, and there for some years scattered with abundant fruit those seeds of sacred and profound learning which he had gleaned in the schools of Ireland; but, subsequently, continuing his pilgrimage to the Continent, he was chosen abbot of Walciodorum, now Wassous, on the Meuse, between Dinant and Givet, and died in the year 975, in the seventieth year of his age, and the thirtieth of his Continental pilgrimage.[1]

In the eleventh century St. Dubthach renewed the fame of Ireland for sanctity in the extreme north of Scotland. St. Dubthach, whose name has been corrupted Dutach, and Duac, is styled in the Annals of Ulster, "præcipuus confessarius Hiberniæ et Alban," and his death is marked on the 8th of March, 1068. At Tayne, in the diocese of Ross, his body was found incorrupt seven years after his death, and was translated to a precious shrine. Loch Duich and Kilduich derive their names from him. He was also honoured at Arbroath, and at Kilduthie, near the Loch of Leys, and at Arduthie, close to Stonehaven.

---

[1] The Life of St. Cadroe has been published by *Colgan*, Acta, pag. 494; and by the *Bollandists*, Mart., tom. I., pag. 468.

I will close this series of Irish saints with the name of Saint Malachy, for, as late as the twelfth century, the friendly bonds of religion which united the churches of Ireland and Scotland remained still unbroken. St. Malachy O'Morgair, Archbishop of Armagh, twice visited Scotland. During his first visit he proceeded to the royal mansion of King David, where by his prayers he restored that monarch's son to health. It was during this visit that he constructed an oratory of wattles and clay, on the sea-shore near Portpatrick, and blessed the adjoining cemetery, which, after the manner of the Irish raths, he inclosed within a deep fosse. St. Bernard, in his life of Saint Malachy, writes that he not only gave directions to those that were engaged in this work, but that he laboured at it with his own hands. His second visit was just before he left Ireland to die. He had set his heart on building a monastery in Scotland, at a place called Viride Stagnum, *i.e.*, the Green Lake, and he now conducted thither some of the religious brethren from one of his own Irish communities, and marked out the foundations of the new monastery, which soon became famed for holiness, and was known in after times as Saulseat (*Sedes Animarum*). It is only from the records of the past that we learn the existence of this foundation of St. Malachy. The Viride Stagnum, with its green waters, still abides, but not a trace of the venerable monastery now remains. It was probably at this monastery that St. Malachy placed as abbot a holy man named Michael, who, when a monk at Bangor, in the county of Down, had been freed by the prayers of St. Malachy from a grievous infirmity, which affected him both in body and mind, and of whom St. Bernard says, "He now rules a monastery in Scotland, which was the last one founded by the saint."[1]

I cannot conclude this portion of our subject without some reference to the four fanciful legends on which Scottish writers of the last three centuries have so loved to dwell, and by which they have endeavoured to prop up their cherished theories regarding the early origin and the special tenets of their church. These theories, however, will not detain us long. The learned archæologists of the present day have mercilessly torn from them the mask of history under which they were disguised, and when the false features have been laid aside, all that remains is found to be in perfect accord with what we have stated in the preceding pages, and serves to further illustrate in a remarkable way the close connection between the churches of Scotland and Ireland of which we have been speaking.

(*A*.) The first legend regards St. Regulus, or St. Rule, who is supposed to have flourished in Greece in the fourth century, and to have been invested at Patras, in Achaia, with the charge of the relics of the apostle St. Andrew. Being divinely admonished, he carried away a portion of these precious relics to Scotland, and deposited them at Rigmond, which thenceforward bore St. Andrew's name, and was honoured as the primatial see of Scotland. Modern research, indeed, has proved that it is most true that Rigmond, or Kil-Rigmond, was the ancient name of St. Andrew's, but it has also proved that it continued to bear that name and none other till the eighth century. The first mention which we find of

[1] *St. Bernard*, Vit. S. Malach., cap. xii.

Kilrigmond points it out as a monastery of Irish religious, and, among other saints, the patron of Kilkenny, St. Canice, pursued there a life of holy seclusion for some time. Even St. Regulus himself is found to have been one of those Irish saints, and his name is none other than the Irish Riaghail. He was a contemporary of St. Canice, and famed in our early church as abbot of Muicinish, in Lough Derg, on the Shannon, and, like many of our saints, it is probable that he made North Britain the theatre of his missionary zeal, and closed his days at Kil-Rigmond. It was only in the year 736 that the Pictish monarch, in gratitude to God for a great victory which he had achieved, erected there a church in honour of his patron, St. Andrew, which he enriched with vast possessions, and which in the course of time became the royal and primatial church of the whole kingdom. At the time that St. Andrew's was thus founded, Kil-Rigmond had the Irishman, Tuathal, for its abbot, whose demise is recorded in the Annals of Tighernach under the year 747.[1]

(*B.*) The second legend is connected with St. Boniface, whom it represents as born at Bethesda, and ordained at Antioch, and promoted to the supreme dignity of the Tiara of Rome. Quitting the holy city, he is supposed to have proceeded to North Britain, and to have died at Rosmarkey after converting its king, Nectan, and his people, and ordaining no fewer than one thousand bishops. The Scottish antiquaries, however, are now agreed that St. Boniface was an Irish saint, who is otherwise known by his Celtic name of Curitan. He

---

[1] *Skene*, Chronicles, &c., pag. 76.

accompanied St. Adamnan to Ireland, and assisted at the Convention of Tara in the year 697, and he is honoured in the Irish Martyrologies on the 16th of March as bishop and abbot of Rosmarkyn in Scotland. Among those who accompanied St. Boniface to Scotland was the virgin saint who is only known to us by the latinized name Triduana. Her oratory and tomb, close to the tomb of the Blessed Virgin at Lestalrig, in Lothian, became one of the most famous pilgrimages of Scotland. The destruction of this church and sanctuary was the first act of official iconoclasm which marked the sad era of the triumph of Calvinism in Scotland; and on the 21st December, 1660, was published the decree in Edinburgh that the church of Lestalrig "be razed and utterly cast down and destroyed,"[1]

(*C.*) The next legend sets before us St. Adrian, who, it asserts, was of royal birth and a native of Pannonia, in Hungary, and about the middle of the ninth century came with six thousand six hundred and six companions to preach the faith in Alba, and after some years retired to the island of May, where he and his companions received the crown of martyrdom at the hands of the Danes in the year 875. Modern research has shown that St. Adrian is a Latin form of the name of the Irish saint, St. Odhran; and it is probable that, with his Celtic community, he received the martyr's crown from the Danes in the year 875. The Pictish chronicle marks an incursion of the Danes in that year, and adds that they put many to death. The victims, however, are described not as *Hungari*, but as *Scoti*, which name in

---

[1] Book of the Univ. Kirk of Scotland, I., 5.

the Pictish chronicle designates the natives of Ireland.[1] The Breviary of Aberdeen attests that great honour was shown to our martyred countrymen in the isle of May in later times. A monastery "of fair coursed masonry" was erected there, but was soon after destroyed by the Saxons, "the Church, however," it adds "remains to this day, much visited for its miracles by the people; and there is a celebrated cemetery there where the bodies of the martyrs repose." Boece writes that the island of May was rendered illustrious by these martyrs, "as well on account of the number of pilgrims who resort thither, as of the miracles which the goodness of God had superadded." One of St. Odhran's companions was St. Monan. Before his martyrdom he had laboured at Inverary in Fife. His relics were in later times translated thither, and King David the Second erected a noble church in his honour. Dr. Forbes writes that at present he is chiefly honoured at St. Monan's in the parish of Abercromby, in Fife, where there is a fine church erected to him, picturesquely standing on the sea-shore.[2]

(*D.*) The last of the Scottish legends refers to the Culdees, who, we are gravely told, formed a flourishing church in Scotland in the second or third century of the Christian era. Boece even adds the names of some of these early Culdee saints: "Modocus, Calanus, Ferranus, Ambianus, et Carnocus." Polemical writers engrafted their own theological fancies on this historical fiction, till at length throughout the Scottish Kirk it

---

[1] "Scoti qui nunc corrupte vocantur Hibernienses." *Pictish Chronicle*, ap. Skene, Chronicles, &c., page 1, and clxii.
[2] *Forbes*, Kalendars. pag. 412.

was religiously received as an axiom that those ancient Culdees were the pioneers and missionaries of the Presbyterianism of our own days. All this, however, has melted away before the light of authentic history. Of the Culdee saints, who are named by Boece, Dr. Reeves writes: "Modocus is our Modoc of Ferns, who died in 624. Calanus, Ferranus, and Ambianus were no men if they were not Caelan, Forrannan, and Abban, Irish saints of the sixth century; while Carnoc, the South Briton, adopted Ireland as his home."[1] Pinkerton was one of the first who gave a serious blow to the foolish Culdee theory of his countrymen. In his "Inquiry into the History of Scotland," published in 1789, he did not hesitate to write that: "The Culdees were surely only Irish clergy;" and again, "The Culdees united in themselves the distinctions of monks and of secular clergy; being apparently, from Columba's time to the eleventh century, the only monks and clergy in Scotland, and all Irish, as formerly shown."[2] It was reserved, however, for Dr. Reeves to set at rest for ever this Culdee controversy, by his learned "Essay on the Culdees of the British Islands, as they appear in History," read before the Royal Irish Academy in 1860, and published in its Transactions, vol. xxiv.; and further light has since been added regarding some of the details of the question by the Scottish historian, Skene, in the second volume of his "Celtic Scotland," published in Edinburgh in 1877. The following are the conclusions which, through the labours of these learned writers, have been placed in the clearest light. First, that the

[1] *Reeves*, "The Culdees of the British Islands," pag. 67.
[2] *Pinkerton*, vol. 2, pag. 272.

religious brethren known by the name of Culdees proceeded from Ireland to Scotland, and thus serve as an additional link uniting together the early churches of these sister countries. Second, that it was not until the eighth century, and after the time of St. Maelruan of Tallaght, that the Culdees formed their first communities in North Britain. Third, that they followed in Scotland the rules which they had brought with them from their parent monasteries in Ireland; that is to say, the religious rules which were drawn up for the Celidés by St. Carthage and St. Maelruan, and as these rules have happily been preserved to us, we are able to place beyond the reach of doubt their perfect orthodoxy, for they set before us, in the clearest light, the minutest details as well of the faith which was professed as of the religious observance and exact discipline, and fervour of spirit, and love of holy church, which characterized the missionaries and the saints of our country in the golden ages of her history.[1]

[1] For the text of the Rules of St. Carthage and St. Maelruan, see "Irish Ecclesiastical Record," vol. i., and Reeves on "The Culdees," pp. 82 and 84.

CHAPTER VIII.

FIRST MISSIONS TO THE ANGLO-SAXONS.

St. Gregory the Great sends the first Missionaries to the Anglo-Saxons :—The Anglo-Saxon Kingdoms :—Conversion of Ethelbert, King of Kent, and his People :—The Kingdom of Essex also converted :—Archbishop Laurentius and St. Dagan of Inverdaoile :—Four points of difference between the Irish and the Continental Churches :—The British Clergy unable to evangelize the Saxons :—Kent and Essex fall away from the Faith :— Conversion and Apostacy of the Northumbrians :—King Oswald's victory at Heavenfield :—Religion restored in Northumbria.

It was in A.D. 597, the very year in which St. Columba rested from his labours in peace, that the first missionaries to the Anglo-Saxons, sent by the Holy Pontiff, St. Gregory the Great, landed on the coast of Kent. This great Pope had long sighed and prayed for the conversion of England. A few years before his elevation to the See of St. Peter, as he proceeded one day from his monastery on the Coelian hill to the city, passing through the Roman forum, he observed some fair-haired youthful slaves standing in the market for sale. Struck by their comeliness and graceful mien, he inquired whence they had come. He was told they were *Angles*, and that they were still in the darkness of Paganism. "Not Angles but Angels," was Gregory's reply, " if only they were Christians," and he sighed deeply as he added: " Oh! grief of griefs, that the author of darkness holds their nation so enslaved, and whilst such beauty shines forth in their countenances, their souls are deprived of heavenly light." In reply to further inquiries, he was told that they were natives of Deira, and that *Aella* was the king of their territory; and with playful reference to these names, he said: "They must be rescued from the anger of God (*de ira*), and then alleluja shall be hymned in their native land in praise of the one Sovereign Lord of all." Through Gregory's charity the young Angles were at once purchased by the monastery, and instructed in the truths of religion, and thus they were, at the same time, freed from the slavery of Satan and from material bondage.

St. Gregory, as Sovereign Pontiff, set his heart on perfecting the work thus happily begun, of bestowing on the Anglo-Saxon kingdoms the blessings of the Faith of Christ. He chose a numerous body of missionaries from his own monastery of St. Andrew's, and placing at their head the holy prior St. Augustine, who was already famed for his many virtues, sent them forth with his blessing on their errand of mercy. They set out with great ardour, but as they tarried for a time at Lerins and Marseilles, accounts reached them of the savage ferocity of the Saxon barbarians, whom they were sent to convert, sufficient to deter the stoutest hearts. The Saxons were more ferocious than wild beasts, it was said; they preferred cruelty to feasting; they thirsted for innocent blood; they held in abhorrence the Christian name; and torture and instant death were sure to await the Christian missionaries. Disheartened by such reports, they sent back Augustine to St. Gregory to make known to him the true state of things, and to ask what course, under the circumstances, he wished them to pursue. The Pontiff replied that they were to continue their journey: the greater the toil, the greater would be their eternal recompense. Gladly would he himself share their perils, but he hoped at least to partake in some measure of their reward.[1] Thus encouraged, they resumed their journey, and shortly after Easter, in the year 597, landed in the Isle of Thanet, at a sandy creek between the modern towns of Sandwich and Ramsgate, a memorable spot which is traditionally marked out as the landing place of Hengist, with his Saxon bands, a century and a half before. For a time heaven seemed to smile upon their missionary labours. Every year the Jutes and Angles and Saxons in thousands approached the baptismal font, and the Christian name was honoured throughout the greater part of England. In the mysterious ways of God, however, the spiritual edifice, built up with so much toil, was destined to be in a few days almost entirely overthrown. St. Augustine and his brother missionaries had indeed laid deep and solid the foundations of the future church; but it was reserved for vigorous Celtic hands to complete the structure. The great work of the permanent conversion of the Anglo-Saxon people, on which St. Gregory had set his heart, was to be one day happily achieved, but it should reward the toil, not of the fervent religious from the Coelian hill, but of the devoted missionaries from Ireland.

Before we proceed further it may be well to state in a few words the political condition of England at this eventful period. Only a few years ago we were accustomed to speak of the Anglo-Saxon Heptarchy as com-

---

[1] St. Gregory Epist. vi., 51. Bede, i., 25.

posed of seven clearly defined kingdoms, all united under the supremacy of one Bretwalda or Chief-King. Now, however, the ablest writers on the Anglo-Saxon period teach us that this stereotyped notion must be abandoned; and it seems to be placed beyond the reach of doubt that the early Anglo-Saxon kingdoms were ever fluctuating as well in their number as in their mutual relations to each other. The title of Bretwalda, too, unlike the Celtic Ard-righ, or Chief-King, was not a necessary element in their organization. It was only granted when some one of their princes by his superior power or military skill forced the rest to acknowledge his rule, and it was even then only accorded so long, and to such an extent, as he was able to enforce his authority. Hence it is that the venerable Bede names only seven kings, who, down to his time, had been invested with this title of supreme sovereignty.[1]

The three kindred tribes of the Angles, Jutes, and Saxons constituted the main strength of the armed bands, who, in the fifth century, had invaded and subjugated Britain. They did not, however, blend together to form one great nation. The Jutes settled in Kent, and formed there a small but powerful independent kingdom. The Saxons occupied almost the whole of the rest of the territory south of the Thames, with a few districts to the north of that river, and divided themselves into three distinct kingdoms, viz.: Essex, or the kingdom of the East Saxons, deriving its chief importance from the city of London, which was situated in its territory; Sussex for the South Saxons; and

---

[1] *Bede*, Hist. Eccles. ii., 5.

Wessex for the West Saxons, which gradually grew in extent and influence till it absorbed the other kingdoms. The Angles subjugated most of the northern territory extending from the Thames to Edinburgh, and founded there three kingdoms, viz.: East Anglia, south of the Humber, and extending from the Midland Fens to the German Ocean; Mercia, or the Marches, that is, the territories bordering on Wales; and Northumbria, extending from the Humber to the Firth of Forth. The Princes of Northumbria soon wrested the supremacy from Kent, and their kingdom continued for a long time the most powerful of all the Anglo-Saxon nations. It was more than once, however, divided into two distinct principalities, that of Bernicia, which extended from the Tyne to the Firth of Forth, and Deira stretching southward from the Tyne to the Humber. These chief divisions will serve at least as so many rough landmarks to guide us whilst following our Celtic fathers in their wonderful missionary career among the Anglo-Saxons.

At the time that St. Augustine and his companions landed in the isle of Thanet, off the English coast, Ethelbert, King of Kent, had won for himself the title of Bretwalda, and thus enjoyed considerable influence throughout all England. He had some years before taken to wife Bertha, a Christian princess, daughter of Charibert, King of Paris. As a condition of the marriage it was stipulated that the queen should be allowed the free exercise of her religion, and accordingly a French bishop accompanied her to the Kentish court, and the ruined church of St. Martin, a relic of Christianity from early British times, was allotted to him for divine worship. Ethelbert was in consequence favourably disposed to welcome the missionaries from Rome, and soon Augustine and his companions, with a silver cross borne before them, and a banner on which was painted the figure of the Crucified, were seen proceeding in processional order, chanting the Litanies "for their own salvation and the salvation of those to whom they came," and slowly wending their way to meet the monarch at the appointed place of audience. He received them with kindness; nor was his conversion long deferred, for he publicly received baptism at the hands of St. Augustine on the Feast of Whitsunday, the 2nd of June, in the year 597. In those days the conversion of a king was the signal for the conversion of his kingdom; and on the Christmas Day following the baptism of Ethelbert, ten thousand of his subjects[1] imitated his example, and renouncing idolatry sealed their acceptance of the Christian Faith by being baptized in the waters of the River Thames, at the mouth of the Medway, opposite the Isle of Sheppy. All Kent soon espoused the faith, and through the influence of Ethelbert an opening was gained for the Christian missionaries in the neighbouring kingdoms. The King of Essex was the first of the other kings to ask for baptism, and in 604 St. Mellitus was appointed Bishop of London. Some years later the King of Northumbria and his people also embraced the faith. St. Augustine died in the year 605, and was succeeded by Laurentius, who had also come from St. Gregory's monastery on the Coelian hill, a man of great learning and piety, and a truly devoted missionary. In the fulness of zeal he wished, as Bede informs us, not

---

[1] Epist. S. Gregorii Papæ, lib. viii. ep. 30, edit. Jaffe.

only to exercise his pastoral solicitude among the
Saxons, but also to extend his care "to the ancient
inhabitants of Britain, and to the Scots who inhabit the
island of Ireland, which is next to Britain."[1] The Irish
and the Britons had heard with joy the tidings of the
conversion of the Saxons, and there can be no doubt
that they were ready to extend the hand of fellowship to
the missionaries, whose labours had been so far crowned
with success; but when Laurentius attempted to interfere with their time-honoured traditional usages, handed
down to them by their fathers, they not only refused
to be guided by his words, but they further broke off all
communication with him, for thus they thought he
exceeded his authority, and was unnecessarily intermeddling in their affairs. He was particularly mortified
by the course pursued by the Irish Bishop Dagan,
who seems to have proceeded to Canterbury about the
year 610, deputed by some of the great monasteries of
Ireland and Wales, to confer with Laurentius and
his brother bishops. St. Dagan is commemorated in
our calendars as Bishop of Inverdaoile, in Wexford, and
as being remarkable for his meekness.[2] He had more
than once visited Rome. He had further been the bearer
to St. Gregory of the Monastic Rule of St. Molua, and
merited to receive for it from the lips of that great
Pontiff the most emphatic words of commendation and
approval. None could have been better chosen to
disabuse St. Laurentius of his erroneous notions regard-

[1] *Bede*, ii., 4.
[2] Marianus O'Gorman in his Martyrology styles him "Daganum praeplacidum de Inverdaoile." Inverdaoile is situated on the coast of Wexford, at the mouth of the river Daoile. *Colgan*, Acta, 586; *Lanigan*, ii. 365.

ing the ancient usages of the Irish and British churches. Of this conference, however, with the Archbishop of Canterbury we know nothing except its result. The Irish Bishop, finding that St. Laurentius persisted in regarding the disciplinary practices of the Britons and his own countrymen as erroneous, with genuine Celtic frankness refused to hold further communication with him, and shaking the dust from his sandals, would not even partake of food in the house in which the Archbishop dwelt. It was in consequence of this that St. Laurentius, with his suffragan bishops, Mellitus of London, and Justus of Rochester, addressed to the Irish Church a letter of remonstrance, of which the following fragment is preserved by Bede :

"To our most dear Brothers, the Lords Bishops and Abbots throughout all Ireland: Laurentius, Mellitus and Justus, servants of the servants of God.

"When the Apostolic See, according to the universal custom which it has followed elsewhere throughout the whole world, sent us to these western parts to preach to pagan nations, we came to this island, which is called Britain, without possessing any previous knowledge of its inhabitants. We held the Britons and Irish in great esteem for sanctity, believing that they followed the custom of the universal church; but after becoming acquainted with the Britons we supposed that the Irish should be more observant. We have been informed, however, by Bishop Dagan coming into this aforesaid island, and by the Abbot Columbanus in Gaul, that the Irish in no way differ from the Britons in their observance; for Bishop Dagan coming to us, not only refused to eat with us, but even to take his repast in the same house where we were entertained."[1]

This is the only part of the letter given by Bede, but he tells us that in the rest Laurentius exhorted them to

[1] *Bede*, Hist. Eccl., ii., 4.

conform in the matters of Catholic discipline with their brethren throughout the world. Surely it is not thus that he would have addressed them if, as some Protestants of the present day pretend, they had fallen away from the true faith.

From the letters of SS. Augustine and Laurentius, and the other documents connected with this period, we learn that the difference between the Roman missionaries and the Irish and British churches was confined to four heads, all of them pertaining to discipline, and tolerated elsewhere by the supreme authority of the Holy See. I will make for the present only a few brief remarks on each of these heads. The first point of difference was the form of Tonsure used by the clergy; but on this head it will, perhaps, suffice to say that the Irish Catholic usage of the present day differs more from the custom in Rome than it did in the days of St. Laurentius. Owing to the special circumstances of this country the Tonsure is not at present used at all by our clergy, whilst its use is imperative for the clergy of Rome. Yet no one will dare to affirm that the Irish Catholic church of to-day is not most closely united in the bonds of spiritual union with Rome. The second difference regarded the time for celebrating Easter. Here again the discrepancy arose, not from a diversity of faith, but merely from the varying cycles which were used in computing the time for the Easter festival. The cycle of eighty-four years, which was followed by the British and Irish churches, had been for a long time adopted in Rome itself; and though the Holy See had gradually perfected the Easter computation, yet, even as at a later period in the introduction of the Gregorian calendar, it did not seek to force an abrupt change on other churches, but wished that the adoption of the more correct rule should proceed from their own voluntary act. The third difference regarded the manner of Baptism. We learn, however, from St. Gregory's letters that such ritual variations in regard to the Baptismal ceremonies—for instance, the triple or single immersion, and so forth—existed in Spain and elsewhere, and when the Pontiff was interrogated about them he wisely ruled that each church might be permitted to follow its own disciplinary usage.[1] The fourth and last difference between the churches was the use of several Collects in the Sacred Liturgy; but even in this the wise Pontiff who had himself done so much to perfect the Liturgy of the Church, advised a wise moderation. So far was he indeed from condemning the Gaulish or the Celtic Liturgy, that in a letter to St. Augustine he counselled him to study carefully not only the Roman but also the other various Liturgies, and to select whatever he would find best in each of them for his Saxon converts, as yet young in the faith; and he adds the golden maxim, "Where the Faith is one, differences of custom do no harm to Holy Church."[2]

But beside these trivial points of difference, which only serve to place in bolder relief the perfect harmony of the Churches in all matters appertaining to faith, we find a complaint made by Laurentius, and which was again and again repeated—viz., that the British and Celtic clergy had neglected to evangelize the Saxon pagans, and that even now, when the missionaries from Rome had entered on that sacred work, they stood aloof

---

[1] St. Gregory, Epist. i., 43.   [2] St. Gregory, Epist. i., 43.

and would not come to aid in gathering in the spiritual harvest. Perhaps it would be difficult to find a stronger argument to prove the union of our British and Celtic Churches with the Mother Church of Rome than that involved in such a complaint, for surely it is not the agents of heresy or of schism that the representative of the Holy See would invite to join him in preaching the doctrines of Divine Faith. But Laurentius in making such a complaint had not reflected on the embittered feeling of national hatred with which the Saxons regarded their British neighbours. They were not satisfied with conquest unless it was accompanied by the extermination of the natives. They trampled down and destroyed every vestige of Roman and British civilization, and they put to death or sold into slavery any of the inhabitants that fell into their hands. A contemporary Gaelic Bishop, Sidonius Apollinaris, describes them as the "most truculent of all enemies," who made it a point not only of honour but of religion "to torture their captives rather than to put them to ransom," whilst they sacrificed the tenth part of them to their gods (epist. viii. 6). Such, too, is the terrible picture of the Saxon invasion presented by Gildas, which is probably exact in all its details, when he tells us of ruined sanctuaries, and fallen towers, and shattered altars, and priests and bishops with their people slain in the streets, and their corpses clothed with blood, left without burial, and the miserable remnant of the inhabitants being slaughtered in the mountains, or selling themselves as slaves to the invaders.[1] When Anderida, now Pevensey,

---

[1] *Gildas*' History, chap. 24.

was taken, not a Briton was left alive; and again, a little later, when the Isle of Wight was surrendered to the Saxons, every Briton found on the island was put to death in cold blood. The British chieftains on their part fought against the Saxons with almost the same ferocity, and when victory for the last time seemed to smile on their arms, their king, Cadwallon, avowed his resolve to exterminate the whole Saxon race within the bounds of Britain. With such national antipathies it was vain to look to the British Church for the conversion of the Saxons.[1] As preserved in the traditions of Wales, the following was the Abbot of Bangor's reply to St. Augustine: "No, we will not preach the Faith to the cruel race of strangers who have treacherously driven our ancestors from their country, and robbed their posterity of their inheritance." For a time, too, the Saxon princes seem to have regarded the Irish race with the like hostility, considering them at first as their rivals in the plunder of Britain, and subsequently as the allies of their hated foe. The Irish missionaries however cherished no such national hatred against the Saxons. At Iona St. Columba received with open arms some Saxons who had proceeded thither, and having instructed them in the truths of Faith enrolled them among the brethren of the monastery. St. Fridolin's mission in Helvetia, St. Columba's labours among the Picts, St. Columbanus's wonderful toil in the Vosges, are sufficient proof that there was no lack of missionary zeal among the Irish Bishops and Priests. In fact, they only awaited a favourable opportunity in

---

[1] *Myfyr*, Archaeol. ii. 365; *Geoffrey of Monmouth*, xi. 12.

order to bring the blessings of civilization and religion to the benighted Saxons. In the designs of Providence the long wished for opportunity was soon to be presented, and we will see with what zeal and with what success they at once devoted themselves to labour in this field of God.

In the meantime, however, by the death of Ethelbert, in the year 616, the Christianity of the Saxons became well nigh extinct : as an English historian has quaintly expressed it, "it appeared as though much of the Kentish Christianity was buried in the king's grave." His worthless son, Eadbald, who succeeded him on the throne of Kent, cast off the Christian name, and most of his people, following his example, relapsed into paganism. In the same year the Christian king of Essex also died ; and his three sons, who were pagans, set themselves to restore the worship of the false gods, and compelled Bishop Mellitus and his companions to depart from their kingdom. Venerable Bede adds : "Being forced from thence, Mellitus came into Kent to advise with his fellow-bishops, Laurentius and Justus, what was to be done in that case; and it was unanimously agreed that it was better for them all to return to their own country, where they might serve God with a free mind, than to continue without any fruit among those barbarians who had revolted from the faith."[1] This sudden relapse of the Saxons to paganism, after the example of their wicked princes, has only a parallel in the falling away of the English nation into heresy, nine hundred years later, after the evil example of Henry

---

[1] *Bede*, ii. 5.

the Eighth. What is the more striking in this first national apostacy, we do not read of a single one having received the martyr's crown, or of any of the professing Christians being even imprisoned for the faith. The King of Kent, indeed, soon after repented, and gave full authority again to Laurentius and Justus, but for a considerable time little fruit repaid their labour, and the Venerable Bede adds, "the Londoners would not receive Bishop Melitus, choosing rather to be under their idolatrous high priests."[1]

The same fate attended the first preaching of Christianity in Northumbria. In the year 617, Edwin succeeded to the throne of Northumbria, and at once grasped the supreme dignity of Bretwalda, which he continued to hold with an iron hand till his death. This powerful monarch received the grace of the true faith through the preaching of St. Paulinus, who, on a plot of ground now covered by the glorious Minster of York, erected a wooden chapel, dedicated to St. Peter, and there, on Easter Eve, in the year 627, administered baptism to Edwin. The whole kingdom of Northumbria joyfully followed the example of the king, and Paulinus was gladdened by the abundant fruits which repaid his toil. Nevertheless the storm was not to be long delayed. The united forces of Cadwallon and Penda attacked and overthrew Edwin at the battle of Hatfield, in South-east Yorkshire, in the October of 683, the king himself being slain, and his whole army destroyed or dispersed.[2] Deira and Bernicia became separate kingdoms on his death, and their kings, the better to secure the favour

---

[1] *Bede*, ii. 6. [2] *Bede*, ii. 20.

of the pagan Penda, disowned their Christian belief, and relapsed into paganism. The people followed their example, and St. Paulinus, with his companions, was obliged to seek safety in flight, a deacon, Justus, alone remaining to keep alive the sacred spark till the day of mercy would again arise on that unhappy nation.

The apostate kings of Deira and Bernicia both fell very soon by the terrible sword of Cadwallon, and then the eyes of all were turned, as their only hope, to the brave Oswald, the son of Ethelfrid. Oswald was now in his thirtieth year. From his childhood he had lived an exile in Ireland, and had been regenerated there in the waters of baptism. In after years he never forgot the lessons of wisdom and piety which he had learned in the Irish schools, and amidst all the dangers of the Northumbrian court, he proved himself as religious as he was brave, and it is no small glory for Ireland that she prepared for the throne this valorous champion of religion, the first of the long roll of Anglo-Saxon princes who was found worthy of the honours of the altar. Strength and sweetness were blended in his character, and, during his short reign of eight years, his life presents to us almost a perfect ideal of a Christian monarch. Among the Saxons he enjoyed the title of Bretwalda, and he also compelled the nations north of the Firths of Clyde and Forth to acknowledge his supremacy. On the other hand, he was so devout that oftentimes he spent half the night in prayer, and, in the words of Bede, "while guiding a temporal kingdom, was wont to labour rather for an eternal one."[1] Amid

---

[1] *Bede*, iii. 12.

all that could lift him up to arrogance, he was gentle and humble, and he was generous and beneficent to the poor and to strangers. In a word, he was "a prince of men, one born to attract a general enthusiasm of admiration, reverence, and love."[1]

With a small army Oswald, in December, 634, took up his position within a few miles of Hexham, near the spot called Heavenfield, on a rising ground, where now stands the humble chapel of St. Oswald's. In the night preceding the battle, St. Columba, for whom he cherished a tender devotion, appeared to him radiant with heavenly light, and, promising him victory, desired him to take the cross for his standard. At morning's dawn the king caused a cross of wood to be made after the manner of those which he had seen so often erected on the green hills of the land of his exile, and with his own hands he held it whilst his men fastened it in the ground. He then commanded his soldiers to kneel with him, and to pray to the one true and living God, who knew how just was their cause, and around whose standard they were now gathered, to be with them against their proud and cruel enemy. They rose full of courage, and charging the superior forces of Cadwallon, broke their ranks and gained a complete victory, Cadwallon himself being numbered among the slain.

It was one of the first cares of Oswald to send messengers to Iona to pray the abbot to provide a bishop and devoted missionaries who would restore the faith in his kingdom, and gather in the harvest now

---

[1] *Bright*, 'Early English Church History' (Oxford, 1878), pag. 133.

ripe for the sickle. The first person chosen was Bishop Corman, a religious remarkable for his austerity and exemplary life; but after a few weeks' experience in Northumbria he withdrew in despair from the rude and indocile heathens, whom he was sent to minister to, and returned to Iona. The community being assembled, he recounted the motives of his return, and assured them that it was idle to think of converting such a savage people. From among the seniors, a voice was raised in gentle remonstrance: "Perhaps, brother, the fault is not theirs, but yours. Did you deal mildly with them, as the apostle exhorts, giving milk to the infants? Did you not rather show severity towards them, and expect them to cultivate all at once those virtues which could only be the crowning fruit of your missionary labours." All eyes were at once turned to the speaker, and the seniors, with one accord, cried out that to him the arduous mission should be entrusted.

It was an Irish monk, Aidan by name,. who thus opposed the counsel of Bishop Corman, and who, succeeding to his place, is now honoured in our Kalendars as the Apostle of the Kingdom of Northumbria.

CHAPTER IX.

ST. AIDAN, FIRST BISHOP OF LINDISFARNE, APOSTLE OF NORTHUMBRIA.

Early Life of St. Aidan:—Lindisfarne:—Virtues of St. Aidan:—His efforts to train up a Native Clergy:—His Apostolic Labours:—King Oswald interprets his Sermons for the People:—Aidan at the Royal Table:—His care for the Poor:—He adheres to the Irish Customs:—Foundation of Mailros:—Coldingham:—St. Aidan's Hermitage in Farne Island:—Death of Oswald:—Character of this pious Prince:—The Fortress of Bamborough saved by the prayers of Aidan:—Oswin, King of Deira:—Death of St. Aidan.

VENERABLE BEDE gives us no details regarding the early years of St. Aidan's life, but we are able to glean from the ancient Irish records that in his youth he enrolled himself among the religious of the island-monastery of St. Senanus, at Inniscattery, in the Shannon, and that he lived there for many years in the fervent practice of every virtue. We do not know in what precise year he proceeded to Iona, but it is a venerable tradition that before his departure from Ireland he was raised to the Episcopate. In the old register of the diocese of Clogher, he is named among the bishops of that see, and Dr. John Lynch, in his MS. History of the Irish Bishops, as also Ware and Cotton, and others of our ablest historical writers, following the testimony of this authentic record, have placed St. Aidan fifth in succession from St. Molaisse, whose death is recorded in the Annals of Ulster in the year 563.[1] Perhaps we may find in this an explanation of the otherwise strange fact that, whilst the Abbot of Iona and the other seniors received in silence the report of Bishop Corman, St. Aidan, relying on his own episcopal experience, should raise his voice to declare that it was only by long endurance and mildness the pagan hearts of the Saxons could be softened to receive the doctrines of faith.

It was in the summer of the year 635 that Aidan, at the bidding of the abbot and community of Iona, set out for the royal residence of Oswald. Welcomed with open arms by that pious monarch he was free to choose for his Episcopal See any spot he might select from the Firth of Forth to the Humber. St. Aidan, however, chose for his cathedral and for his monastic home the small island of Lindisfarne, lying off the eastern coast of Britain, a few miles above the strong castle of Bamborough, and known in later times as 'the Holy Island.' This small island is twice every day united with the mainland, and twice again is encircled by the sea, according to the ebb and flow of the tide:—

> "Dry shod, o'er sands, twice every day
> The pilgrims to the shrine find way;
> Twice every day the waves efface
> Of staves and sandall'd feet the trace."

In this Island-sanctuary St. Aidan was enabled, amid

[1] The Reg. Clogherense adds: " Juxta verbum Domini exivit de Hibernia in Britanniam quem honorifice recepit Usualdus (Oswald) rex; et tunc fuit Episcopus Linfarensis, cujus animam vidit sanctus successor ejus postea, deferri per angelos ad regnum coeleste." (MS. T.C.D., E. 3 13.) Some have identified him with Aiden-mac-Aengusa, from whom Kilmore Aedhan, near Monaghan, is supposed to take its name. This, however, has been ably refuted in Shirley's 'History of Monaghan' (London, 1878), pag. 315.

his episcopal cares, to cultivate that retirement and solitude which had such an attraction for him, whilst at the same time it reminded him of his first religious home at Iniscattery, and of the glorious Iona, whose fruitfulness and whose fame he was henceforth to emulate among the Anglo-Saxon nations. There was, however, yet another reason for his choice, one not to be overlooked amid the ever-recurring conflicts between the rival kingdoms of the Anglo-Saxons: his church and monastery would there be specially secure under the shelter of the royal castle of Bamborough. This fortress-rock, situated high up on the coast of the present Northumberland, would seem to be marked out by nature for the stronghold and palace of some brave chieftain. It was called Dingueirin by the Britons, and was fortified at first with a fosse, and afterwards with a wall or rampart by the valorous Ida, who was called the "flame bearer" on account of his terrible ravages throughout all that territory, and it subsequently received from the Saxons the name of Bebbasburgh, which was gradually corrupted to Bamborough. Impregnable by position, and strengthened by art, it continued for a long time to be the favourite residence and the chief castle of the kings of Northumbria.

But to return to Lindisfarne: "No sacred spot in Britain," writes the present professor of Ecclesiastical History in Oxford, "is worthier of a reverential visit than this Holy Island of Aidan and his successors:"[1] and more than a thousand years ago the same sentiment was uttered by Alcuin, when he styled this chosen sanctuary, "locus cunctis in Britannia venerabilior."[2]

---

[1] *Bright*, p. 137.   [2] *Alcuin*, ep. 12. ap. Haddan and Stubbs, iii. 493.

The eloquent Montalembert has given the following glowing description of this Celtic monastery, which for so long a time was destined to be the great centre of piety for the Anglo-Saxon race: "Amid the waves of the Northern Sea, opposite the green hills of Northumberland, and the sandy beach which extends between the border town of Berwick on the north, and the imposing ruins of the feudal fortress of Bamborough on the south, lies a low island, flat and sombre, girt with basaltic rocks, forming a kind of a square block, which terminates to the north-west in a long point of land, stretching towards the mouth of the Tweed and Scotland. This island bears the impress of melancholy and barrenness. It can never have produced anything but the sorriest crops and some meagre pasturage. There is not a tree, not an undulation, not one noticeable feature, save a small conical hill to the south-west, now crowned by a strong castle of picturesque form, but recent construction. In this poor islet was erected the first Christian church of the whole district, now so populous, rich, and industrious, which extends from Hull to Edinburgh. This was Lindisfarne, that is to say, the Mother Church, the religious capital of the North of England and south of Scotland, the residence of the first sixteen bishops of Northumbria, the sanctuary and monastic citadel of the whole country round,—the Iona of the Anglo-Saxons. The resemblance of Lindisfarne to Iona, of the colony to the metropolis, the daughter to the mother, is striking. These two isles, once so celebrated, so renowned, so influential over two great and hostile races, have the same sombre and melancholy aspect, full of a wild and savage sadness. Religion

Q

alone could people, fertilise, and tranquillise these arid and desolate shores."[1]

Such was the place chosen by St. Aidan to be the Episcopal See and the monastic capital of his vast diocese, extending from the Humber to Edinburgh.

In sketching the career of St. Aidan we need do little more than compendiate the pages of Venerable Bede, who pays a just tribute of admiration to the virtues of this great Irish missioner; and it has been remarked that the chapters which he devotes to his life are unsurpassed for earnestness and eloquence by any other passages of his history. And this should not surprise us, for Bede was born less than a quarter of a century after St. Aidan's death, and his monastic life was passed in Northumbria, still fragrant with the virtues of its great apostle.

St. Aidan was remarkable for his humility, piety, and meekness: he was a pontiff "inspired with a passionate love of virtue, but at the same time full of a surpassing mildness and gentleness."[2] He despised vain pomp and applause, trampled under foot avarice and anger, and was earnest in promoting peace and charity. Constant in study and persevering in prayer, he was a marvel of self-denial and austerity, and a model of entire unworldliness; he was always the first to practice what he taught, and none could ever reproach him with having failed to fulfil, to the best of his ability, all the evangelical precepts. He was so indifferent to worldly possessions that he expended in alms the gifts, no matter how precious, which he daily received from the king and the wealthy

---

[1] *Montalembert*, Monks of the West, vol. 4, pag. 20.
[2] *Bede*, iii. 3.

noblemen of Northumbria. He showed true compassion and tenderness to all who were in suffering, but exercised stern justice towards the wicked, especially if they were invested with power and authority and refused to repent.

In his daily life he performed diligently the works of faith and charity which religion commands, and as far as his Episcopal duties permitted, rigorously observed all the rules and religious exercises of the monastic community of Lindisfarne. After the manner of the Irish monks his dress was white, and consisted of a thick woollen cowl and a tunic; when travelling he wore sandals. His only drink was water or milk. It was not till a hundred years later, when Ceolwulf, King of Northumbria, laid aside his crown to enter the monastery of Lindisfarne, that leave was, for the first time, given to the monks of Lindisfarne to taste either wine or ale.[1] St. Aidan also established the custom of fasting on all Wednesdays and Fridays until three o'clock, p.m., Easter time alone being excepted from this penitential exercise. He loved to meditate on the Sacred Writings; he was never wearied in breaking to those around him the spiritual food of heavenly knowledge, and it was his special delight to instruct children in the truths of eternal life. That his mission might be more fruitful, he summoned to his aid a number of zealous priests from Ireland, who shared in all his missionary enterprises. This is attested by Bede, but

---

[1] *Roger de Hovenden*, Annales, page 403; *Sim. Dunelmen.*, p. 139 —" Antea enim nonnisi lac vel aquam bibere solebant, secundum antiquam traditionem Sancti Aidani primi ejusdem Ecclesiæ antistitis, et monachorum qui cum illo de Scotia veniebant."

unhappily the names of these his fellow-workers have not been handed down to us. He founded in every district churches or oratories, and he multiplied the monasteries, which became at once so many centres of piety, and schools where the Anglo-Saxon youth received from the Irish monks an education as complete as any that could be supplied in that age in the greatest monasteries of Ireland or the Continent.[1] Following the example of St. Patrick in his apostolate of Ireland, it was his first care to train up a native priesthood, thus to perpetuate the blessings of Divine faith among this newly converted people. For this purpose he selected twelve Anglo-Saxon youths whom he wished to be instructed and prepared for the sanctuary under his own immediate guidance, and we will see in the following chapters how they proved themselves worthy of their great master, and emulated his zeal in preaching the faith to their fellow-countrymen. He expended in the redemption of slaves a great deal of what he received from the munificence of his noble converts, and he was particularly desirous. as Bede records, to free from captivity those who had been "unjustly sold," that is, who without any fault or crime had been condemned to slavery.

St. Aidan carried on his missionary work on foot, penetrating into the wildest forests and marshes, visiting his scattered flock in town and country, entering the houses as well of the poor as of the rich, and instructing all alike in the truths of Divine faith; even those whom he met as he journeyed along he was wont to exhort (writes

---

[1] *Bede*, iii. 3, "imbuebantur praeceptoribus Scotis parvuli Anglorum."

Bede), "if not already Christians, to embrace the faith, and if Christians, to show forth their faith by almsgiving and good works."[1] While he travelled he meditated on some passages of the sacred Scripture, or with his companions recited the Psalms. In the first years of his episcopate a great difficulty in the way of the conversion of the Anglo-Saxons was their language, but in this Aidan and his converts were happy in having an Oswald for their king. This pious prince, during the years of his exile in Ireland, had perfectly learned the Irish language, and thus the sufferings and the troubles of his early years were found in the ways of God to have prepared a blessing for his subjects; and well may Bede style it "a sight truly beautiful," giving joy to the angels in heaven, when Aidan instructed the crowds of Anglo-Saxons who were gathered around him on the beach at Lindisfarne, whilst Oswald, humbly seated at his side, interpreted to them the words which fell from the holy bishop's lips. This religious devotedness of Oswald reveals to us a depth of solid virtue, and whilst it anticipated the piety of Alfred the Great and St. Louis, had hitherto but few examples in history. "The tender friendship and Apostolic brotherhood which thus united the king and the bishop of the Northumbrians has, perhaps, more than anything else, contributed to exalt and hallow their memory in the annals of Catholic England."[2] With such devoted zeal of St. Aidan, and such earnest solicitude on the part of King Oswald, it is not to be wondered at that the preaching of the faith produced an abundant fruit, and that the whole nation of Northumbria was in a short time restored to the fold of Christ.

[1] *Bede*, iii. 5.   [2] *Montalembert*, iv. 28.

The king at times invited Aidan to the royal table, but, well knowing the self-denying habits of the holy bishop, he did so much less frequently than he would wish. Bede relates that when Aidan accepted such invitations, he proceeded to the royal residence accompanied by one or two clerics, and "when he had taken a little refreshment, he would make haste to leave that he might pursue his study with his companions or continue his prayers," for through the munificence of Oswald a church and a cell had been provided for him near the royal city of Bamborough.[1] On an Easter Sunday we read of his sharing the king's forenoon meal, but when a silver dish, full of royal dainties, had been set before them, and Aidan had stretched forth his hands to bless it, a thane entered, whose care it was to relieve the poor, and informed Oswald that a great crowd of poor people had assembled from all the country-side, and were sitting in the street begging some alms from the king. Oswald at once ordered the contents of the dish to be carried to them, and the dish itself to be broken and divided for their benefit. On this Aidan seized the king's right hand, and with eyes raised to heaven prayed "May this hand never decay." The saint's prayer was heard, for in after times St. Oswald's right hand was preserved in St. Peter's Church at Bamborough in a silver shrine; and Bede writes that in his time it was still undecayed.

In his dealings with the rich St. Aidan showed himself superior to fear or favour. Far from sparing any of their excuses, he rebuked them with the greatest frankness. He made it a rule to present no gifts to the chiefs

---

[1] *Bede*, iii. 17.

or thanes, that thus their friendship might rest solely on religion. If a Saxon nobleman came to Lindisfarne he was hospitably entertained, but the poorest of the poor received the same welcome. If money or lands were given to the monastery, all were promptly distributed to the poor, for "like a true father of the afflicted, and a cherisher of the needy," Aidan was ever intent on relieving their distress.[1] For himself and the community of Lindisfarne he retained nothing, being content with the scanty crops of the island of Lindisfarne cultivated with their own hands. The only gift which he elsewhere retained was when in the domains of the king or noblemen, a site for a church or oratory, and a small cell attached to it, was offered him, that there he might find repose in his prolonged missionary excursions.

Whilst Bede can scarce find sufficient words of eulogy to commend the piety and devoted zeal of St. Aidan, one thing alone he regards as a fault, and this was the unflinching firmness with which he adhered to the special disciplinary usages of the Irish Church, particularly in the celebration of Easter. We will have to return in the next chapter to this erroneous computation of Easter time, which Rome itself for a long time shared with our Celtic fathers, and in which the astronomical science, and not the faith of Ireland, was at fault. Suffice it at present to learn from Bede himself, that in this old Irish usage no doctrinal error was involved, contrary to what some pretentious Protestant writers of the present day would wish their readers to believe.

---

[1] *Bede*, iii. 14.

Again and again Bede proclaims that St. Aidan was a man of God, adorned with sanctity, and a true missioner of the faith, " so that he was deservedly loved by those who differed from him about the Pasch," and was honoured by Archbishop Honorius and Bishop Felix, and all those who were most observant of the Continental rule. "His keeping the Pasch out of its time I do not approve nor commend," writes Bede, "but this I do approve of, that what he kept in thought, reverenced, and preached in the celebration of his paschal festival, was just what we ourselves do, that is, the redemption of mankind through the passion, resurrection, and ascension into heaven of Jesus Christ, the Mediator between God and man."[1]

Before St. Aidan closed his apostolic career he had the consolation to see the Christian Faith firmly planted throughout the length and breadth of the Kingdom of Northumbria. A devoted clergy were everywhere engaged administering the blessings of heaven to his spiritual children, and though many of his fellow-labourers in the sacred ministry had come to him from Ireland, many too there were chosen from his own flock, and trained by his own care during his episcopate of sixteen years. Though he followed the disciplinary rules of Iona, the faith which he preached was the same as that which had been announced by St. Paulinus at York, and by St. Augustine at Canterbury. The churches which he built were rude wooden structures, but the same divine sacrifice was solemnly offered up in them as in the nobler edifice of Whitherne; and "the usual language

[1] *Bede*, iii. 17.

about the mysteries of the Sacred Eucharist was as familiar to a disciple of Hy or of Lindisfarne as to the churchmen of Gaul or Italy,"[1] Among the peculiarities of his ritual may be mentioned the manner of sanctifying, by prayers and fastings, the places which were granted him for a church or a monastery. One of his disciples was requested by the son of Oswald to choose a site on which to erect a monastery. Yielding to his desires he searched out a solitary spot amid the wild and barren hills, which seemed, says Bede "better suited as lurking places for robbers, and retreats for wild beasts, than as habitations for men," and he requested the royal permission to purify the place from the contagion of its former crimes, by prayer and fasting, which was "the custom of those from whom he had learned the rule of regular discipline."[2] He accordingly proceeded thither to spend the whole time of Lent, fasting every day except Sunday, with no other sustenance than a very little bread, one egg, and a little milk mixed with water. When there were ten days of Lent still remaining there came a messenger to summon him to the king, and he, that the religious rite might not be intermitted on account of the king's affairs, requested another priest to complete the fast which had been so piously begun; and, as Bede adds, the time of prayer and fasting being ended, he built there a monastery, which is now called Lastingham, and he established there the religious rule according to the model of Lindisfarne.[3]

Among the monasteries founded by St. Aidan there are two which deserve particular mention. The first

---

[1] *Bright*, page 145.   [2] *Bede*, iii. 23.   [3] *Bede*, iii. 23.

of these is Mailros, or Melrose, which sometimes, to distinguish it from the later Cistercian abbey of the same name, has been called old Melrose. It was situated on a gentle slope in the small and at that time barren[1] projection of land, which is seen from the upper road that leads from Dryburgh to Melrose, a little below the point where the Leader pours its scanty waters into the Tweed, and about two miles to the west of the modern town of Melrose. The river here takes a bold semi-circular sweep, and encloses the old monastery on three sides, the fourth being protected by a wall. The land is now fertile and richly planted, and the opposite banks to the north of the Tweed are high, rocky, and overhung with the woods of Bemerside. Here Aidan erected a monastery on the model of those wherein he had lived in Ireland, and he placed there as abbot the Anglo-Saxon Eata, one of his own first and most beloved disciples. It continued to flourish for two hundred years, a great centre of piety and of Christian life for all Lothian, till an invasion of the Scots in the year 839, when it was utterly destroyed. The other monastery was for a time equally famous for its fervour and its religious spirit, but becoming relaxed in its discipline after the death of Aidan, was memorable for the chastisement which fell upon it. It is called by Bede *Urbs Coludi*, that is, Coldingham, and was built on a rock overhanging the sea, a short way south of the promontory termed Saint Abb's Head. The neck of land on which it was built stretched out into the sea, and had at three sides perpendicular rocks of great elevation. The fourth side was

[1] "The name *Mailros* is Celtic, formed from *Moel* and *Ross*, and means "the bare promontory."

cut off from the mainland by a high wall and deep trench. It was a double monastery, and contained two distinct communities of men and of women. Its first abbess was St. Aebba, and from her the promontory of Saint Abb's Head takes it name. Among its inmates there was an Irishman, by name Adamnan, who for a long time had led a most penitential life, fasting on all but two days of the week—Sunday and Thursday. One day as he returned to Coldingham with a brother monk, looking towards the monastery from afar, he predicted that it would at no distant day be consumed by fire. Being afterwards questioned by the abbess, he reluctantly told her that he had learned this in a vision, but that the doom would not be accomplished in her days. Soon after St. Aebba's death, while the inmates flattered themselves, says Bede, on the peace and safety which they enjoyed, the whole monastery was burned to the ground, "as all who knew the case could well perceive, by a heavy vengeance from heaven."[1]

St. Aidan was accustomed to retire at times to a hermitage which he erected for himself on the rocky island of Farne, nearly opposite Bamborough, and there to spend some days in perfect retirement, his thoughts fixed on God alone : "thither," writes Bede, "he was wont often to retire to pray in private, that he might be undisturbed; indeed his solitary cell is to this day shown in that island." This island is bordered around with basaltic rocks, which rise abruptly from the ocean, and at the south-west extremity attain the height of eighty feet above the level of the sea. In the 'Hermit Saints' this little island is described as "a circle of solid

[1] *Bede*, iv. 25.

rocks, the top of which is thinly strewn over with a layer of barren soil. On its south side it is separated by a channel of about two miles in breadth from the shore; to the east and west a belt of rocks protect it from the fury of the sea; while on the north it lies open to the whole force of the waves, in the midst of which it lies like the broken and defenceless hull of a shipwrecked vessel. Sometimes when the tide rises higher than usual, and the wild storms of that rugged coast come to its aid, the waves make an inroad on the land, and the salt foam is blown over the whole island, wetting the shivering inhabitant to the skin, and penetrating the crevices of his habitation." Besides being most sterile, this island had the bad repute of being the abode of evil spirits, and hence was shunned by the inhabitants of the mainland. Such was the place which Aidan chose for his hermitage, and which by the practices of penance and the sweet exercises of prayer became delightful to him as the threshold of Paradise.

From the outset of his episcopate, St. Aidan was not without anxieties and sorrows.[1] Above all he was overwhelmed with affliction by the death of Oswald, on the field of battle, in 642. This dire calamity fell upon the Northumbrian church and kingdom at the hands of Penda, the pagan king of Mercia. For two years war had raged between Northumbria and Mercia, and Oswald had been so far successful that he added the district of Lindsey, with its chief town of Lincoln, to his dominions. It was on the 5th of August, 642, that the decisive battle was fought, at a place called Maserfield, near the Shropshire town, which still commemorates Oswald in

[1] *Bede*, iii. 9, 14, 16.

the name of Oswestry.¹ The brave prince fell fighting for his religion and his country, as Bede takes occasion to mention, and "seeing himself hemmed in by armed assailants, he ended his life with words of prayer for his own soldiers: whence arose the proverb, 'O God, have mercy on their souls, as Oswald said when falling to the ground.'"² Another proverbial saying is recorded by Henry of Huntingdon: "The plain of Mesafeld was whitened with the bones of the saints." 'Thus perished, at the age of thirty-eight, Oswald, marked by the Church among her martyrs, and by the Anglo-Saxon people among its saints and heroes of most enduring fame.'³ Ireland may well be proud of having trained to piety this first royal saint and martyr whom the Anglo-Saxon kingdoms added to the Calendar of Holy Church. The ferocious Penda caused the head and hands of Oswald to be cut off, and exposed on wooden stakes, but after some months they were rescued, and the hands were placed in a silver box, at St. Peter's Church, on the summit of the rock of Bamborough, whilst the head was consigned to St. Aidan, and interred with due solemnity in the monastic chapel at Lindisfarne. Of his other relics, we learn from Bede, that thirty years after the battle of Maserfeld the niece of Oswald brought them with great state to the Lincolnshire monastery of Bardney, which was in the Mercian kingdom, but the monks received them with coldness, saying that he was an enemy of Mercia, and left the wain, which had arrived with them in the evening, to stand outside their doors

---

[1] *Giraldus*, "id est, Oswaldi arborem." Itin. Camb. 11, 12. In Welsh the town is called Cross-Oswald.
[2] *Bede*, iii. 12.   [3] *Montalembert*, iv. 32.

with a pall thrown over them. All that night a pillar of light, reaching from earth to heaven, shone over the remains, and was seen throughout the whole surrounding district of Lindsey. At the dawn of morning eagerly were the doors thrown open, the remains were reverently encased, and over them was suspended the gold and purple royal banner which had been borne before Oswald on the field of battle.

The spot on which King Oswald fell long continued greener and fairer than the ground around, and pilgrims, even from remote parts, flocked thither to pay the tributes of their devotion to God. Both places were indeed honoured, where he first planted the standard of the Cross entering on his career of victory, and where he ended his course, pouring out his life-blood for the cause of God. The latter, however, seems to have borne away the palm :—" The monks of the great and magnificent Church of Hexham (writes Montalembert), went in procession every year to celebrate the day consecrated to Oswald at the site of the cross, which he had planted on the eve of his first victory. But the love and gratitude of the Christian people gave a still greater glory to the place of his defeat and death. Pilgrims came thither in crowds to seek relief from their sufferings, and had each a miraculous cure to relate on their return. The dust which his noble blood had watered was collected with care and conveyed to great distances as a remedy for disease, or a preservative from the evils of life. By dint of carrying away this dust a hollow was scooped out, of a man's size, which seemed the ever-open tomb of this martyr of his country. On seeing the turf around this hollow clothed with an unwonted verdure, more delicate and beautiful than elsewhere, travellers said that the man who had perished there must needs have been more holy and more pleasing in God's sight than all the other warriors who rested beneath that sward. The veneration of which his remains were the object spread not only among all the Saxons and Britons of Great Britain, but even beyond the seas in Ireland and among the Greeks and the Germans. The very stake on which the head of the royal martyr had been fixed was cut up into relics, the fragments of which were regarded as of sovereign efficacy in the healing both of body and of mind."[1] One of the miracles narrated by Bede is given on the authority of St. Willibrord, Archbishop of the Frisians, and happened when that apostolic man, "being as yet only a Priest, led a pilgrim's life in Ireland, for love of the eternal country." A certain Irish scholar, "a man indeed learned in worldly literature, but in no way solicitous or studious of his own eternal salvation," was reduced to the last extremities, having caught the contagion which then prevailed. Willibrord coming to him, and finding that he cherished a great devotion to the holy Oswald, said to him that he had "a portion of the stake on which Oswald's head was set up by the pagans when he was killed: and if you believe, with a sincere heart, the Divine goodness may, through the merit of so great a man, both grant you a longer term of life here, and render you worthy of admittance into eternal life. He answered immediately that he had entire faith therein. Then I blessed some water (adds St. Willibrord) and

---

[1] Montalembert, iv. 35.

put into it a chip of the aforesaid oak, and gave it to the sick man to drink. He presently found ease, and recovering of his sickness, lived a long time after, and being entirely converted to God in heart and actions, wherever he came he spoke of the goodness of his merciful Creator, and the honour of his faithful servant." St. Willibrord added, that even in his distant mission among the Frisians miracles were wrought through the relics of Oswald.[1]

I have dwelt thus on the memory of this holy prince on account of his being trained to piety in the Irish schools, his zealous co-operation with St. Aidan in sanctifying his people, and the devoted affection which he ever displayed towards his Irish masters. He bequeathed a bright example of Christian heroism to the royal families of the Anglo-Saxon kingdoms, and many were those who sought to emulate his perfect life. His festival was kept throughout England " with joyous and blessed gladness "[2] on the 5th of August, and his name is entered in the Irish, Scottish, and Roman martyrologies on the same day. A foreign historian of England has well appreciated his true chararcter when he writes that " as his life was distinguished at once by activity and by a spirit of fervid Christian beneficence, so his Christian merits and his martyrdom rendered him a hero of the Christian world ; "[3] and we may add with Montalembert, that, " crowned by the love and devotion of the people on whom he bestowed the blessings of peace and of divine truth, spending his life for its sake; gentle and strong, serious and sincere, pious and intel-

---

[1] *Bede*, iii. 13. [2] Sarum Collect, 5th August.
[3] *Lappenberg*, i. 161.

ligent, humble and bold, active and gracious, a soldier and a missionary, a king and a martyr, slain in the flower of his age on the field of battle, fighting for his country and praying for his subjects. Where shall we find in all history a hero more nearly approaching the ideal, more richly gifted, more worthy of eternal remembrance, and, it must be added, more completely forgotten ?"[1]

On the death of Oswald the Kingdom of Northumbria was divided ; Oswy, a younger brother of Oswald, was proclaimed king in Bernicia, whilst Oswin of the race of Ella was raised to the sovereignty of Deira. Aidan's diocese now comprised two kingdoms. Both princes were Christians, and both were desirous to co-operate with the holy bishop in consolidating the conversion of their subjects.

The victorious Penda, not content with the triumph over Oswald, resolved to add Bernicia to his Mercian Kingdom, and marched straight to the royal citadel at Bamborough. Baffled in his attempt to storm the ramparts of that impregnable position, he pulled down the wooden huts of the neighbouring villages, and piling an immense mass of dry timber and straw close to the gates, set it on fire, whilst a favourable south-west wind carried the smoke and flames into the city. All seemed lost for Oswy, but he found safety in the prayers of Aidan. The saint was at this time in his place of solitary retreat on the small island of Farne, when looking up he saw the flames of fire and smoke rising high above the city which he so loved, and raising his eyes and hands towards heaven he cried out with tears, " See, O Lord, all the evil that Penda is doing." At the

[1] Montalemb., iv. 33.

moment the wind changed, and the flames being driven back on the assailants, destroying many of them, Penda and his forces speedily retired, deeming it useless to attack a city which they plainly saw to be divinely protected.[1]

But though Aidan thus guarded Bamborough by his prayers, his esteem and affection were specially fixed on Oswin the King of Deira. This prince presented to his subjects a royal example of singular loveliness. Bede writes that he was remarkable for his stature and graceful mien, being at the same time eminent for piety and winning the love of all who approached him "by the royal dignity of his mind, his countenance, his conduct." His gentleness, his charity, his humility were universally extolled, and the thanes of noblest birth deemed it a privilege to serve his household. He venerated Bishop Aidan as a father, and religion flourished under his wise rule. One fact recorded by Bede will serve to illustrate the charity of Aidan and the character of this noble prince. Oswin had seen with anxiety that the holy bishop made his missionary circuits on foot, and knowing how severe such journeys would be, especially amid the hilly districts and marshy fens of Yorkshire, made him a present of one of his best steeds splendidly caparisoned. Aidan accepted the gift, but very soon afterwards meeting with a poor man who asked an alms, he dismounted and gave to the poor man the horse with all its goodly trappings. Oswin was told of this, and the next time that Aidan came to dine with him said, "What do you mean, my lord bishop, by giving away the horse that was to be all your own?

[1] *Bede*, iii. 16.

Had I not many other horses of less value, or other things that could have been given in alms?" But Aidan replied, "What do you say, O king? Is that son of a mare worth more in your eyes than the son of God?" Oswin was silent for a while, and stood at the fire with his thanes whilst Aidan and his companion cleric took their seats; then laying aside his sword, he cast himself at the feet of the saint, asking forgiveness, and said: "Never again will I say a word about this, nor shall I again complain as to what or how much you bestow on the sons of God;" and then reassured by the kind words of the bishop, he joyously seated himself at table. Aidan, however, was filled with sadness, and turning to the Irish priest who sat by his side, said to him in their native tongue, which Oswin did not understand: "I am now convinced that this king will not live long. I never before knew a king so humble. I know that he will soon be hurried out of life, for this people does not deserve to have such a ruler."[1] This little tale, writes Ozanam, presents to us a perfect picture; it discloses in those barbarous times a sweetness of sentiment, a delicacy of conscience, a refinement of manners, which more than knowledge is the sign of Christian civilization.

The prophecy of Aidan was too soon to be fulfilled. Occasions of dissension soon arose between the kings of Bernicia and Deira. Oswin, seeing himself unable to meet Oswy in the field, disbanded his army, and resolved to reserve himself for better times. He was betrayed, however, into the hands of Oswy, and was mercilessly put to death on the 20th of August, 651.

[1] *Bede*, iii. 14.

This act of cruelty, for which the necessity of state policy could alone be pleaded, is the one blot on the career of Oswy, the one great crime which during the remaining years of his reign he laboured unceasingly to atone for.

It was within twelve days from the murder of Oswin that St. Aidan went to his reward. He was at the time in the royal residence, not far from Bamborough, "for having a church and cell there, he was wont often to go and stay there, and to make excursions thence to preach in the country round about."[1] Being taken suddenly ill, his attendants set up a tent for him close to the west end of the church and there, on the 31st of August, leaning on the wooden buttress that propped up the church-wall, he breathed his soul to God.[2] "It was a death which became a soldier of the faith on his own fit field of battle."[3] The little town of Bamborough has much to attract tourists by the ruins of its noble castle, and its associations with Northumbrian royalty, but interesting above all else to the Christian traveller will be the little church still bearing the name of St. Aidan, and the spot on which that great saint died. His remains were solemnly borne to Lindisfarne, and interred in the cemetery of the brethren of the monastery, but when a little later a noble church was erected on that island, his relics were translated thither and deposited at the right of the altar.

The wooden prop upon which Aidan had rested in death was long held in veneration by the faithful. "It

---

[1] *Bede*, iii. 17.
[2] "Quies Edani episcopi Saxonum." *Tighernach.*
[3] *Montalembert*, iv. 46.

happened," writes Bede, "that Penda, king of the Mercians, coming some years later into these parts with a hostile army, destroyed all he could with fire and sword, and burned down the village and church above mentioned, where the bishop died; but it fell out in a wonderful manner that the post which he had leaned upon when he died could not be consumed by the fire, which consumed all about it. The church being rebuilt, the same post was set up on the outside, as it had been before, to strengthen the wall. It happened again, some time after, that the same village and church were burned down the second time, and even then the fire could not touch that post; and when, in a most miraculous manner, the fire broke through the very holes in it, wherein it was fixed to the building, and destroyed the church, yet it could do no injury to the said post. The church being, therefore, built there the third time, they did not, as before, place that post on the outside as a support, but within, as a memorial of the miracle; and the people coming in were wont to kneel there, and implore the Divine mercy. And it is well known that since then many have been healed in that same place, as also that chips being cut off from that post, and put into water, have healed many from their distempers."[1]

[1] *Bede*, iii. 17

CHAPTER X.

THE IMMEDIATE SUCCESSORS OF ST. AIDAN.

St. Finan, Bishop of Lindisfarne :— Monasteries founded by King Oswy :—The Paschal controversy :—St. Colman, Bishop of Lindisfarne :—Anglo-Saxons flock to the Irish Schools :— SS. Wigbert and Willibrord :—The Conference at Whitby in A.D. 664 :—Decision of King Oswy :—Character of the Irish Monks of Lindisfarne :—St. Colman withdraws to Iona :—He founds Monasteries at ' Mayo of the Saxons ' and Inisbofin.

ST. FINAN, who is honoured in the Irish Kalendars, on the 9th of February, was chosen to succeed St. Aidan in the See of Lindisfarne. He was an Irish monk of St. Columba's monastery of Iona, and was selected by that community[1] on account of his piety and his zeal, that he might consolidate and complete the great work of the conversion of the Northumbrian Kingdom, so auspiciously begun by St. Aidan. He made it one of his first cares to erect in Lindisfarne a new cathedral, in some way worthy of his see. There were as yet, however, no skilled masons to rival the noble structure of Whitherne, so he built it, as Bede records, "in the Irish fashion, not of stone, but entirely of hewn oak, with an outer covering of reeds."

Under the guidance of St. Finan, King Oswy resolved to expiate the crime of Oswin's murder, and so sincere was his repentance, and so many were the virtues and heroic deeds which distinguished the latter portion of

---

[1] *Bede,* " a Scottis ordinatus ac missus." Ecc. Hist. iii. 25

his reign, so ardent and consistent was his zeal for the advancement of the Christian religion, that in after times the Anglo-Saxon Church numbered him among her saints. The remains of the murdered Oswin were deposited in a chapel dedicated to the Blessed Virgin, and situated on a granite headland, almost entirely surrounded by the sea, at the mouth of the river Tyne, which formed the boundary between Deira and Bernicia. The Northumbrians now began to venerate as a saint and martyr him whom hitherto they had honoured as their prince, and around his remains soon grew up a double monastery, which—amid all the vicissitudes of centuries—continued till the Reformation period one of the greatest sanctuaries of England. The ruins of its conventual church, enclosed within the fortress which defends the entrance of the Tyne, still retain some traces of the beauty and magnificence which once characterized that sacred structure: "the seven great arcades, whose time-worn relics rise majestically against the sky, from the height of their rock, produce a vivid effect on the traveller who arrives by sea, and nobly announce England's adoration of the ruins she has made."[1] Another great monastery was erected on the spot where Oswin had perished. Eanfleda, the wife of Oswy, was its founder, and its government was entrusted to Trumhere, himself indeed a scion of the royal family of Northumbria, but trained for the priesthood, and ordained in the Irish Church.[2] The purport of this foundation was that prayers might be offered

---

[1] *Montalembert*, iv., 47.
[2] *Bede*, " de natione quidem Anglorum, sed edoctus et ordinatus a Scottis," ii. 24.

there for ever for the spiritual welfare of the repentant king, and of his saintly victim.

The most remarkable foundation, however, which marked the Episcopate of Finan was that at Streaneshalch, better known by its Danish name of Whitby. Oswy had secured the supreme dignity of Bretwalda, and ensured the peace and freedom of his kingdom, whilst at the same time he sealed the triumph of Christianity among the Anglo-Saxons, when he achieved the complete overthrow of the fierce pagan Penda, king of Mercia. In token of gratitude to God, he made to the abbess Hilda a gift of ten hides of land to establish a monastery. She chose the precipitous headland of Streaneshalch (that is, the bay of the lighthouse), and erected there the greatest of England's convents, which, whilst it guided the mariners on that stormy sea, served also for a thousand years as a pharos of light and peace for the whole of that territory. We will allow the eloquent Montalembert to describe this noble monastery of St. Hilda : " Of all the sites chosen by monastic architects, after that of Monte Casino, I know none grander and more picturesque than that of Whitby. It is even, in certain aspects, still more imposing than the Benedictine capital, as being near the sea. The Esk, which flows through a hilly country, unlike the ordinary levels of England, forms at its mouth a circular bay, commanded on every side by lofty cliffs. On the summit of one of these rocks, three hundred feet above the sea, Hilda placed her monastery, on a platform of green and short seaside turf, the sides of which slope abruptly to the northern ocean. From this spot the eye wanders now over the uplands, valleys, and vast heaths of this part of Yorkshire, now along the rough precipices which line the coast, now on the wide horizon of the sea, whose foaming waves break against the perpendicular sides of the great rocky wall which is crowned by the monastery. The dull roar of the tide accords with the sombre tints of the rocks, which are rent and hollowed out by its force; for it is not here, as on the shores of the Channel, where the whiteness of the cliffs has gained the name of Albion for the island of Great Britain. The precipices of the Yorkshire coast are, on the contrary, as dark in colour as they are abrupt and rugged in outline. Nothing now remains of the Saxon monastery; but more than half of the abbey church, restored by the Percies in the time of the Normans, still stands, and enables the marvelling spectator to form to himself an idea of the solemn grandeur of the great edifice."[1] This monastery was long famed for the fervour of its inmates, and for its strict religious observance; and it became a proverb among the Northumbrians that the image of the primitive church, wherein there was neither rich nor poor, and where all things were common among the Christians, was to be seen realized at Whitby.

It was mainly during the episcopate of St. Finan that the light of religion spread from Northumbria to the other Anglo-Saxon kingdoms, but we will have more to say on this subject in another chapter. The Paschal question, too, began to be agitated with great ardour. The practical inconvenience of having, in the same kingdom, two different systems for the calculation of Easter,

---

[1] *Montalembert*, iv., 62.

became sorely felt, when, on one occasion, King Oswy and his court were keeping the Easter feast with the Irish bishop, whilst the queen and her attendants, who followed the Continental computation, were still observing the strict fast of Lent, and celebrating "their day of Palms."[1] There were not wanting among the Irish missionaries some warm supporters of the correct Continental usage. One Irish priest, in particular, named Ronan, whom Bede designates as "a very ardent upholder of the true Easter," entered into the controversy with the greatest ardour. His reasoning, and the forcible language with which he denounced the Celtic computation, led many to renounce their traditional observance, but only served to exasperate more and more the bishop and many of the clergy whose desire it was to walk according to the traditions of their fathers. This Ronan is supposed by Mabillon to be the same who, a few years later, appears as "a pilgrim of Irish birth,"[2] in a charter of foundation of an ecclesiastical establishment at Mazerolles, on the banks of the river Vienne, in Picardy, and of which it is only recorded that he and his brother pilgrims from Ireland were its first occupants.

The Paschal controversy was still raging when St. Finan was summoned to his reward. He died in the year 661, and his hallowed remains were laid beside those of his predecessor, in the church of Lindisfarne. In the Breviary of Aberdeen, he is styled "a man of venerable life, a bishop of great sanctity, an eloquent teacher of unbelieving races, remarkable for his training in virtue

---

[1] *Bede*, iii. 25.
[2] "Peregrinus ex genere Scottorum." *Mabillon*, Annal. ord. S. Bened. i., 474. See 'Gallia Christ.' ii., 1222.

and his liberal education. While he surpassed all his equals in every manner of knowledge, as well as in circumspection and prudence, he chiefly devoted himself to good works, and presented in his life a most apt example of virtue."

He was succeeded in the See of Lindisfarne by St. Colman, another Irishman, who had embraced the religious life at Iona. His episcopate in England was short, for we will just now see that, in the year 664, he chose to return to his own country rather than relinquish the Paschal computation which he had received from those who had gone before him. Bede pays him a just tribute of eulogy when he styles him a man of simple and austere piety, and of an innate prudence, and greatly beloved by Oswy.

At this time several of the Anglo-Saxon nobility, and many too of the middle class, struck by the wondrous piety and learning of the Irish bishops and clergy, who had come to preach to them the truths of eternal life, "forsook their native island," and proceeded to Ireland, the better to ensure their sanctification, and to perfect themselves in the salutary knowledge of Divine faith. Some of these entered the Irish monasteries, and in the austerity of their lives emulated the heroism of their masters. Others went about from school to school, and from cell to cell, enriching themselves with a precious store of truth, wherever they found teachers, famed for their skill in science, human or divine.[1] From the words of Venerable Bede it would appear that these Anglo-Saxon youths went in crowds to Ireland thus to satiate their thirst for sacred truth, and he adds: " The

[1] *Bede*, Ecc. Hist. iii. 27

Irish most willingly received them all, and took care to supply them gratuitously with daily food, as also to furnish them with books to read, and with their teaching, without making any charge." So many were these foreign students at the school of Armagh, that one district of the city was known as the "Saxon quarter:" numerous bands of them were also found at Clonard, Bangor, Glasnevin, Lismore, Mellifont, Clonmacnoise, and the other great monasteries and schools, and many of them, following the bright example of their Irish companions and masters, embraced the missionary life, and laboured in Friesland and other nations of the Continent to win innumerable souls to Christ.

Two of these Anglo-Saxon missionary saints merit particular mention. St. Wigbert, whilst as yet a youth, left his Anglo-Saxon home to walk in the footsteps of the saints in Erin. Bede tells us that he lived for many years in Ireland, and he became famed in the Irish schools for his piety and learning. Filled with the desire of bringing the light of the Gospel to those nations of Northern Europe, from whom the Saxons themselves were sprung, he set out on his missionary enterprise in the year 688, and landed in Friesland. This territory, which is divided into two provinces by the Issel and the Zuyder Zee, stretches along the northern coast of Europe from the Rhine to the Ems, and, at the period of which we speak, extended its frontiers to the Elbe, and probably to the Eyder. It was inhabited by the Frisons, a barbarous people, "living like fish in the water, and holding intercourse with other nations only by sea."[1] They were regarded by the

[1] *Pertz*, 'Monumenta Germ.' II., pag. 341.

Romans as an indomitable race, and hitherto the Christian missionaries had failed to lead them captive to the truth. Their king, Rathbod, at one time avowed his desire to become a convert, but when the baptismal water was about being poured upon his head, he turned to the priest and asked: 'Are the brave Frisons, that are dead, in heaven or in hell?' The priest replied that none but those who were baptized could enter heaven: 'Well, then,' said the wild chieftain, 'I wish rather to be with my brave Frisons than to be in heaven with strangers,' and he at once stepped back from the font. Among these people Wigbert laboured with untiring zeal for two years, but his efforts were fruitless, and, despairing of success, he returned to Ireland, which he now regarded as his home, and during his remaining years devoted himself there "to edify his neighbours by his example, since he had failed to win strangers to the faith."[1]

About this time Pepin of Heristal, the mayor of the palace, who had been filled with admiration at the devotedness and zeal of the Irish bishop, St. Kilian, during the trying period of Ebroin's tyranny, sent messengers to Ireland[2] to solicit missionaries for Neustria, the modern Netherlands, and for that portion of Friesland which he had lately conquered from Rathbod. The eyes of all were turned to Willibrord as the man best suited for this arduous mission. This greatest of the Anglo-Saxon missionaries was born about the year 657, in the neighbourhood of Ripon, and soon after his birth his father embraced a solitary life, and built for

---

[1] *Bede*, Eccl. Hist. v. 9.
[2] *Le Cointe*, Ann. Ecc. Fr. iv. 214, ad. an. 690.

himself a cell on the banks of the Humber, where he served God in watching and prayer. In his twentieth year Willibrord proceeded to Ireland, partly from desire of leading a strict religious life, and partly in order to profit by the sacred learning of its schools; as Alcuin expresses it, "like an active bee, he desired to suck honey from its flowers." For thirteen years he made Ireland his home, and now matured in sanctity, he was chosen to carry out the pious wishes of Pepin. With twelve companions, some Irish, some Saxons, whom he selected from the Irish schools, he set sail on his sacred mission before the close of the year 690, and landed at Caturic, at the mouth of the Rhine. Willibrord found the harvest, through the mercy of God, now ripe for the sickle, and the people came to him in crowds to be instructed in the faith. The saint, true to his Irish training, resolved to ensure the blessing of heaven on his missionary toil, and hastened to the feet of the Vicar of Christ to receive his sanction and authority for the mission in which he was thus about to engage. "At their first coming into Frisia" *(primis quoque temporibus)* writes Bede, "he made haste to Rome, to Pope Sergius, who then presided in the Apostolic See, that he might undertake the much-desired work of preaching the Gospel to the Gentiles with his license and blessing; and hoping to receive from him some relics of the blessed apostles and martyrs of Christ."[1] Strengthened by the Pope's benediction, and enriched with sacred relics, Willibrord preached with the zeal of an apostle, and heaven smiled upon his labours. In 696 it was deemed expedient that he should be raised to

---

[1] *Bede*, Ecc. Hist. v. 11.

the Episcopate, and again he made the journey to Rome, where, on St. Cecilia's Feast, in the church of that great virgin-martyr, he was consecrated by the Pope, and Utrecht was assigned to him as his Episcopal See. St. Willibrord is justly styled the apostle of Friesland and of the Netherlands. He ceased not from his missionary toil till his death, in his 82nd year, in A.D. 789 : in the words of his venerable biographer, "so long as he lived, he ceased not to labour in the love of Christ."

But to return to St. Colman, the chief event of his episcopate was the famous conference, held at Whitby, in the year 664, for the purpose of introducing uniformity in the Paschal celebration throughout the kingdom. It was, indeed, a foregone conclusion, and it was well it should be so. Already the Continental computation had been enforced by the sub-king of Bernicia. The queen, too, and her household, and several of the clergy, had learned that such was the usage of Rome and of the greater part of the Christian world. It was vain to expect that they would lay aside this more perfect computation for the older but less correct cycle that from time immemorial had been followed in the churches of Ireland and Wales. It was at the request of Oswy, the common benefactor of all, that the conference was held. The place chosen was the Abbess Hilda's new monastery of Whitby, "elevated on that proud seaward height which is now crowned by the ruined church of a monastery, founded two centuries after her minster had been laid desolate."[1] Colman, with a few Irish priests, seems to have stood alone in defending the claims of the Celtic computation, but there were present Bishop Cedd, and

[1] *Bright*, 194.

the Abbot Eata and others, who had studied at Lindisfarne or Iona, and had hitherto joyfully followed the tradition of Ireland. On the other side the leading disputant was St. Wilfrid, and with him were two venerable bishops, Agilbert and Tuda. It is strange that all three are representatives of Irish schools. Bishop Tuda was himself an Irishman, and, as we learn from Bede, had been consecrated bishop in the south of Ireland, where the correct celebration of Easter was already adopted, and having lately come into Northumbria laboured assiduously there in preaching the faith, and setting forth its divine teachings, "both by word and work."[1] Agilbert was consecrated in France, but attracted to Ireland by the fame of its schools, "had lived a long time there for the sake of studying the Scriptures."[2] He had subsequently laboured in the kingdom of Wessex, and soon after the Whitby conference returned to France where he was appointed to the See of Paris. Wilfrid, too, had begun his religious life at Lindisfarne. He entered that monastery in his fifteenth year, and for three years was trained to piety and to sacred learning by its Irish monks. He learned there by heart the Psalter in St. Jerome's correct recension, and he was loved by the other students as a brother, by the seniors as a son.[3] With the approval of St. Finan and the monks of Lindisfarne, he had quitted the monastery to visit Rome, to gain the blessing of the successor of St. Peter, and to glean whatever might be learned in the Continental schools. He was now in his thirtieth year, and had only a few weeks before the conference received the Holy Order of Priesthood from Bishop Agilbert.

[1] *Bede*, iii. 26. [2] *Bede*, iii. 7. [3] *Bede*, v. 19.

King Oswy opened the proceedings by saying that as they all served the same God, and hoped for the same heavenly rewards, it was advisable that they should all follow the same disciplinary rules, and the same observance of the holy time of Easter : and then stated the question for discussion : Of the two different traditions regarding the celebration of Easter which was the more correct ? He called on Bishop Colman first to explain his ritual and to justify its origin.

It will be well to bear in mind that two distinct questions were involved in this Paschal computation. First, what cycle of years must pass before the Paschal full moon will fall on the same day ? Second, on what day of the Paschal month should the Easter festival be kept ; that is to say, if the Sunday immediately following the Paschal full moon happened to be " the fourteenth moon " could the Easter feast be celebrated on that day ?

The Irish church had received from our apostle, St. Patrick, the cycle of eighty-four years. It was the cycle followed in Rome at the time that he was sent by Pope Celestine to evangelize our people, but during the two centuries that had intervened, Rome had gradually perfected the Easter computation, whilst Ireland continued to observe the first cycle unchanged. The first alteration in Rome was in the year 444. The cycle of eighty-four years would place Easter, in that year, on March 26th: whilst the Alexandrian computation, which was considered the most accurate in the East, marked Easter day on the 23rd of April. Pope Leo, without fixing on any permanent change, wished the Roman church for that year to follow the Alexandrian rule. In the year 455, he again observed the Easter time in accordance with the Alexandrian computation. His successor, Pope Hilary, adopted the cycle of Victorius of Aquitaine, which continued in use till a more perfect system was proposed, in the year 527, by Dionysius Exiguus, which was completely in accordance with the Alexandrian calculations, and was finally accepted in Rome and throughout the Catholic world. Nevertheless, the Victorian cycle held its ground for a time, and continued to be followed in France, even as late as the mission of St. Columbanus, towards the close of the sixth century.[1]

The Celtic computation of Easter also included "the fourteenth moon," when it fell on Sunday, within the days on which Easter might be celebrated. The Quartodecimans had been condemned by the Church, for they held that on whatever day of the week "the fourteenth moon" might happen to fall it should be observed as the Easter feast. But the Irish and British churches were quite free from this error, for they never celebrated Easter except on Sunday: and in their observance they relied on the authority of the illustrious bishop, St. Anatolius, who was equally revered in Rome and in Alexandria, but whose Paschal canon had come to the Irish and British churches—as, indeed, it had been published all through the West—in a corrupt form.[2]

Having premised so much for the clearer understanding of the controversy, we may now return to the

---

[1] *Columbanus*, epist. opp. S. Gregorii, ix. 127.
[2] See this Canon of Anatolius in *Gallandi*, Biblioth. iii. 545. Bucherius says of it: "Paschae Dominicam luna xiv. nullo scrupulo indicit"; and, as published in the West, it fully justified the Irish usage.

disputants at Whitby. St. Colman stated his case with calm and tranquil dignity, and scrupulously avoided every shadow of exaggeration: "My usage is that which was followed by my predecessors; all our fathers observed it; they were men of God, and we read that their usage was derived from the apostle St. John. In reverence for these holy men, I dare not change it, and I will not change it. We hold it as a venerable tradition that the fourteenth moon, being Sunday, is to be kept as Easter Day. Let the other side state the reasons on which they ground their usage." Oswy called on Bishop Agilbert to reply, but he requested that Wilfrid, who could explain the matter better in the English tongue, might be allowed to speak in his stead. Then Wilfrid said: "We keep Easter as we have seen it kept by all Christians at Rome, where the blessed apostles, SS. Peter and Paul, lived, taught, suffered, and are buried. We have seen the same rule observed throughout Italy and Gaul: we know that it is so in Africa, in Asia, in Greece, and throughout Christendom, in spite of all difference of language and of country. It is only these (*i.e.*, Colman and his companions), and their partners in obstinacy, the Picts and Britons, who, inhabiting some parts only of the two most remote islands of the world, are acting foolishly in seeking to fight against the whole world."[1]

Colman replied: "It is strange that you speak of our acting foolishly, when we follow the rule of the great Apostle who reclined on the Lord's breast." Wilfrid,

---

[1] "De duabus ultimis oceani insulis, et his non totis." *Bede,* iii. 25. Cummian had said the same. "Britonum, Scotorumque particula, qui sunt paene extremi." *Usher,* Sylloge, p. 21

in his answer, argued that St. John might have found it necessary to adhere for a time to Jewish observances; but that the true Christian celebration of Easter, as taught by the Sacred Scriptures, was that which St. Peter preached in Rome, and which the churches of the whole world now followed. The Irish, he added, did not follow the old Asiatic custom, which celebrated Easter on whatever day the fourteenth moon happened to fall, and hence they agreed neither with Peter nor John, neither with the Jewish Law nor with the Gospel. In this Wilfrid was in manifest error, for he supposed that the Easter rule then adopted by the successors of St. Peter was the one which from the beginning had been followed in Rome, whereas it had only been introduced there about one hundred years before.

Colman next appealed to the Paschal Canon of Anatolius, according to which the Paschal limits should be "the fourteenth and twentieth moons," and then he asked, "Are we to be told that our most venerable father, Columba, and his successors, men beloved of God, have acted contrary to what the Divine Word teaches? Many of these holy men have given proof of their sanctity by miracles; and as for me, who believe in that sanctity, I choose to follow their teaching and their example." Wilfrid, in his reply, entered into a long statement regarding the Anatolian Canon, proving, as the learned Patavius remarks, that he was quite ignorant of the true Canon of Anatolius, and assigning to that holy bishop opinions which he had never dreamt of.[1] But then he very sensibly added:

[1] *Petavius*, De Ratione Temp. " opinionem quam ne somniavit quidem unquam."

"As to your father Columba, and his disciples, I do not deny that they were servants of God and beloved by Him; no doubt they loved Him in their rustic simplicity with the most pious intentions. I do not think there was much harm in their observance of Easter, because no one had told them of more perfect rules. If a Catholic computation had been presented to them, I believe they would have followed it, as they followed the commandments of God which they knew. But as for you, without doubt you are in fault, if, after having heard the decrees of the Apostolic See, and of the universal church, confirmed by the Holy Scripture, you still despise them. Even admitting the sanctity of your fathers, how can you prefer, to the Church, spread over the whole earth, this handful of saints in one corner of a remote island? Your Columba, and I will say also our Columba, so far as he was the servant of Christ, however holy or powerful by his virtues he may have been, is he to be placed before the chief of the Apostles, to whom our Lord himself said: 'Thou art Peter, and upon this rock I will build my Church, and the gates of hell shall not prevail against it; and I will give unto thee the keys of the kingdom of heaven.'"

We must make allowance for the ardour and impetuosity of the youthful Wilfrid, while we recall the many errors into which he fell in this argumentation. There was no decree of the universal church, or of the Apostolic See, condemning the Celtic usage, and there was nothing in Sacred Scripture that he could legitimately claim as supporting one usage rather than another. The Paschal system, then in use in Rome, was a matter of disciplinary observance, in which the

Roman church had herself abandoned her original tradition. The successors of St. Peter had gradually perfected the manner of calculating the Paschal time, but with wise and prudent moderation had allowed its general acceptance to be the result of its own intrinsic merits, without enforcing it by any special decree. The last words of Wilfrid, however, were those which came home to the heart of Oswy. They set before him the majesty of the Apostolic See, and the reverence which even in matters not essential should be shown by the faithful to the key-bearer of heavenly authority. Addressing himself to Colman: "Is it true" he said, "that these words were addressed by our Lord to St. Peter?" "It is true, O king," was the answer. "Do you claim any similar authority for your father Columba?" rejoined the king. "No," said the bishop. "You are then both agreed in this that the keys of heaven were given to St. Peter by our Lord," added Oswy. "Yes, assuredly," they both replied. Then with a smile the king pronounced his decision: "I say to you both that this is the doorkeeper of heaven, whom I do not choose to gainsay, and that I will not oppose him, but as far as I know and am able, I desire in all things to obey his rulings, lest when I reach the doors of the celestial kingdom, there be no one to open them for me, if I am the adversary of him who carries the keys. In all my life I will neither do or approve anything or any person that may be contrary to him."

The assembly applauded the king's decision, but Colman, ever ready to obey the monarch in temporal matters, refused to recognise his authority in things spiritual. To remove, however, all danger of dissension he resigned his See of Lindisfarne, and accompanied by those who still adhered to the Celtic usage, withdrew from Northumbria and repaired once more to his loved parent monastery of Iona. Strange to say, some Protestant writers find in this conduct of St. Colman a pretence for asserting that he rejected and disobeyed the authority of the successors of St. Peter. But surely that authority had not been exercised, how then could it be rejected or disobeyed? Wilfrid, or those who sided with him, had not been invested with any power to speak in the name of the Sovereign Pontiff, and Oswy in his decision only proclaimed a secular enactment. Far more just would it be for us to conclude that St. Colman and his opponents were alike obedient to the successors of St. Peter. Both recognised his supreme authority; both admitted that to him, and to him alone, were addressed the words, "Thou art Peter, and upon this rock I will build my Church;" and both declared that to him alone the keys of Christ's Kingdom were consigned, and that he was the divinely strengthened rock on which the whole church should rest. But St. Colman considered that till the successors of St. Peter exercised in this matter their supreme authority, and prohibited the usage which he defended, it was his privilege, and it was a duty to which he would not prove unfaithful, to follow the tradition of his fathers.

Most of the Irish monks departed from Lindisfarne with Colman, and with them also went some thirty Anglo-Saxons who had been instructed in that monastery, and were united in the closest bonds of affection with their spiritual father. One parting request the holy Bishop made to Oswy. He feared lest the brethren who remained at Lindisfarne might be disturbed on his account, and he asked that Eata, who had been one of Aidan's first pupils, and was now abbot of Melrose, would be set over that monastery. To this Oswy readily assented, and before the close of A.D. 664, Colman, accompanied by the religious brethren, and bearing with him a portion of the relics of St. Aidan, bade a last farewell to Lindisfarne.

The Venerable Bede takes occasion from his departure to review the career of Colman and his predecessors, and his words present a golden eulogy of these illustrious Irish Bishops :—" How great was Colman's austerity," he writes, " how great his continence, the place which they governed shows for himself and his predecessors; for there were very few houses, besides the church, found at their departure; indeed no more than were barely sufficient for their daily residence. They had also no money, but some cattle, for if they received any money from rich persons they immediately gave it to the poor, there being no need to gather money or provide houses for the entertainment of the great men of the world, for such never resorted to the church except to pray and hear the Word of God. The king himself, when opportunity required, came only with five or six servants, and having performed his devotions in the church departed. But if they happened to take a repast there they were satisfied with only the plain and daily food of the brethren, and required no more—for the whole care of those teachers was to serve God, not the world, to feed the soul, not the flesh. For this reason the religious habit was at that time held in great veneration, so that wheresoever any cleric or monk happened to come he was joyfully received by all persons as God's servant; and if they chanced to meet him, as he was upon the way, they ran to him, and bowing, were glad to receive the sign of the cross from his hand, or words of blessing from his lips. Great attention was also paid to their exhortations, and on Sundays the people flocked eagerly to the church or the monasteries, not to feed their bodies, but to hear the Word of God; and if any priest happened to come into a village the inhabitants flocked together forthwith to hear from him the Word of Life. For the priests and clerics went into the villages on no other account than to preach, baptize, visit the sick, and, in few words, to take care of souls; and they were so free from the curse of worldly avarice that none of them received lands and possessions for building monasteries unless they were compelled to do so by the temporal authorities; which custom was for some time after observed in all the churches of the Northumbrians."[1] We could not desire a more authentic testimony to the disinterestedness and piety, as well as to the devoted zeal with which the Irish bishops and priests had cultivated the spiritual vineyard in the kingdom of Northumbria, building up, by their labours, churches of fairest proportions and marvellous strength, and training a native clergy to perpetuate among the Anglo-Saxon nations the salutary teaching and the blessings of divine faith. The Professor of Ecclesiastical History in Oxford at the present day is not less eloquent than the first father of Anglo-Saxon history in his praise of these illustrious bishops. Their mission in Northumbria, he writes, "brought religion straight home to men's hearts

[1] *Bede*, iii. 26.

by sheer power of love and self-sacrifice: it held up
before them, in the unconscious goodness and nobleness
of its representatives, the moral evidence for Christianity.
It made them feel what it was to be taught and cared
for, in the life spiritual, by pastors who, before all
things, were the disciples and ministers of Christ—
whose chief and type was a St. Aidan." (Page 204).

St. Colman remained for some time in Iona, resting
there from his past labours and enjoying the sweets of
the observance of the religious life. He then proceeded
to the Island of Inisbofin, off the coast of Mayo, and
erected a monastery, in which he placed the former
community of Lindisfarne; but after some time dissensions arising between the Celtic brethren and the
Saxons, he conducted the latter to Mayo, where he had
received a noble site for a monastery under the condition of prayers being offered in it for the repose of the
soul of the donor. Around this monastery a city
sprung up, which in the course of time became an important Episcopal See; many religious from England
continued for about a hundred years to flock thither, and
from them it derived the name, by which it long continued to be known in the Irish schools, of "Mayo of
the Saxons." Bede tells us that in his day it was still
possessed by the English brethren, whom he styles "a
distinguished congregation of monks, who live by their
own labour in great strictness and holiness under a
canonical rule and abbot."[1]

Our writers are not agreed as to the precise year of
the foundation of the monastery of Inisbofin. Usher and
others placed it in the year 664, and, indeed, it is diffi-

[1] *Bede*, iv. 4.

cult to suppose that Colman would permit the island community of Iona to be for any lengthened period burdened with the support of the large body of monks who had accompanied him. Others, however, adopt a later date, relying on the authority of the Annals of Ulster, which mark, under the year 667, ' the sailing of Colman to Inisbofin, and his founding a church there ;' and on the Annals of Tighernach, which in 668 have a somewhat similar entry:—"A.D. 668, navigatio Colmanni Episcopi cum reliquiis sanctorum ad insulam *vaccae Albae* (Inisbofin) in qua fundavit ecclesiam." Perhaps these jarring opinions may be reconciled by supposing that the community proceeded at once to enter on its labours in the island of Inisbofin, but that it was only in the year 667 or 668 when the church was built and the community consolidated, that St. Colman translated thither the precious relics of St. Aidan and the other sacred treasures which he had brought with him from Lindisfarne.

At all events this holy bishop was not idle during his sojourn at the parent monastery of Iona, and it was during this interval that he founded the churches of Fearn in Angus, and of Tarbet in Easter-Ross, the former of which was dedicated to St. Aidan, and probably enriched by a portion of that saint's relics, whilst the other in after times bore the name of its founder, St. Colman. St. Cummian, who wrote the first life of St. Columba, was at this time abbot of Iona, and it is not improbable that he was moved to undertake this work by the request of St. Colman, who must not have concealed from him what he had fully realized at the conference of Whitby, that very little was known, even by the clergy across the borders, of the name, and the sanctity, and the miracles of their great founder.

St. Colman governed the two monasteries of Mayo and Inisbofin till his death, which took place at the latter monastery, in the year 676, on the 8th of August, on which day his feast is marked in our ancient Martyrologies.[1] The ruins of his church may still be seen at Knocktownland, in the island of Inisbofin.

CHAPTER XI.

ST. CUTHBERT.

SS. Tuda and Eata:—St. Cuthbert born in Ireland:—His early years —He tends flocks on the Lammermoor:—His life in the monastery of Mailros:—His hermitage at Dull:—His austerities:—Succeeds Boisil as Prior:—His charity to pilgrims:—Apostolic zeal:— St. Cuthbert in Lindisfarne:—He retires to Farne Island:—Is appointed Bishop:—Death of King Egfrid:—St. Cuthbert's virtues and miracles:—His friendship for Herbert of Derwentwater:—He protects the home of his foster-mother:—Visits the monasteries of Coldingham, Whitby, and Tynemouth:—St. Cuthbert's death:—Popular veneration for his memory:—Character of King Aldfrid of Northumbria.

THE influence of the Irish Church on the Kingdom of Northumbria did not cease with the withdrawal of St. Colman from the Episcopate of Lindisfarne. Another Irish Bishop, whose name has already been before us, was appointed to succeed him. This was Tuda. Trained

---

[1] His life is given by the Bollandists in tom. iii. Februarii, pag. 82.

in the southern monasteries of Ireland, he had adopted
the correct Easter computation, and it was hoped that
under his wise rule peace and concord would be soon
re-established, and religion would continue to prosper as
hitherto it had prospered under his Celtic predecessors.
His Episcopate, however, lasted only a few months, for
he was carried off by the plague before the close of the
year 664. Bede compendiates his history in a few words:
" he was a good and religious man, but governed the
church only a very short time." [1] The plague which
raged at this time was known as the *Buidhe Connaill*,
or the yellow pest, on account of the ghastly yellow hue
of those whom it attacked. It made its appearance in
the south of England in the beginning of May, 664, the
King of Kent and the Archbishop of Canterbury being
among its first victims. Before the close of Autumn it
spread to Ireland, and our annals give a long list of the
illustrious princes and holy men whom it carried off.[2]
It was whilst visiting the monastery of Paegnalech,
supposed to be Finchale, on the western bank of the
Wear, at Durham, that Tuda was hurried out of this
world, and his remains were interred in the church of
that monastery. A few years later the abbot, Eata, was
appointed bishop of this See. He was one of the first
Saxons whom St. Aidan had trained for the sanctuary
in Lindisfarne. He had subsequently been appointed
by the same holy bishop to govern the monastery of
Mailros, and after the conference of Whitby, at St.
Colman's request, he took charge of the parent house of

---

[1] *Bede*, " permodico tempore ecclesiam regens." iii. 26.
[2] The Ulster Annals have the entry "Innumerabiles mortui
sunt."

Lindisfarne. He faithfully preserved, and handed on the traditions of Celtic piety, and had for his successor in this See St. Cuthbert, the most illustrious and the most beloved of the many saints whom Ireland has given to the English church.

Venerable Bede has given us two lives of St. Cuthbert. He had gleaned the facts which he relates from those whose privilege it was to be disciples and companions of the saint, and he himself may be considered a contemporary, for he was thirteen years old at the time of St. Cuthbert's death. Nevertheless of the early life of Cuthbert, Bede gives us no details.[1] He is silent as to his country, his parents, his childhood, and he first introduces us to St. Cuthbert when he was in his eighth year, and living with a pious widow named Kenspid, whom he regarded with such affection that he used to call her 'mother,' and under whose care he grew up to manhood, tending the herds and flocks entrusted to him on the banks of the Leader, or along the southern slopes of the Lammermoor hills.

Other authorities, however, supply for this deficiency of Bede, and it is an immemorial tradition, to which no impartial inquirer can refuse to give his assent, that

[1] Some recent writers have thought that they could find in Bede's Metrical Life of St. Cuthbert a reference to his birthplace, when he writes that Britain

" Temporibus genuit fulgur venerabile nostris,"

but the context clearly shows that these words refer not to Cuthbert himself, but to the fame of his sanctity and his holy rule of life. In the same way Rome is said in the preceding verses to be rendered illustrious by the heroism of the Apostles SS. Peter and Paul, and Constantinople by the eloquence of Chrysostom. All the ablest editors of Bede and the other ecclesiastical historians of England admit that Bede is silent as to St. Cuthbert's birthplace.

St. Cuthbert was a native of Ireland. This was the tradition of the Cathedral of Durham, where for six centuries his sacred shrine was the great centre of pilgrimage for the faithful from all parts of England. Under the figure of St. Cuthbert on the altar screen was preserved the inscription down to the Reformation period, " St. Cuthbert, Patron of the Church, City, and Liberty of Durham, an Irishman by birth, of royal parentage, who was led by God's providence to England."[1] The rich-stained glass windows which once adorned this Cathedral recorded the whole series of the Saint's life. They were demolished indeed in Edward the Sixth's reign, the Protestant Dean " breaking them all to pieces, for he could never abide any ancient monuments, acts, or deeds that gave any light of, or to, godly religion ; " but the scenes which they represented have happily been registered, and first amongst them was " the birth of the Saint at Kells," with " the bright beams shining from heaven upon the mother and child, where he did lie in the cradle, so that to every man's thinking the Holy Ghost had overshadowed him."[2]

Such, too, was the tradition of the Irish Church, and this has been attested to us in a most authoritative way. In the year 1838, the Surtees Society for illustrating the history and antiquities of Durham, published

[1] "Sanctus Cuthbertus, patronus ecclesiae, civitatis, et libertatis Dunelmensis, natione Hibernicus, regiis parentibus ortus," &c. *The ancient Rites of Durham*, pag. 112.

[2] Ibid., pag. 65. The writer adds: "The Bishop baptized the child, and did call him Mulloche in the Irish tongue, the which is in English as much as to say Cuthbert . . . The name of the city that the child St. Cuthbert was baptized in is called Hardbrecins (Ardbraccan)."

for the first time from the MSS. of the Dean and Chapter of York, a valuable Tract on the Life of St. Cuthbert, which had been compiled about the year 1200, from earlier authentic sources.[1] This Tract of such venerable antiquity expressly attests that the Saint was born in Ireland, and gives in detail the narrative of his royal descent and Irish parentage. The writer, moreover, assigns the sources whence he had derived the facts which he narrates, and he appeals to Irish MSS. which had been explained to him by most trustworthy Irish Priests, disciples of St. Malachy, and to most ancient Annals of Ireland, 'Hyberniensium annalibus vetustissimis.' He further cites the oral testimony of an Irish Bishop named Eugene, a man of high repute and of holy life, with whom he had often conversed[2] on the matter, and who, being a native of Meath, assured him that the tradition relative to St. Cuthbert's birth in Kells was vividly cherished in that then flourishing city. As if all this did not suffice, he had further received the written attestation of four other Irish Bishops who, by

[1] It is entitled: "Libellus de nativitate sancti Cuthberti, de Historiis Hybernensium exceptus et translatus." Publications of the Surtees Society, 1838, pag. 61.

[2] "Sanctae opinionis et conversationis virum," pag. 63. The name of this bishop's see is at first very corruptly given *Harundinonensis*: however at page 87 he is called *Episcopus Hardmonensis*, which points to Ardmore in the county Waterford as his See. From Cotton's "Fasti," pag. 212, we learn that at the close of the 12th century a Bishop Eugene held this See. The Tract on the Life of St. Cuthbert adds that the holy patron of this See was "novem mortuorum suscitator magnificus," and famous for miracles: this belongs to the Life of St. Declan, the patron of Ardmore. Bishop Eugene further described that part of Ireland as "patriae provinciam regionibus caeteris Hyberniae praeclariorem et praestantiorem omnibusque rebus fertiliorem," pag. 73

the seal of their authority, authenticated this tradition of our country, and he gives the names of these four Prelates—St. Malachy, Archbishop of Armagh; Gillebert, Bishop of Limerick; Albinus, Bishop of Ferns; and Matthew O'Heney, Archbishop of Cashel. Now these are some of the brightest names that adorn the Irish Church in the twelfth century;[1] and I will add that, in regard to St. Cuthbert, the testimony of O'Heney, Archbishop of Cashel, brings with it special weight. It is not only that whilst he held the See of Cashel, he was also the delegate or representative of the Holy See for all Ireland, and that in the Annals of St. Mary's Abbey, he is styled, "the wisest and most religious man of the Irish nation," but further it is known that he applied himself in a particular manner to the study of the History of the Irish Church, and, as Ware informs us, he even composed a Life of St. Cuthbert, which unfortunately is not now known to exist.

In addition to all this evidence, there is a fragment of a Latin Metrical Life of St. Cuthbert in the British Museum, beginning :

"Si cupis audire, Cuthberti miraque scire,"

which expressly refers to his Irish birth :—

"Regis erat natus, et Hybernicus est generatus."[2]

Fordun is further a witness that such, too, was the tradition of Scotland; and the testimonies of John of Tinmouth and Capgrave and the English Martyrology

[1] The writer of the Tract most justly adds: "quisquis ipsorum sanctitatis vestigia noverat, de verbis illorum et veritatis protestatione dubitare non poterat." Surtees. Public. pag. 78.
[2] MSS. Brit. Mus. Titus, A. ii., 2, 3.

should suffice to prove that the general tradition of England was favourable to the same opinion, for they are all found to agree in this, that St. Cuthbert was born in Ireland.[1]

We may now resume our narrative of the saint's life. He was born at Kells, in the County of Meath, about the year 625, and he was brought to Ardbraccan to be regenerated in the waters of baptism. "There is a very large city in Ireland (thus runs the narrative in the Tract, written about the year 1200), which in the Irish tongue is called Kenanás (Kells), and it is situate in the province of Meath, which is most rich in game and corn, in pasturage and woods, and is abundantly supplied with streams and rivers: the river Boyne, which flows through it, is full to overflowing with several varieties of fish. This city, which is both rich and beautiful, is stated to have been the birthplace of the holy youth, and the inhabitants still point out the place where he was born, and it would appear from the ruins, which still remain, that a convent of nuns was in later times erected there, and through the memory of the sanctity of the child, the spot is exceedingly honoured by the people of the whole province."[2] In baptism St. Cuthbert received the name of *Mo-uallog*, which may be interpreted "my privileged one," but in England this name was exchanged for the Saxon Cudberct or Cuthbert, which, as, indeed, one of the ancient records

---

[1] In Butler's "Lives of the Saints" it is said "St. Cuthbert, according to his MS. Life in the Cottonian Library, was born at Ceannanes, or Kells, in Meath. By his mother, Saba, a princess who led a holy life, he was grandson of Murertach, King of Ireland, A.D. 533," vol. xii., pag. 399, ed. Dublin, 1845.

[2] *Surtees*, pag. 72.

expressly mentions, corresponds in meaning with the Irish name.[1] Soon after his birth, a brilliant light from heaven encompassed the house in which he lay, and, beaming brightly around his cradle, foreshadowed that he would be a chosen instrument in the designs of heaven. Sabina, his mother, was of noble birth, but in one of those intestine wars, which so often rendered desolate the most favoured portions of the kingdom, most of her family had been slain, and she herself had been overwhelmed in misfortune and ruin. The bishop of Kells, indeed, had undertaken the charge of instructing Mo-uallog, and so bright was the intelligence of the child that he soon was able to repeat the Creed and the Psalms. But this good bishop was too soon summoned to his reward, and Cuthbert's mother, knowing the danger to which her son would be now exposed, taking him with her, entered a little coracle, and sailed for North Britain. They landed at Portpatrick, in the

[1] Colgan, having before him only the corrupt text of Capgrave, in which the saint is called *Nulluhoc*, gave a different interpretation of the name. However, in Cormac's Glossary we find the word *Uall* used for pride or excellence (Public. of I.A.S., 1868, pag. 165): and *Uallach*, which is derived from it, is still used as a female proper name, as we learn from O'Donovan in preface to Irish Topographical Poems (Public. of I.A.S., 1862, pag. 62). The endearing Celtic epithet *Mo* being prefixed, as is so common in the old Irish names, we have *Mo-uallog*, or by contraction *Muallog*, which would mean "My proud or privileged one," and thus fully corresponds with the Anglo-Saxon name; for, *Cudberct*, or *Cuthbert*, in Saxon, means "one eminently skilful," or "illustrious for skill." It has been suggested that, perhaps, St. Cuthbert's name was confounded with that of Columba, "who was born at Kells in Meath." (The History of St. Cuthbert, by Very Rev. Monsignor Eyre, pag. 4). However St. Columba was not born at Kells, but in the county of Donegal, and there does not seem to be much similarity between the names Moualloc and Columba.

Rinns of Galloway, and, finding there a vessel about to proceed towards the north, continued their journey, and landed on the cost of Argyll. There they were beset by robbers, who were attracted by the rich ornaments which Sabina wore, but they were saved by the prayers of Cuthbert. Having tarried here for a time, they crossed the Scottish frontier into Lothian, where the pious Oswald now held sway, and where St. Aidan was so zealously tending the flock of Christ. The Tract adds that in Lothian a church was in after times "erected in St. Cuthbert's honour, which is to this day called Childeschirche," in which we find a strong corroboration of the accuracy of its narrative, for such was indeed "the old name of the parish, now called Channelkirk, in the upper part of the vale of the Leader,"[1] the precise district in which we meet with Cuthbert, when Bede begins the narrative of his life. Sabina here consigned the child to the care of a virtuous widow, who lived at a village called Wrangholm, on the banks of the Leader,[2] in Berwickshire, and pursued her pilgrimage to Rome, where she lived for some time, and was held in great repute for sanctity,[3] and dying there was

[1] *Skene*, Celtic Scotland, vol. 2, pag. 205.

[2] This stream pours its waters from the north into the Tweed, two miles below Melrose.

[3] We find frequeut mention in our Annals of pilgrimages to the Continent by Irish females of royal birth : for instance, St. Mingarda, sister of St. Siadhuil, who is honoured in Lucca; and St. Syra, sister of St. Fiacre ; and St. Osanna, who entered the convent at Jouarre. Darras, in his "Histoire Generale de l'Eglise," writes that in the crypt of Jouarre are preserved several monuments of the merovingian period, and among them a statue of "Sainte Ozanne, une Irlandaise de royale origine," who had been an inmate of the monastery under the holy abbess, St. Thelchide, and who "a laissé dans la tradition du pays le souvenir toujours vivant de ses vertus," vol. 16, pag. 73.

honoured as a saint in some of the churches of the Marches, her festival being kept on the 5th of November.[1]

Among the companions of his childhood, Cuthbert was foremost in every boyish game, as well as in their various exercises of agility and strength. As he advanced in years, however, he loved labour, and guarding the flocks entrusted to his care, he grew to manhood on the southern slopes of the Lammermoor. From the whole narrative of Bede it would seem most probable that his foster mother ranked among those rich vassals to whom the higher Saxon lords gave the care of their flocks on those extensive pasturages which, under the name of *folcland*, were left to their use. A somewhat similar custom, we are told, exists in Hungary at the present day. Among our Celtic saints the shepherd's life was often the prelude to sanctity. So it was with St. Carthage, the younger, who, though of noble birth, tended his father's flocks on the banks of the Mang, but when one day the king of the territory offered him the sword and other insignia of knighthood, he replied that he desired rather the monk's cowl, and the insignia of the servants of God. So, too, it was with Cuthbert, who, leading a shepherd's life, began to cherish a love of solitude, whilst the spirit of prayer grew every day more perfect in his heart. One instance will suffice to show with what fervour he prayed even at this early period. Not far from the mouth of the river Tyne, towards the south, there was a monastery, known in after times as Tiningham. Some of the religious were

---

[1] *Fitzsimons*, in Catal. SS. Hib. Fitzsimons, however, calls St. Sabina the *avia*, and not the mother, of St. Cuthbert, being led astray in this by the statement of Capgrave.

engaged conveying upon the river a supply of wood for the monastery, on rafts, but a sudden tempestuous wind, arising from the west, drove the rafts far out to sea, and the religious gave themselves up for lost. The monks launched some boats with the view of assisting them, but such was the force of the current, and the power of winds, that their efforts were unavailing. They had then recourse to prayer, but nevertheless the storm continued to rage, and now the rafts were so far out at sea that they appeared like little birds upon the waves. Some of the people, who were gathered on the opposite bank of the river, began to ridicule the monks because their prayers were fruitless, but Cuthbert, who was in the midst of them, checked their reproaches, saying it was more meet that they too should pray for those who were in such peril, and then bowing down his head to the ground in prayer, the wind at the moment changed, and soon the rafts, and those that guided them, were safely wafted to the beach.[1]

One night as Cuthbert was tending his flocks, he saw a brilliant light streaming down to the earth, and choirs of angels descending from heaven, and after a little while again they ascended, bearing with them a soul of exceeding brightness to the heavenly country.[2] Next day he learned that precisely at that moment Aidan of Lindisfarne had passed to his reward. Cuthbert had often had serious thoughts of embracing the religious life: this vision decided his choice, for he yearned to

---

[1] *Bede*, Vit. Cuthb., chap. 3.
[2] For the details of St. Cuthbert's Life, we must refer the reader to "The History of St. Cuthbert," a most interesting work, published in 1849, by the present Archbishop of Glasgow.

secure for himself the blessedness of such happy souls. Without delay he set out for the monastery of Mailros, and there consigning his horse and spear to an attendant, entered the church and gave himself to God.

This must have been soon after the death of St. Aidan in the year 651, and since Cuthbert is presented to us by Bede as full grown in years, and, acting as his own master, we may suppose him to have attained his twenty-fifth year.[1] Boisil was at this time prior of the monastery, and seeing Cuthbert approach said to those around him: "Behold a true servant of the Lord": a prediction which was soon verified by the earnestness with which he applied himself to all the exercises of the religious rule. For ten years he thus pursued the peaceful paths of the monastic life, outstripping the most fervent of his companions in austerities[2] as well as in prayer, and study, and manual labour.

In the year 661, Eata, the holy abbot of Mailros, received a gift of an estate of thirty or forty hides of land at Ripon, and resolved at once to open a monastery there. Cuthbert was one of those chosen for the new foundation, and the special office of provost of the guest-chamber was entrusted to him. In this office he gave abundant proof of how fully the true charity of the religious life had taken root in his soul. When

---

[1] Bede nowhere assigns the precise age of St. Cuthbert. In his Ecclesiastical History, however, he says that at the time of his death he had attained " senilem aetatem" (iv. 27). This would scarcely be true unless he were at least sixty years of age at the time of his death, which took place in 687. He must, therefore, have been in his 24th year at least when he entered Mailros.

[2] It is particularly recorded of Cuthbert that he abstained from wine and every other intoxicating drink.

travellers arrived fatigued from their journey, and famished or fainting with cold, he himself washed their feet, and warmed them in his bosom, and then hastened to prepare the food which they might require. Eata, however, and Cuthbert, and their brother religious, were soon obliged to retire from Ripon, for, even before the conference of Whitby, the sub-king of Deira, to whom they were indebted for this foundation, insisted on their laying aside the Celtic observances, to which they clung with fond affection. With this royal injunction they refused to comply, and hence all returned to Mailros. And now began the missionary life of Cuthbert, which was to produce such abundant fruit, whilst at the same time he applied himself to the heroic practice of penitential austerities, which excited the admiration and wonder of the holiest men of his age. " Not a village was so distant, not a mountain side so steep, not a cottage so poor that it escaped his zeal. He sometimes passed weeks and even months out of his monastery, preaching to and confessing the rustic population of these mountains. The roads were very bad, or rather there were no roads; only now and then was it possible to travel on horseback; sometimes when his course lay along the coast of the districts inhabited by the Picts, he would take the help of a boat. But generally it was on foot that he had to penetrate into the glens and distant valleys, crossing the heaths and vast table-lands uncultivated and uninhabited, where a few shepherds' huts, like that in which he himself had passed his childhood, and which were in winter abandoned even by the rude inhabitants, were thinly scattered. But neither the intemperance of the seasons, nor hunger, nor thirst, arrested the young and valiant missionary in his apostolic travels to seek the scattered population, half Celts and half Anglo-Saxons, who, though already Christian in name and by baptism, yet retained an obstinate attachment to many of their former superstitions."[1]

It was probably at this time that St. Cuthbert lived for a while as a solitary near the village of Dull, in Atholl. About a mile from the village there was in the woods a steep mountain, now called the Rock of Weem, on the summit of which he erected a little cell. Here at his prayer a spring of pure water gushed forth from the hard rock, and here, too, he erected a large stone cross, and close to it an oratory of wood. The cliff of Weem still rises to a height of about six hundred feet, and in many places it is so steep as to be almost perpendicular. At its foot is the Church of Weem, and about the middle of the rock there is a spring of water now called St. Dabi's Well,[2] for St. Dabius, too, came in after times to live here, and to him is dedicated a little oratory which stands on a shelf of the rock, now called Craig-na-Chapel. St. Adamnan founded a monastery here soon after the death of St. Cuthbert, and thus these three illustrious Irish saints combined to sanctify this chosen spot, and to prepare the way for the first foundations of what in after times was to become the great University of St. Andrew's.[3] In the eleventh century the comharb, or lay abbot of this monastery, was the ancestor of the royal house of the Stuarts.

---

[1] *Montalembert*, "Monks of the West," iv., 384.
[2] See, for this Saint, page 184.
[3] *Montalembert* calls it the "Cradle of the University of Saint Andrew's," iv., page 385.

Bede gives us many instances of the great austerities of St. Cuthbert at this period of his life, and he more than once refers to his habit, so peculiar to our early Celtic saints, of plunging into the running stream or into the waves, and remaining there whilst reciting the Psalter. On one occasion he was so fatigued by this penitential exercise that when he left the water he fell exhausted and benumbed upon the sea-shore, and the tradition still lingers among the peasants of Northumberland, and of the Scottish borders, that two otters came to lick his frozen feet, and to hug them until life and warmth were restored.

About this time England, as well as Ireland, was visited by that terrible scourge known as the *Buidhe Conaill*, or the Yellow Pest, which carried off several of our greatest saints. Boisil, the prior of Mailros, was one of those attacked by it. Summoning Cuthbert to his bedside he said, "I have but seven days to live," and then he told him to take and read for their mutual instruction a copy of the Gospel of St. John, which was in seven quaternios, that thus reading and commenting on one each day they would have it ended before his death.[1] Six hundred years afterwards that copy of the sacred text was still laid on the altar in Durham on our saint's festival, and was kissed with devotion by pious pilgrims through reverence for the holy prior and for St. Cuthbert. Cuthbert was himself attacked by the plague, but the monks prayed earnestly for his recovery. When it was told him that the community had spent the night in prayer for him, he cried out, "What am I doing in bed?

---

[1] *Bede*, Vit. Cuthb., 8.

It is impossible that God should shut his ears to such prayers: give me my staff and sandals," and he at once arose.

Cuthbert was appointed prior in room of Boisil, and during the several years that he held this office at Melrose, or at Lindisfarne, "he performed its functions with so much spiritual zeal, as became a saint, that he gave to the whole community not only the counsels, but also the example, of a monastic life."[1] It is particularly recorded how his charity to the poor and to the pilgrims merited for him the privilege of ministering to an angel, who presented himself under the disguise of a stranger, and who, on taking his departure, left for Cuthbert three loaves of surpassing beauty, "such as this world cannot produce," writes Bede, "excelling the lilies in whiteness, the roses in perfume, and the honey in sweetness." At the same time Cuthbert displayed the zeal of an apostle in breaking the Bread of Life to the faithful of the surrounding territory, and ministering to their spiritual and temporal wants. The details which have been preserved by Bede show that his labours extended over all the hilly district between the two seas, from the Solway to the Forth. Visiting these remote districts "he often did not return to his monastery for an entire week, sometimes for two or three, yea, occasionally, for even an entire month, remaining all the time in the mountains, and calling back to heavenly concerns these rustic people by the word of his preaching as well as by his example of virtue."[2] How different is

[1] *Bede*, Vita S. Cuth., 9.
[2] *Bede*, Ibid. "In viculis qui in arduis asperisque montibus." Hist. Eccl. iv. 27.

the aspect of that district now-a-days from what it presented to St. Cuthbert: " To-day the land is a land of poetry and romance. Cheviot and Lammermoor, Ettrick and Teviotdale, Yarrow and Annan-water, are musical with old ballads and border minstrelsy. Agriculture has chosen its valleys for her favourite seat, and drainage and steam-power have turned sedgy marshes into farm and meadow. But to see the lowlands as they were in Cuthbert's day we must sweep away meadows and farm again, and replace them by vast solitudes, dotted here and there with clusters of wooden hovels, and covered by boggy tracts, over which travellers rode spear in hand and eye kept cautiously about them."[1] On one occasion Cuthbert, accompanied by two of the brethren, proceeded by sea to visit the Picts, who were called Niduari. Their boat reached the shore in safety, but no sooner had they landed than a tempest arose which detained them for several days exposed to hunger and cold. They took refuge under a cliff, where Cuthbert was wont to pass the night in prayer, and there, at the prayers of the saint, food was miraculously supplied to them, till the tempest ceased, and they returned home with favourable wind and tranquil sea.

When, in 664, after the conference at Whitby, St. Colman and several of the brethren, unwilling to lay aside the usages of their fathers, were compelled to depart from Lindisfarne to seek another home where they might serve God in peace, that monastery, at St. Colman's request, was given in charge to the community

---

[1] *Green*, English People, i., 53.

of Melrose. Eata ruled both monasteries as abbot, and Cuthbert was by him transferred to Lindisfarne, "there to teach the rules of monastic perfection with the authority of a superior."[1] For twelve years St. Cuthbert with untiring energy, devoted himself to this religious work. He composed a rule for the brethren, which centuries later still held its place, and was observed, together with the rule of St. Benedict; he was wont to blend severity towards sin with infinite tenderness towards the sinner; and nothing could disturb his meekness, which often triumphed when every argument had proved of no avail. One of his monastic regulations is specially recorded. He imposed on the brethren of Lindisfarne the obligation of wearing the habit in undyed wool, as was usual in the Irish monasteries. Crowds flocked to his island monastery to listen to his counsels of heavenly wisdom, and to receive the sacraments at his hands. "So great was his skill in speaking," as Bede attests, " so intense his eagerness to make his persuasions successful, such a glow lighted up his angelic face,[2] that no one of those present dared to hide from Cuthbert the secrets of his heart; all fully made known in confession what they had done, for in truth they supposed that he was already aware of these very deeds of theirs; and after confession they, at his bidding, repaired by worthy fruits of repentance the sins they had committed. . . . He knew how to refresh the mourner with pious exhortation, to remind those that were in tribulation of the joys of heavenly life, and to

---

[1] *Bede*, Vita, 16.
[2] *Bede*, "Tale vultus angelici lumen." The anonymous Life repeats the same, "erat aspectu angelicus."

show that both the smiles and the frowns of this world are equally transient."[1] When he offered the Holy Sacrifice " it was rather his heart than his voice " that was uplifted at the *Sursum Corda;* and he could never celebrate Mass without shedding abundant tears. He sought in every way possible to shun the respect and the applause of those who crowded to Lindisfarne, and to the brethren he used to say, " were it possible that I could hide myself in ever so narrow a cell, upon a cliff where the waves of the swelling ocean should gird me round on every side, and shut me out from the sight, as well as the knowledge of all men, not even there should I think myself free from the snares of this deceitful world."[2]

Cuthbert allowed nothing to disturb the serenity of his confidence in God. One day he wandered far from the monastery with a youthful companion. Night was approaching, and they had nothing to eat. "Where shall we lodge," asked his companion, "where shall we find food?" "Learn, my son," replied Cuthbert, "to have faith and hope always in God. No one who serves him faithfully shall ever perish for want of food." As he spoke, an eagle which hovered overhead, laid a fish at a short distance from them on the bank, which the prior told his companion to cut in two. One half they kept and made a meal of at a village which they soon after reached; the other half the saint bade his companion to put back upon the bank that the eagle might have some return for its service to them. Another time when he was with the brethren in an open boat, a

---

[1] *Bede*, Vita, 22. [2] *Bede*, Vita, 8.

blinding storm came on which drove them on the coast of Fife. Some whispered in alarm, 'the road is closed by the snow along the shore;' others said, 'our way by sea is barred by the storm;' 'the way to heaven is not closed,' was the calm reply of Cuthbert. He used to say to the religious that with the assistance of God they should despise their spiritual enemies, whose snares were only as the threads of a spider's web; and he would add, "How often have they sent me headlong from the lofty cliffs? How often have they thrown stones at me, as if to slay me? How often have they raised up fantastic temptations of one kind or another to frighten me and attempted to drive me from this place of contest? Yet, nevertheless, they have never been able to inflict any injury upon my body, nor to touch my mind with fear."[1]

The soul of Cuthbert, however, was not yet content; he yearned for still higher perfection, and he resolved to enter on more rugged paths of penance and self-denial. He first chose for himself a solitary cell on a detached portion of the basaltic line of rock which runs in front of the ruins of the monastery of Lindisfarne, and becomes an islet at high-water, while at low-water it is accessible by a ridge of stone covered with seaweed. It still bears St. Cuthbert's name, and in olden times there was a small chapel there, dedicated to him, which was called 'the chapel of St. Cuthbert on the sea.'[2] He soon resolved, however, to select a spot of greater solitude. A few miles to the south of Lindisfarne, and about two miles from the mainland, there is a group of seven small

---

[1] *Bede*, Vita, 22.   [2] *Raine*, North Durham, p. 145.

and desert islands, called the Farne Islands. He proceeded to the central island of this group, where none before, save St. Aidan, had ever dwelt. It was supposed to be the haunt of demons, but Cuthbert took possession of it as a soldier of Christ, victorious over the evil one. Here, with the deep sea rolling at his feet, he constructed an anchorite enclosure, of which Bede gives a minute description. It was nearly circular, and it measured from wall to wall about four or five perches. The wall itself externally was higher than the stature of a man, but inwardly it was much higher, the living rock being scooped out by the saint, so that he could see nothing from his mansion but heaven, that thus the whole bent of his mind might be turned to heavenly desires. The wall was constructed, not of hewn stone, nor of brick and mortar, but of turf and unwrought stones. Within this wall there were only two compartments—an oratory and a cell. At the landing-place of the island, however, there was a large house for the convenience of the brethren and strangers who might come to visit him, and close to it there was a fountain of fresh water. Here St. Cuthbert lived for eight years, subsisting on the wild roots that grew upon the island, and on the produce of a little field of barley, sown and cultivated by his own hands, but so insufficient was this supply of food that the tradition grew among the inhabitants of the coast that he was fed by angels with heavenly bread. The life of Cuthbert was not less productive of spiritual fruit in this solitary island than when he had been engaged in missionary toil. From all parts of England pilgrims came to the servant of God to seek light in their doubts, guidance in their difficulties, comfort in their sorrows.

On the greater feasts the religious from Lindisfarne paid him a short visit. Even then, however, he used to interrupt the conversation from time to time to remind them of the necessity of watchfulness and prayer: and, as Bede relates, the monks used playfully to answer him: 'Nothing is more true; but we have so many days of vigil, and of fasts and prayers, let us at least to-day rejoice in the Lord.' The legends of Northumbria linger lovingly upon this period of the saint's life. From him they name the little shells, which are only found on their coast, "St. Cuthbert's Beads," for with them, as the tradition runs, he numbered his prayers. From him, too, the sea fowl, which are found nowhere else in the British isles, are known as "St. Cuthbert's Birds:" they are most gentle, allowing themselves to be stroked and caressed, and it is the popular belief that they derived their gentleness from being the companions of St. Cuthbert in his solitude.

These years of the saint's penitential austerities, on his solitary island, were to him the sweetest of his life, and, whilst he emulated on earth the perfection and the heroism of the heavenly citizens, he seemed to enjoy a foretaste of the joys of Paradise. They were years, however, of storm and strife throughout Northumbria. Wilfred had been obliged to fly from his see, the faithful were torn by dissensions, and factions were multiplied. Lindisfarne, indeed, and its immediate district, continued to enjoy comparative peace, for it had been now erected into a separate see, and was governed by Eata as Bishop. At length, in 683, a great synod was held at Twyford, on the Alne, in the presence of King Egfrid, and presided over by Theodore, Archbishop of Canterbury. All were

unanimous in the resolution that Cuthbert should be
raised to the Episcopal dignity. From the synod, the
king, with several of his magnates, and accompanied by
some of the brethren from Lindisfarne, proceeded to the
saint's island-hermitage, and there on bended knees
prayed him not to refuse the proffered dignity. Cuthbert
yielded only after a long resistance, and weeping when
he did so. He wished, however, that his consecration should be delayed six months, which time he passed
in his dear solitude, till the Easter of 684, when he was
consecrated in York by Archbishop Theodore and seven
bishops, in the presence of the king and all the
magnates of the kingdom. The see of Hexham had
been assigned to him, but this he at once exchanged
with Eata for Lindisfarne, and thus he returned once
more to administer as bishop that cherished territory of
St. Aidan, where he had already so long laboured in past
years. By the donation of the king, Cuthbert received
at his consecration, with other gifts, the district of
Cartmell, "with all the Britons who dwelt on it," and
it was decreed that his jurisdiction would extend to
Carlisle and all the surrounding monasteries. Two
months later the saint made a journey to Carlisle. On
Saturday, the 20th of May, the inhabitants of that old
Roman city, which was now an Anglo-Saxon stronghold,
went out in procession to welcome their saintly bishop.
They led him to their walls, shining bright on that
sunny day, and thence they conducted him to the city
fountain, "the wondrous work of Roman hands," when
on a sudden Cuthbert, leaning on his pastoral staff,
seemed to be overcome with the strongest emotion.
Then, after a while, lifting up his eyes towards heaven,

he exclaimed, " even now the contest is decided." Interrogated by a priest, who stood beside him, he made some evasive answer. Two days later the mystery was explained to them, for there arrived a man who had escaped from the Scottish borders, and brought tidings which overwhelmed them with anguish. Egfrid and his army, invading the territory of the Picts, had crossed the Firth, and penetrated beyond the Tay, and destroyed two forts, the native forces, by feigned retreats, luring them into a defile at Dunnichen, near Forfar. There the king had fallen, with nearly all his men, on the very day and at the very hour when Cuthbert was standing by the Carlisle fountain, like one who saw what he durst not reveal.[1] This defeat of Egfrid was most disastrous to Northumbria: "the hope and force of the Anglian Kingdom," thus Bede writes, " began to retreat like an ebbing tide."[2] St. Cuthbert had done everything in his power to dissuade Egfrid from this fatal expedition, and now he sought by his prudent counsel to repair as far as possible the ruin that had fallen on the kingdom. Aldfrid, who was in Ireland, and was famed for his wisdom and valour, though by his birth not entitled to the throne, was summoned home and invested with the royal dignity. His rule proved a blessing to the whole kingdom, and his grateful subjects decreed to him the title of Aldfrid the Wise.

St Cuthbert as bishop pursued the same life which he had led in the monastery of Lindisfarne and at Mailros, displaying the same lowliness of heart, the same fervour of piety, the same ardour of charity. Each time he

---

[1] *Bright*, page 335.   [2] *Bede*, iv., 26.

offered the holy sacrifice he melted into tears; in the words of Bede, "The grace of compunction kept his mind fixed on things heavenly, and above all, there glowed within him the fire of divine love."[1] He was at the same time most active in every work of charity, giving food to the hungry, and clothes to those who were exposed to the cold, ransoming captives, protecting the widows and orphans, rescuing the poor from the oppressor. In his sermons he had in this an advantage over the other Celtic bishops of Lindisfarne, that having grown up among the peasants on the banks of the Leader, he could use their homely language and speak as his own their native tongue. His infirmities did not deter him from visiting the most distant parts of his diocese, penetrating, as of old, into the poorest hamlets and the remotest villages. On one occasion he had arranged to hold a confirmation in a remote district, and in default of a church the people spread tents near a woodland spot, and cut down boughs of trees to afford some shelter. For two days he ministered without ceasing to the piety of these devoted people. Before his departure a poor woman brought her son, wasted with fever, and set him on a rude pallet at the entrance of the wood, and asked the bishop to bestow his blessing upon him. Cuthbert bade the boy be brought near, and having prayed over him, blessed him, whereupon the boy rose up restored to health, and being refreshed with food, gave thanks to God, and returned in joy to his home. During the same episcopal tour, having laboured for some time in a certain village,

---

[1] *Bede*, Ecc. Hist., iv. 28.

he inquired if there were other sick that required his ministrations. One woman presented herself, who a little before had lost one son by the pestilence, and now she held his sick brother in her arms, whilst the tears, which furrowed her cheeks, gave proof of her affliction. Cuthbert went up to her and kissed the child, and comforted the mother saying : " Fear not, your child shall live, neither shall any other of your household die of this pleague." And his words came true, and both mother and son lived long afterwards to attest his words.

Several of his other miracles are recorded by Venerable Bede. One of the ealdormen of King Egfrid came in haste to Lindisfarne, overwhelmed with grief, his wife, a woman most pious and charitable, being seized by a demon. He feared to disclose the nature of the attack ; he merely said that she was approaching death, and he begged that a priest might visit her, and that when she died he might bury her in the holy isle. Cuthbert heard his story, and said to him, " This is my business, I myself will accompany you." As they went on their way together, Cuthbert, seeing the cheeks of the rough warrior wet with tears, comforted him with the assurance that the trial from which the pious woman suffered was permitted by God for her own greater merit ; and he added, " when we arrive we will find her cured." And so the event proved, for the demon did not dare to await the coming of the man of God. On another occasion Cuthbert was asked by a nobleman attached to the court to visit his house, and to give his blessing to a poor servant, who for a long time had been afflicted with a painful malady. St. Cuthbert, not being able to go thither, blessed some water, and giving it to a young man named Baldhelm, said, "Go, let the poor patient taste it." Baldhelm proceeded to the house, poured a little of the blessed water three times on the lips of the sick man, who was thereby restored to health. And Venerable Bede adds: "Baldhelm is still living. He is a priest in the Church of Lindisfarne, and adorns the priestly office by his virtues. He takes delight in narrating the miraculous powers of St. Cuthbert, and told me with his own lips this prodigy."[1]

St. Cuthbert cherished a special affection for a holy priest named Herbert, "who lived as an anchorite in an island of Lake Derwentwater, one of those fine lakes which make the district of Cumberland and Westmoreland the most picturesque part of England. Every year Herbert came from his peaceful lake to visit his friend in the other island, beaten and undermined continually by the great waves of the Northern Sea; and upon the wild rock, to the accompaniment of winds and waves, they passed several days together in a tender solitude and intimacy, talking of the life to come."[2] When Cuthbert came for the last time to Carlisle to ordain priests, and to give the veil to some nuns, and to establish some schools,[3] this friend came to visit him. Before they parted Cuthbert said to him, "My brother, you must now ask me all that you want to know from me, for we shall not meet again here below." At these words Herbert burst into tears—"I conjure you," he cried, "do not leave me on this earth behind you; remember my

---

[1] *Bede*, Vita, 25, "qui nunc usque superest."
[2] *Montalembert*, iv. 417.
[3] "In profectum divinae servitutis scholas instituit." *Sim-Dunelm*, cap. 9.

faithful friendship, and pray God that as we have served Him together in this world, so we may pass into His glory together." Cuthbert threw himself on his knees, and after praying for some minutes, said to him, "Weep no more, my brother, God has granted to us that which we have both asked from Him." And so it happened. They never saw each other again here below, but they died on the same day and at the same hour, the one in his tranquil isle, bathed by the peaceable waters of the lake; the other upon his granite rock, fringed by the foam of the Northern Ocean; and their souls reunited by a blessed death, were carried by the angels into the eternal kingdom.[1] Seven centuries later, in 1374, the bishop of Carlisle appointed that a Mass should be said on the anniversary of the two saints, in the island of the Derwentwater, where the Cumbrian anchorite had died, and granted an indulgence of forty days to all who crossed the water to pray there in honour of the two friends.

We have seen how Cuthbert used to salute as mother the pious widow, who, on the southern slopes of the Lammermoor hills watched over him in his younger years. He continued ever grateful to her for her maternal care, and whenever in his apostolic journeys, as missionary or as bishop, he had occasion to visit that district, he made sure to call on her in the village where she lived. During one of his visits a fire broke out in the village in a neighbouring house, and the flames, driven by the wind, threatened her with ruin. But Cuthbert said to her, "Fear nothing, dear mother, this fire shall not harm you;" then falling prostrate on the

[1] *Bede*, "unius ejusdemque momento temporis egredientes de corpore spiritus eorum," &c. Vita, 28.

ground before the door, he prayed silently, till suddenly the wind changed, and by his prayers the humble roof was saved, which sheltered the old age of her whom he loved to call his mother.

There were at this time in Northumbria several monasteries of nuns, and Cuthbert laboured assiduously to encourage the pious inmates in their life of holocaust, and to stimulate them to piety by his instructions. We find him, for instance, remaining for some days at Coldingham to impart lessons of heavenly wisdom to its two communities; and the narrative adds, that he preached both by word and example, and all were edified by the wonderful harmony between his life and his doctrine. The monastery of Whitby was governed by Elfleda, the niece of the pious King Oswald. St. Cuthbert, who had a special devotion for that holy founder of Lindisfarne, repeatedly visited the monastery to comfort Elfleda in her sorrows, and to cheer her on in the works of piety, which were multiplied by her religious zeal. An incident of one of his visits has been recorded. When Cuthbert was about to celebrate Mass, the royal abbess approached him, saying she had to ask for a special favour. Word had just been brought that a Saxon servant of the monastery, named Haduald, had been killed the day before by falling from a tree, and the favour which she desired was that the holy bishop would make a memento for him in the Holy Sacrifice. Her words are preserved by Bede: "Precor, domine mi episcope, memineris, ad Missas, Hadualdi mei qui heri cadendo de arbore defunctus est."[1] The last visit which he paid was to the Abbess Verca, whose monastery was

---

[1] *Bede*, Vita, 34.

situated at the mouth of the Tyne, the river which formed the southern boundary of Bernicia. Here he became faint. They offered him wine and beer, but he would taste nothing but water. The water which he had thus tasted was preserved by the religious sisters of Tynemouth, and seemed to them as the most delicious wine. St. Cuthbert made known to them that he would see them no more, and he accepted from them, as the last pledge of spiritual friendship, a piece of fine linen to serve as his shroud.

Cuthbert celebrated the feast of Christmas, A.D. 686, with the monks of Lindisfarne, but, feeling the approach of death, he immediately afterwards withdrew to his former hermitage in the little island of Farne, exulting that he had regained his loved solitude, and intent only on preparing for the heavenly reward which awaited him. The monks would fain have him to remain at the monastery, but their prayers were in vain: and when they asked "when may we hope for your return?" they received the reply, "when you shall bring back my body to your monastery." In sadness they accompanied him to the beach. "It must have been an affecting sight to have seen the venerable bishop on the beach, surrounded by his children and fellow-monks, who, to the respect due to a bishop, loved him with the affection due to a father, and taking his leave of them. It must have been as affecting a scene as when Jacob called his sons together, and blessed them, before he was gathered to his people."[1] When the abbot of the monastery came a little later to visit him in his hermitage, he expressed a wish to be interred near the oratory which he had erected

[1] *Abp. Eyre*, History, page 68.

there, and at "the foot of the holy cross," which he had himself planted: "I would fain repose in this spot," he said, "where I have fought my little battle for the Lord, whence I hope that my merciful Judge will call me to the crown of righteousness:" and then he added: "You will bury me, wrapt in the linen which I have kept for my shroud, out of love for Verca, the friend of God, who gave it to me." At the request, however, of the brethren of the monastery, he gave permission that he should be interred in their church of the blessed apostle Peter, at the right side of the altar, where he had so often offered the Holy Sacrifice and administered the sacraments of life. A little time before his death, being unable to walk, he asked to be carried to his little oratory, and there the abbot, as a last request, prayed him to give a farewell message[1] as a legacy to all the brethren. The saint, in reply, faintly and at intervals pronounced his last words, " Keep peace one with another, and preserve heavenly charity: maintain mutual concord with other servants of Christ: despise not those of the household of the faith who come to you seeking hospitality; receive them with affection, entertain them, and send them away with friendly kindness: be not puffed up, as if you were better than others of the same faith and conversation; but have no communion with those who err from the unity of Catholic peace." The evening of the 19th of March, 687, was passed in tranquil expectation of future bliss, and the saint continued his prayers till past midnight. At length, "when the usual time for nocturn-prayer was come," he received from the

---

[1] *Bede*, "quem haereditarium vale fratribus relinqueret." Vita. 39.

abbot's hands "the communion of the Lord's Body and Blood to strengthen him for his departure," and then his eyes gazing towards heaven, and his hands lifted high above his head in attitude of prayer, his soul departed for the joys of heaven. Eleven years after St. Cuthbert's death, his body, when translated to a shrine in the church, was found uncorrupt, and more like one that was asleep than one who was dead. Again, it was found fresh as a living body when it became the treasure of the church of Durham at the close of the tenth century: and so, too, at the beginning of the twelfth century it was still unchanged when placed in the new cathedral of that city, which was destined to be for three centuries its resting place : " From this time," writes Montalembert, " the name and memory of Cuthbert hovered over the magnificent cathedral of Durham, one of the most beautiful in the world. This magnificent building, with its three stories of arched windows, its two towers, its five naves and two transepts, forms, with the ancient castle of the bishop, built by William the Conqueror, a monument at once of religion and art, as admirable as it is little known. It can be compared only to Pisa, to Toledo, to Nuremberg, or Marienburg. It has even a great advantage over all these celebrated places, in the beauty of the landscape which encloses it. It is the sole existing example of a splendid cathedral, situated in the midst of an old wood, and on the height of a rock, the abrupt descent of which is bathed by a narrow and rapid river."[1] The wicked agents of Henry the Eighth, in 1537, when desecrating the shrines of Durham, and plundering their rich treasures, found to their dismay

[1] *Montalembert*, iv. 422.

that St. Cuthbert's body was as entire, and the limbs as flexible, as though it were still living. It is a well-grounded tradition that his sacred remains were at that time religiously interred by faithful hands, and it is said the secret as to the spot where they lie has been jealously handed down to the present day in the English branch of the Benedictine Order.

Throughout the whole Saxon period St. Cuthbert continued the most popular of the national saints. Kings and people alike cherished his memory, and they vied with each other in offering at his altar the tributes of their piety. King Alfred the Great honoured him as his special patron, and when hidden in the marsh of Glastonbury, preparing for his decisive struggle against the Danes, he was favoured with a vision of St. Cuthbert, who promised him victory and the deliverance of his country. Canute, too, when master of England, went barefooted to St. Cuthbert's tomb to invoke the protection of the saint most venerated by the people he had subdued. Even the Norman Conquest did not diminish the saint's popularity. William the Conqueror himself made his offerings at the saint's tomb, and for centuries during the border warfare it was around the 'standard of St. Cuthbert' that the Anglo-Normans won their proudest victories. The famous copy of the Gospels known as St. Cuthbert's Gospels, is one of the priceless gems of the British Museum. As we might expect, its text and its ornamentation are all in the Irish style, and it is justly reckoned among the most perfect monuments of early Celtic literature that have been preserved to our times. "The chief features of its ornaments and letters are extreme delicacy and intricacy of pattern, the most ingenious interlacing of birds, knots of various geometrical forms, composed of bands crossing each other in all directions, sometimes terminating in the heads of serpents or birds. These intricate initial letters are divided into compartments filled with rich interlacing work, formed by coloured threads and slender attenuated animals. The four pages opposite the commencement of the four Gospels are almost inconceivably elaborate, yet most pleasing in effect both from excessive beauty and accuracy of execution, and from the judicious arrangement of colours."[1]

St. Cuthbert was the last Irish Bishop of Lindisfarne, yet the Irish Church did not cease for some time to exercise a salutary influence in Northumbria. Aldfrid, surnamed the Wise, had been sent for safety to Ireland in his youth, and had grown to manhood in the Irish schools. It would appear from the narrative of Bede that if he so desired he might have returned to England before the death of Egfrid, but such was his ardour in the pursuit of knowledge that he remained in Ireland in voluntary exile, " ob studium literarum exulabat."[2] Hence, on his accession to the throne he was not only skilled in every martial exercise, but was also " most learned in the Scriptures and in knowledge of all sort."[3] And as Oswald by his Irish training became the first saint of the Anglo-Saxon kings, so Aldfrid, as the fruit of his long study in the Irish schools, became the great promoter of literature throughout his kingdom, and the first of the literary kings of England.[4] Whilst in exile

---

[1] *Eyre*, History of St. Cuthbert, page 306.
[2] *Bede*, Vita, 24.   [3] *Bede*, Ecc. Hist. iv. 26.   [4] *Bright*, p. 338.

Aldfrid seems to have lived for some time at Lisgoole on the west bank of Lough Erne, and to have also visited Arranmore and Inniscattery, and the other great monasteries of Erin. He also composed a poem in Irish, of which a literal translation, made by the learned Celtic scholar O'Donovan, may be seen in the notes to the new edition of Archdall's Monasticon.[1] The following are a few of its strophes :—

> "I found in Armagh the splendid,
> Meekness, wisdom, circumspection,
> Fasting in obedience to the Son of God,
> Noble, prosperous sages.
>
> "I found in each great church,
> Whether inland, on shore, or island,
> Learning, wisdom, devotion to God,
> Holy welcome and protection.
>
> "I found in the country of Tirconnel
> Brave,' victorious heroes,
> Fierce men, with fair complexion,
> The high stars of Ireland."

The reign of Aldfrid was the golden period for the schools of Jarrow, Ripon, Canterbury, Malmesbury, and Lindisfarne. With his death on the 14th December, 705, their decay set in, and half a century later, through the incursions of the Danes, their light became well nigh extinguished.

---

[1] *Archdall*, edition of 1876, vol. II., page 164.

CHAPTER XII.

IRISH MISSIONS IN THE OTHER ANGLO-SAXON KINGDOMS.

Influence of Northumbria on the other Anglo-Saxon Kingdoms:— Conversion of the Mid-Angles:—SS. Diuma and Cellach:— St. Chad:—Sigebert, King of the East Saxons, embraces the Faith:—St. Cedd:—Bishop Jaruman:—The East Angles:— Virtues of St. Fursey:—His Monastery at Cnobbersburg:—The Visions of St. Fursey:—His labours among the East Angles:— His life in France:—He visits Rome:—His Death:—His Relics:—The Companions of St. Fursey:—Irish Monks the Pioneers of the Faith in Sussex:—Conversion of the West Saxons: —Agilbert and Mailduff:—St. Aldhelm:—The Irish Missions crowned with success.

WE have hitherto said little of the religious influence exercised by Northumbria and its Celtic missionaries on the other Anglo-Saxon kingdoms. And yet that influence was very great, for throughout this critical period of England's history the power of Northumbria was supreme,[1] and its kings, Oswald and Oswy, successively invested with the high dignity of Bretwalda, were earnest in their desire to see the blessings of the true faith extended to all their pagan countrymen. The Irish missionaries on their part, as soon as an opportunity presented itself, entered with apostolic zeal on the mission beyond the Northumbrian borders, and an abundant fruit rewarded their spiritual labours.

---

[1] *Bright,* "The History of the Church in Northumbria during the larger part of the seventh century is conspicuously the backbone of the history of the Church in England," pag. 154.

1. The Mid-Angles, who dwelt between the Trent and the Bedford district, were at this time subject to Penda, King of Mercia, who placed over them his son Peada, "a youth of excellent disposition," as Bede writes, "and most worthy of the title and dignity of king." During an interval of peace he visited Northumbria, and requested the daughter of Oswy in marriage. Oswy replied: "I cannot give my child to a heathen. If you would wed her, you must prepare for it by yourself and your people accepting the faith of Christ and baptism." Peada listened with docility to Christian teaching: and when the truths of redemption, and the mercy of God, and future immortality, and the heavenly kingdom were unfolded to him, he cried out: "I will be a Christian." Being fully instructed, he openly declared that his final resolve was made, and that even should Oswy refuse him his royal daughter's hand, nothing would turn him aside from the faith which he desired to receive. At length with solemn pomp, baptism was administered to him by the Bishop of Lindisfarne, St. Finan, and at the same time his earls and knights and other attendants were all regenerated in the laver of life. The place chosen for this ceremony was the royal town called "Admurum," situated on the banks of the Tyne, where Newcastle now stands. At the request of Peada, four priests were commissioned to accompany him and his bride to evangelize their people. The missionaries chosen for this new field of labour were Diuma, an Irishman, and Cedd, Adda, and Bettin, three of those Anglo-Saxons whom Aidan had specially instructed and prepared to be the first fruits of the native clergy of England.

Thus in the year 653 was formed the first mission to the Midland-Saxons and the Mercians. The people willingly listened to the words of life taught them by the zealous missionaries, " for these were men of learning and of holy life," and day by day many, as well of the nobles as of the lowest people "renounced the filth of idolatry, and were cleansed in the fountains of faith,"[1] Diuma and his companions did not limit their labours to the Midland-Saxons. They ventured further into Mercia proper, and though the old pagan king, Penda, would not renounce his false gods, yet he permitted the faith to be freely preached to his subjects, declaring that his hatred and contempt would be only directed against "the mean wretches, who having put their faith in Christ, will not trouble themselves to obey him." Among the converts were the other five children of the king, and it is recorded that all these and nearly all his royal grandchildren died in the odour of sanctity.

It was in the autumn of the year 655 that Penda invaded Northumbria for the last time. His army was the most imposing that as yet had been marshalled on the battle-fields of England. There were thirty chiefs of princely rank serving under his banner, and he vowed not to sheathe his sword till he had annihilated Northumbria as a kingdom. Oswy's army was small, but full of courage, relying on Christ for victory. The hostile armies having met on the 15th of November, on the banks of the Winwaed, the Mercians were completely overthrown, and many more perished in the river, swollen by the autumnal rains, than the sword had

[1] *Bede*, iii. 21.

destroyed while fighting. Among the rest, Penda was slain, and with him fell the last pillar of paganism in England. At the request of the young prince Peada, the Irish Diuma was now consecrated by St. Finan Bishop of all the Mercians, the paucity of the clergy, as Bede remarks, rendering it necessary that one bishop should rule over so vast a people. His episcopate lasted little more than two years, but "in a short time he won not a few to the Lord, and died among the Mid-Angles in the country called Infeppingum,"[1] a district which has not been as yet identified. It was during his episcopate that the first monastery was erected among the Mercians, through the combined munificence of Oswy and Peada. The spot chosen for it was known as Medeshamstede, that is, "the dwelling-place in the meadows," and it was dedicated to the glory of Christ, under the invocation of St. Peter. A town gradually formed around this monastery, which has been justly styled the first resting-place of Christianity in central England; the town has now grown into a great city, but it still retains its first name of Peterborough.

Diuma was succeeded by another Irish bishop, by name Cellach, called by the Saxons Ceolla, who like his predecessor was consecrated by St. Finan at Lindisfarne. Towards the close of the year 658, the Mercian chiefs threw off the yoke of Northumbria, expelled the ealdormen of Oswy, and bravely regained at once their boundaries and their freedom. Unlike the earlier revo-

---

[1] *Bede*, loc. cit. Some have supposed that Reppington, in Derbyshire, was the place of his death, but upon no satisfactory authority. Wharton (Anglia Sacra. i., 424) places his death in A.D. 658.

lutions, this did not involve any relapse into paganism. The Christian religion had already taken firm root among the people, and the Mercians "being now free," as Bede relates, "with a king of their own, they rejoiced to serve Christ, the true king."[1] Cellach, however, did not long remain in Mercia. Before the close of 659, he resigned the see, and, having lived for a time in St. Columba's monastery at Iona, returned home to Ireland, and there rested in peace.[2] His successor, Trumhere, was a native of England, but had been trained to piety by the Irish monks, and like his predecessors he, too, proceeded to Lindisfarne to receive consecration at the hands of St. Finan. The next bishop was Jaruman, an Irishman, whose name was rendered illustrious by his apostolic labours among the East Saxons, but of whose Mercian episcopate Bede gives us no details. He held the see till the year 669, when he was succeeded by the illustrious St. Chad.

This holy man was brother of the missionary St. Cedd, of whom we have just now spoken. Like his brother, he was one of the first twelve Saxon youths trained for the sanctuary by St. Aidan. He corresponded to the care of his holy master, and grew in sanctity as in years. After completing his studies at Lindisfarne, his thirst for sacred knowledge led him to Ireland, where

[1] *Bede*, iii. 24.
[2] Montalembert thus sketches the lives of these two Celtic bishops: "The Pontificate of Diuma was short, but fruitful. At his death he was succeeded by another Irishman, Ceolach, who was reckoned among the disciples of Columba, the great Celtic missionary, as coming from the monastery of Iona, to which he returned after some years of a too laborious episcopate in Mercia to seek the peace of cloistered life in that citadel of Celtic monachism." iv. 121.

he lived for some years in the sublimest practice of every virtue.

When Wilfrid, after his appointment to the See of York, remained absent for a considerable time in France, St. Chad, at the request of King Oswy, was consecrated for that see. As bishop, he followed in all things St. Aidan as his model, travelling throughout the diocese on foot, "preaching the Gospel in towns, in the open country, in cottages, and villages,"[1] the faithful everywhere rejoicing on account of the sanctity of their pastor. Eddi, the panegyrist of St. Wilfrid, does not hesitate to style St. Chad "an admirable teacher, a true servant of God, and a most meek man."[2] The consecration of Chad, however, had been irregular, and no sooner did he receive an intimation to that effect, in the year 669, from Theodore, the newly-appointed Archbishop of Canterbury, than he at once joyfully retired to the monastery of Lastingham, which some time before he had governed as abbot. Before the close of the year, however, the episcopate of the kingdom of Mercia becoming vacant, by the demise of Bishop Jaruman, St. Chad was chosen by the Archbishop to fill that See, for, as Bede records, Archbishop Theodore had learned to admire his profound humility and solid virtue, and was unwilling that the labour of so able and so devoted a missionary should be lost to the Saxon Church; and when the archbishop learned that it was the custom of our saint to go about his diocese on foot, he desired him "to ride whenever he had a longer circuit than usual before him." Chad, however, objected out

---

[1] *Bede*, iii. 28.   [2] *Eddi*, Vita, pag. 14.

of "zealous love of pious labour;" but Theodore was not to be overcome: "You shall ride," he said, and with his own aged hands he lifted him on horseback; "because," adds Bede "he had ascertained that Chad was a holy man."[1]

St. Chad fixed his see at Lichfield, where no Mercian bishop had as yet sat, and close to the site now occupied by the beautiful cathedral, erected a church under the invocation of the Blessed Virgin. Near it, at a place which from him took the name of Chadstowe, now Stowe, he built a house, where he dwelt when not engaged in the sacred ministry of the Word, and there seven or eight of his religious brethren shared his studies and devotions. It is recorded of St. Chad that he unceasingly kept his mind fixed on preparing for his last end. If a high wind swept across the moors at Lastingham, or beat around his little church at Lichfield, he gave up his reading to implore the divine mercy. If it increased still more, he would shut his book and prostrate himself in prayer. If it rose to a storm, with rain or thunder, he would repair to the church, and remain there till it ceased, with his mind fixed in contemplation, or engaged in the recitation of Psalms. When questioned about this, he would say that the thunder of the heavens reminded him of that tremendous day when the heavens and earth would be consumed, and the Lord would come in the clouds with great power and majesty to judge the living and the dead. At the same time Chad cherished in his heart a constant love and desire of the heavenly rewards, and "it was no wonder," as Bede writes, "if he rejoiced to behold the day of death,

[1] *Bede*, iv. 2.

or rather the day of the Lord, seeing he had so anxiously prepared for it until it actually came."[1]

One day a brother of the monastery, named Owin, who was remarkable for his great humility and holiness, was at his work in the field adjoining the saint's house, the others having gone to the church, when he heard a sweet sound as of angelic melody coming down from heaven towards the house where St. Chad was, and after half-an-hour it rose again heavenward. Owin, whilst marvelling what this could be, received a signal from the bishop to summon the brethren around him, and when they had come he gave them his last instruction. He bade them to cherish love and peace, and to adhere to all the rules of discipline which they had learned from him, and which were taught by the fathers who had gone before them : " My time is very near," he added: "that lovable guest, who used to visit our brethren, has come to me to-day: go back to the church, and commend to the Lord my departure, and yourselves prepare for the last day, the hour of which you know not." And when the others had returned to the church, Owin, drawing near, besought the bishop to make known to him what were those joyous strains which he had heard floating downwards from heaven, and St. Chad replied, that "the angels had come to summon him to the heavenly rewards, which he had ever loved and longed for, and that they would return in seven days and take him thither with them." The saint that day fell ill, and in seven days, as he had foretold, after receiving the holy Viaticum, he calmly rested in peace, on the 2nd of March, A.D. 672. He was buried in St. Mary's Church, but his

[1] *Bede*, iv. 3.

relics were afterwards removed to the cathedral, which was dedicated to St. Peter. The labours of St. Chad throughout Northumbria and Mercia were those of a true apostle; his episcopate is justly styled by Bede a most glorious one,[1] and to his name has deservedly been allotted a foremost place among the greatest of the Anglo-Saxon saints.

2. It was from Northumbria that the light of faith proceeded also to Essex, the kingdom of the East-Saxons. Thirty-six years had now passed since St. Mellitus had been compelled to fly from London, and a new generation had grown up in the worship of idols and amid the corruption of paganism, when in the year 653, the same in which Peada had received baptism, Sigebert, king of the East-Saxons, paid a visit to the Northumbrian court. Bede relates that Oswy had frequent discourses with Sigebert about the folly of the pagan worship. "Surely," said the king, " that cannot be God which is made by the hands of man; and how can supreme worship be given to material things, which may be burned or broken, or trampled on, or converted to the basest uses, whereas God is the Creator of heaven and earth, infinite in His powers and perfections, the Supreme Ruler and Judge of all men, and His eternal abode is not in poor, perishable metal, but in heaven, where eternal rewards await those who do their Maker's will." These things frequently repeated, with the earnestness of a friend and even of a brother, told upon the heart of Sigebert, and, before the end of the year, he and all his companions entered the waters of the

---

[1] *Bede*, iv. 3.

Tyne, as fervent neophytes, and received baptism at the hands of St. Finan.

Sigebert asked for some Christian teachers who might instruct his people, and Cedd, being summoned from his work among the Mid-Angles, was sent with another priest to evangelize this new nation, now open to the Gospel. After some months Cedd returned to Lindisfarne to give an account to St. Finan of the rapid progress which religion had already made among the people entrusted to his charge, whereupon the holy bishop, calling in two other bishops, consecrated Cedd bishop of all the territory of the East-Saxons. For ten years he laboured with unremitting zeal, building churches, instructing the faithful, and preparing a native clergy to carry on the work of the Gospel. He built two monasteries, as hives of Christian piety, one at Ithancaestir, which is supposed to have been situated at the mouth of the Blackwater, the other at Tilbury, which in after times became familiarly associated with the Spanish Armada, and in them he trained a number of religious, after the manner of Lindisfarne, "in the discipline of the regular life, as far as their untrained minds were able to receive it;"[1] and, as the fruit of his toil, he had the consolation of witnessing that "the teaching of the heavenly life received a daily increase, to the joy of the king and amid the sympathies of his subjects." The holy bishop had the affliction, however, of seeing the good king, Sigebert, hurried away too soon by the hands of assassins. The reason which the

[1] *Bede*, "in quibus collecto examine famulorum Christi, disciplinam vitae regularis, in quantum rudes adhuc capere poterant, custodire docuit." iii. 23.

assassins assigned for their crime shows how rude was as yet the barbarism of the Saxon nations; their only motive they declared was that 'he was too merciful to his enemies.' At the conference of Whitby, in 664, St. Cedd took his place with St. Colman, for he had always observed the Irish usages, and, as he was skilled alike in both languages, he was chosen to act as interpreter for the contending parties. At the close of that conference he paid a visit to his loved monastery of Lastingham, and there in a few days was hurried off by the plague. It would be difficult to find a more touching scene in the Ecclesiastical History of England than that which the death of St. Cedd recalls. As soon as the news of his demise reached Essex, thirty East-Saxons, most of them priests whom he had ordained, started in all haste for Northumbria. They sought the monastery where lay the remains of the Father whom they loved, with the intention of spending the rest of their lives at his holy shrine, and of finding their last repose beside him, if such were the will of God.[1] Their desire was quickly granted. At the end of a few days all but one youth perished from the plague, and they had the consolation of resting in death beside him, whom they revered and honoured as the father of their spiritual life.

Many of the East-Saxons fell away from the faith after the death of St. Cedd. Terrified by the plague, several in the valley of the Tweed had recourse to pagan charms, whilst in other places the temples were restored, and the people publicly worshipped their former idols.

---

[1] *Bede*, "cupientes ad corpus sui patris, aut vivere, si sic Deo placeret, aut morientes ibi sepeliri." iii. 23.

The person chosen to stem this national apostacy was Jaruman, the Irish Bishop of Mercia, and zealously and successfully did he fulfil his mission. Bede gives the account of this bishop's labours in Essex on the authority of a priest, who had been one of his companions and fellow-labourers in that arduous enterprise.[1] Accompanied by priests, he went about throughout the whole kingdom recalling the wanderers to the right path, "so that they abandoned or destroyed their fanes and altars, re-opened the churches, and once more gladly acknowledged the name of Christ, which they had disowned, desiring now rather to die with the sure hope of rising again in Him than to live amid idols in the filth of paganism." These words seem to imply that the deadly plague still raged amongst the people, and that Jaruman and his clergy had faced its perils while indefatigably labouring to win back souls to Christ. Jaruman, however, did not resign his See in Mercia, and having, in the course of the year 665, been the chosen instrument of God in the re-conversion of the East-Saxons, he left some priests to perpetuate among them the work of the sacred ministry, and returned to his own flock.

3. From the East-Saxons we may pass to the East-Angles, where we meet with another king Sigebert, surnamed the learned, zealously co-operating in spreading the faith of Christ. He had in his youth been driven by king Redwald, his stepfather, into Gaul, and there under the guidance of St. Columbanus and his disciples had become a Christian, and fully instructed in the

[1] *Bede*, "juxta quod mihi presbyter, qui comes itineris illi et cooperator verbi exstiterat referebat," iii. 30.

ruths of faith. He was summoned home from exile to ascend the throne of East-Anglia in the year 631, and being, as Bede narrates, " thoroughly imbued with the Christian faith, and very learned, and, moreover, a good and religious man,"[1] he made it the great object of his life to communicate to his subjects the saving knowledge of the divine truths. He brought with him from Burgundy a holy bishop named Felix, who fixed his See at Dunwich, which was then an important city on the Suffolk coast, but has long since been swept away[2] by the encroachments of the ocean, and during his episcopate of seventeen years had the consolation of seeing the whole people freed from paganism, and producing an abundant fruit of Christian virtue.

His chief co-operator in the conversion of East-Anglia was the Irish Abbot St. Fursey, who came to England in 633, accompanied by his brothers St. Foillan and St. Ultan, and two other Irish priests named Gobban and Dicuil, all of whom, through grateful remembrance of his old Irish masters in the Burgundian monasteries, were joyfully welcomed and honourably received by king Sigebert.[3] St. Fursey was remarkable, among the many saints who then adorned Ireland, for his holiness as well as for his missionary zeal, and Bede devotes some pages to the wondrous visions of the other world, with which he was favoured, which for centuries were religiously repeated and carefully handed down in all the monasteries of the West. Several ancient records con-

[1] *Bede*, ii. 15 ; iii. 18.
[2] *Camden* in his ' Britannia' (vol. i. page 448), writing in 1607, describes it as lying " in solitude and desolation," and in great part submerged.
[3] *Bede*, iii. 19.

nected with this Saint's life have happily been preserved, and we glean from them the following particulars.

St. Fursey was of royal birth, and born in the west of Ireland about the year 575. In his youth he embraced the religious life in the monastery of St. Meldan, situated in the island of Insequin in Lough Corrib.[1] The scenery as you sail along this inland sea is some of the finest to be found in the Western province. Its innumerable little islands, whose perennial verdure is reflected in the placid waters of the lake, the undulating hills that mark the horizon, the richly planted demesnes that slope down to the water-edge, the picturesque ruins which are interspersed along the banks, the varied charms with which nature has enriched it on every side, mark it out as a place that religion would wish to sanctify and to dedicate to the service of God. The island of Insequin is the largest of the islands in the lake, and is about half a mile off the shore. "On that island," writes O'Flaherty, "St. Brendan built a chapel and worked divers miracles. There, too, St. Meldan, whose festival day is on the 7th of February, was abbot of a famous abbey about the year 580. He was spiritual father to the great St. Fursey of Peronne in France, who carried the relics of this saint along with him, and enshrined them at Peronne."[2] The religious life of St. Fursey was characterized by the greatest fervour. "From the period of his very youth," writes the Breviary of Aberdeen, "he gave no little attention to sound learning and monastic discipline, and, as eminently becomes the saints, he took care to perform

[1] *Bede*, iii. 19.
[2] See *Monasticon* of Archdall, new edition (Dublin, 1876) vol. ii. page 215.

all that he learned."[1] The language of Bede is almost the same: "He was of very noble Irish blood, but much more noble in mind than in birth. Even from his boyish years he had particularly applied himself to reading sacred books, and following monastic discipline; and, as is most becoming to holy men, he carefully practised all that he learned ought to be done."[2]

As he advanced in years he betook himself for a time to the monastery of Arann, that home of Saints off the western coast, which had been founded by St Enda. One of its oratories in after times was called *Teampull an cheathuir aluinn*, that is "the chapel of the four beautiful saints," for in its dedication were linked together the names of St. Fursey, St. Brendan, St. Conall, and St. Berchan. After some time returning to the shores of Lough Corrib, he erected on the mainland, nearly opposite the island of Insequin, an oratory and cell, the ruins of which, of venerable antiquity, still remain, and are still called Killursa *(Cill-Fhursa)*, 'St. Fursey's Church.' We will not dwell upon his missionary labours throughout Ireland. His life records that he visited every part of the country, reaping everywhere a rich spiritual harvest. Bede in a few words thus compendiates this period of our Saint's life: "After preaching the Word of God many years in Ireland he could no longer bear easily the crowds that resorted to him, wherefore, leaving all that he seemed to possess, he departed from his native island and came with a few brethren through the Britons into the province of the

[1] *O'Flaherty*, 'West Connaught,' Public. of I.A.S., page 22.
[2] *Brev. Aberdonen*, fol. xxxii.

East Angles, and preaching the Word of God there, built a noble monastery." And again : "While Sigebert still governed the kingdom, there came out of Ireland a holy man called Fursey, renowned both for his words and actions, and remarkable for singular virtues, being desirous to live a pilgrim's life for our Lord wherever an opportunity should offer. On coming into the province of the East Angles he was honourably received by the aforesaid king, and pursuing his usual course of preaching the Gospel, by the example of his virtue and the efficacy of his discourse, he converted the unbelievers to Christ, and confirmed in the faith and love of Christ those that already believed." [1]

Receiving from Sigebert a gift of a tract of land at Cnobbersburg, now Burghcastle, in Suffolk, not far from the junction of the Yare and the Waveney, surrounded with wood and commanding a view of the wide expanse of ocean, St. Fursey erected what even Bede styles "a noble monastery," which for twelve years was the centre of his missionary operations throughout East-Anglia. The pious monarch showed boundless affection to St. Fursey, and after a little time resolving to occupy himself no longer with the ambitions of this world, nor to fight except for the Kingdom of Heaven, laid aside the cares of royalty, and entered as an humble monk in the monastery of Cnobbersburg. This was the first example, among the Anglo-Saxons, of a king abandoning secular life and sovereignty to enter the cloister, an example which was followed in after times by more than one of their noblest monarchs. Cressy, in his Church History

[1] *Bede*, iii. 19.

of Brittany thus commemorates this heroic self-denial of Sigebert:—"This year afforded an example of heroical humility and contempt of the world, which had hitherto never been practised in God's Church, but was afterwards frequently imitated: which was that a king, not forced thereto by any calamity, freely abandoned his throne to enclose himself in a monastery, there to be subject to the will of a poor stranger, deprived of all things that might please the senses, mortified with continual abstinence, frequent fasts, watching, cilicies, and scarce ever interrupted devotion. All which he cheerfully underwent that he might more securely provide for another kingdom after this life."[1]

The good king, however, was not permitted to die, as he had hoped, in the cloister. Egric, who had succeeded to the throne, had not reigned two years when, in 636, he was menaced with war by Penda, the fierce pagan king of Mercia. The East-Angles, knowing themselves to be unequal to such a contest, and remembering the former exploits of Sigebert in the battle field, besought him to come forth from his cell and lead them again to victory. Sigebert refused, but they compelled him to show himself at least among the troops, thus to inspire them with courage. He accordingly put himself at their head, but not unmindful of his profession, he armed himself only with a pastoral staff, and he prayed whilst the soldiers fought. All that he could do, however, was to lay down his life for his faith and his country. He and Egric were both slain, and the East Anglians were utterly routed by their pagan enemy.

[1] *Cressy*, Book xv. chap. 7, page 356.

A period of comparative peace ensued, and Anna, the new king, proved himself a zealous helper of St. Fursey in the work of converting his kingdom. Baronius, indeed, justly assigns the chief merit of the conversion of the East-Angles to our saint and his companions.[1] It is particularly recorded of him that he founded throughout East-Anglia various double communities[2] for monks and nuns, a usage which seems to have prevailed in some parts, particularly of the south and west of Ireland. We must not, however, pass over that feature in St. Fursey's life, which is so peculiarly his own, and which served for centuries to bring home to the minds of the faithful the great truths of the eternal rewards and punishments. The late Protestant Bishop of Brechin, Dr. Forbes, in his short notice of the saint, says: "The reputation of St. Fursey extends far beyond the limits of the Scoto-Irish Church. Not only is he one of the most distinguished of those missionaries who left Erin to spread the Gospel through the heathen and semi-heathenised races of mediæval Europe, bridging the gap between the old and new civilizations, but his position in view of dogma is a most important one."[3] The visions of St. Fursey seem to have commenced before he left Ireland, but those commemorated by Bede are said to have been received by him in his monastery at Cnobbersburgh. In the first vision he was admonished to proceed diligently in his ministry of preaching, and to persevere in watching and prayer. In another vision he was found worthy to behold the choir

[1] *Baronius*, Annales, viii. 313.
[2] *Mabillon*, Acta SS., vol. 2, page 296.
[3] *Forbes*, Kalendars, page 352.

of angels, and to hear their blessed canticles. He was wont to declare that he distinctly heard the anthem, "Ibunt de virtute in virtutem, videbitur Deus deorum in Sion," "The just shall advance from virtue to virtue, the God of gods shall be seen in Sion," (Ps. lxxxiii. 7). Again he saw the torments of the damned, and the combats of the evil spirits who sought to obstruct his journey to heaven, but through the protection of his guardian angel all their endeavours were in vain. In another vision, being lifted up in spirit towards heaven, he was told by the angels that conducted him to look back upon the world, and casting his eyes downwards, he saw, as it were, a very obscure valley, in which four fires were raging not far distant from each other. Then asking the angels what fires these were, he was told that they were the fires which would burn and consume the world. One of them was the fire of falsehood, the crime of those who do not fulfil what they promised in baptism, to renounce Satan and all his works. The next was the fire of avarice, of those who prefer the riches of this world to the love of heavenly things. The third was the fire of discord, for those who offend their neighbours even in needless things. The fourth was the fire kindled by the hard-heartedness of those who scruple not to despoil and defraud the lowly and the feeble. These fires, increasing by degrees, united together and became an immense flame, and as they approached, he said to his guardian angel, "Behold the fire draws near." The angel answered, "That which you did not kindle shall not burn you; for though great and terrible is this fire, yet it only tries every man according to the demerits of his works; every man's concupiscence shall burn in this fire, for as every one burns in the body through unlawful pleasure, so when discharged from the body, shall he burn in the punishment which he has deserved." One of his guardian angels then went before him, and dividing the flames, formed a safe passage through which he advanced. Then the sufferings of the wicked in detail were shown to him, and afterwards he was again lifted up to heaven, and he saw the glorious hosts of the blessed ones, and amongst them several priests, "holy men of his own nation," who joyfully imparted to him lessons of instruction and cheering hope. Venerable Bede adds that after these visions St. Fursey took care, as he had done before, to persuade all men to the practice of virtue, as well by his example as by preaching; but as for the matter of his visions he would only relate them to those who, from the desire of reformation, wished to hear them. And when he repeated them, though it were in the sharpest wintry weather, and in severe frost, and he only covered with a thin garment, yet a stream of perspiration would flow down from his face as if it had been in the greatest heat of summer, either through the excess of his fear or the greatness of his spiritual consolation.[1]

St. Fursey continued for twelve years to labour among the East Angles, beloved by all good men, bountiful to the poor, feared by the wicked, whose gifts he persistently refused, and manifesting by miracles the wondrous power of God. He observed the Lord's day with special veneration. From the hour of noon on Saturday till the morning of Monday, he rested from his journey wherever he happened to be, spending the time

[1] *Bede*, loc. cit.

in meditation, offering up the Holy Sacrifice, and imparting spiritual instruction. It is specially recorded that he enriched his monastery at Cnobbersburgh with a precious bell, probably the work of his own hands, and he bestowed another bell on some of his Irish brethren, which was long preserved with religious care in the monastery of Lismore. During a period of famine some of his brethren showed signs of fear lest they might be left without sufficient food for their support. St. Fursey reproached them for their want of confidence in the Divine bounty, and he repeated the instruction which he had often given them, that they who cherish poverty through the love of God, shall never be without the aid of heaven. Within a few days he confirmed his words by a striking miracle. Going forth into a field of the monastery, and attended by his holy companion St. Lactain, who in after times became patron of Freshford in this county, St. Fursey began to cultivate the ground and to cast seed into the furrows. Many incredulously shook their heads at his proceeding, but in three days a smiling harvest repaid his toil, and the ripe corn was ready for the sickle.

At length, in the year 645, the saint, desirous to lead a more solitary life, resigned the care of his monastery into the hands of his brother, St. Foillan, and went to live with St. Ultan, who some time before had retired to a hermitage in a wild desolate spot, and there these devout brothers lived together for a whole year, supporting themselves by the labour of their hands, and spending their time in vigils, fasting, and prayer. Before the close of 646 the Mercian pagans began again to threaten invasion, and the country becoming disturbed, our saint resolved to set out on pilgrimage to visit the sanctuaries of Rome, and to satiate his piety at the shrines of the Apostles and holy martyrs of Christ.

He landed in France at the little port of Quentowic, and soon after by his prayers restored to life the only son of Haymon, Count of Ponthieu. The count, through gratitude, would fain compel the saint to accept a gift of his estate at Mazerolles, where this miracle took place, but this the saint persistently refused, and, after resting there for a short time, continued his journey. Other miracles marked his course at Authville and Grandcourt, and his fame reaching Erchinoald, mayor of the palace, he was asked to baptize the son of that nobleman at his castle of Peronne. Here, too, St. Fursey stopped for some time, praying frequently at the little church of Mont-des-Cygnes, dedicated to the holy Apostles, SS. Peter and Paul, and receiving there many heavenly consolations. In this little church he deposited the sacred relics of St. Patrick and of SS. Meldan and Beoeadh, which he had brought with him, and he prophetically foretold that here, too, he himself would repose in death.[1]

Pursuing his pilgrimage across the Alps, he passed with safety through many dangers, and at length arriving at the walls of the eternal city, cast himself on his knees, and pronounced the beautiful words which are registered in his life: "O Rome! exalted above all cities by the triumphs of the Apostles, decked with the roses of martyrdom, adorned with the lilies of confessors, crowned with the palms of virgins, strengthened by all

[1] "In hac ergo capella, S. Furseus multas noctes ducebat insomnes, et quia Dei colloquiis in ea solitudine dulcius fruebatur," &c. Vita ap. *Colgan*, Acta SS., pag. 270.

their merits, enriched with the relics of so many illustrious saints : we hail thee ! May thy sacred authority never cease, which has been illustrated by the dignity and wisdom of the Holy Fathers: that authority by which the body of Christ, that is the Church, our blessed mother, is preserved in undying consistency and vigour."[1]

Having satisfied his piety in Rome, St. Fursey returned to Peronne, and Erchinoald, having offered him for a monastery any site that he would select, he chose a tract of land at Lagny en Brie (formerly in the diocese of Paris, but now in that of Meaux), on the banks of the Marne, then covered with wood, but now famed for its fruitful vineyards, and here he erected a church and monastery, which Clovis II., and his holy spouse, Bathilde, enriched with many royal gifts, and soon became an important centre of piety and religious observance for all that territory ; and such was the esteem in which the saint was held, that Audobert, bishop of Paris, and his successor, St. Landry, wished him to establish missions and to act as their assistant throughout this important diocese. It was in the exercise of this authority that we find him erecting a church at Compans, in the arrondissement of Meaux, which when finished was consecrated by Bishop Audobert. Another monastery was built for the saint at Mont-Saint-Quentine, in the immediate neighbourhood of Peronne, by Erchinoald, and the same nobleman also undertook to erect a church at Mont-des-Cygnes, instead of the humble oratory which St. Fursey had

[1] *Bollandists* Ianuar. ii., pag. 50, " qua corpus Christi, videlicet beata mater Ecclesia, viget solidata."

enriched with the relics of our Irish saints. The monastery at Peronne was solemnly dedicated by St. Eloy, Bishop of Noyon, in the presence of an immense concourse of the clergy and nobility of France, and St. Ultan, who had come to visit his brother, was installed there as first abbot.

Several religious from Ireland at this time made pilgrimages to the Continent, and many of them, attracted by the fame for piety and miracles of St. Fursey, hastened to Lagny to receive his lessons of heavenly wisdom. Among these was St. Aemilian, who was destined to be the saint's successor as abbot of Lagny. The Life of St. Fursey writes: "His own native land was proud that she had produced so great a saint; and the blessed Aemilian, desiring to see with his own eyes the great sanctity of the beloved Fursey, came with some companions to see him, and after a long journey that happy little band of Irish pilgrims, arriving at Lagny, found the saint of God adorned with more brilliant virtues than even they had heard."[1] When St. Aemilian had tarried a little time at Lagny, St. Fursey, anxious to re-visit his former community in East-Anglia, obliged him to assume the charge of the monastery. On his way towards the coast, Fursey stopped at Mazerolles, where a few years before the Count Haymon had shown him great kindness; here his last illness now came upon him, and in a few days he breathed his soul to God. The precise year has not been recorded, but it was probably in A.D. 653. The count would have wished to retain his relics at Maze-

---

[1] *Colgan*, Acta SS., pag. 574.

rolles, but Erchinoald came in person, accompanied by a royal guard, to conduct them to the new church, which was now almost completed, at Peronne. We may allow Venerable Bede to continue this narrative: "Erchinoald," he writes, "took the body of the saint, and deposited it in the porch of the church he was building in his town, called Peronne, till the church itself should be dedicated. This happened twenty-seven years after, and the body being taken from the porch to be re-interred near the altar, was found as entire as if he had just then died. And again, four years later, a more worthy shrine being built for the reception of the same body, to the eastward of the altar, it was still found free from the stain of corruption, and translated thither with due honour; where it is well known that his merits, through the Divine operation, have been declared by many miracles." "These things," adds Bede, "concerning the incorruption of his body, we have briefly taken notice of, that the sublime character of this man may be the better known to the reader."[1]

Our limits will not allow us to dwell on the veneration which from age to age has been shown in France to the hallowed remains of this great saint. The shrine, which was specially prepared for his remains, was worked by the hands of St. Eloy, who was famed for his artistic skill; it was placed with solemnity on the high altar of the church, and among those who assisted at the joyous ceremony were his brother, St. Foillan, and his cherished friend, St. Aemilian, now abbot of Lagny. Six hundred years later, on the 17th

[1] *Bede*, iii. 19.

September, 1256, St. Louis, King of France, solemnized his return to France, after six years' absence, by the gift to this church of another rich shrine for the relics of St. Fursey. It was of gilt metal, enriched with precious stones, and adorned with statues of the Twelve Apostles, and the king himself, with several bishops, assisted at the translation of the sacred relics. The small portion of the relics saved from profanation amid the demoniac scenes of 1793 was placed in the church of St. John the Baptist, at Peronne, where they are now preserved. On the 12th of January, 1853, the bishops of the ecclesiastical province of Rheims, then assembled in Provincial Synod at Amiens, proceeded to Peronne, and once more enshrined in a rich case the relics of its great Patron-Saint.

The influence of St. Fursey on the Anglo-Saxon Church did not cease with his death. St. Bathilde, who shared the throne of Clovis II., and after his death, governed the kingdom, as Regent, was herself an Anglo-Saxon. She not only extended her royal patronage to the holy missioner who had laboured so many years among her countrymen, but she wished to show him every honour after death. Not far from his monastery at Lagny was the convent of Chelles, founded by St. Clotilde, but which had been for a long time in ruins. Here, through reverence for our saint, Bathilde erected anew a double monastery, after the Celtic manner, for monks and for nuns, and for a long time both were peopled with devout natives of England, and, as Sigebert had laid aside the crown to serve God under St. Fursey, at Cnobbersburgh, so Bathilde expressed her resolve to end her days near the relics of our saint at

Chelles, but it was only after many years that she was enabled to give effect to her pious resolution. One of the daughters of Anna, King of East-Anglia, also followed in the footsteps of St. Fursey, and, forsaking her country, entered the convent of Faremoutier in Brie, near Meaux, where she became abbess, and was famed for her sanctity, and a grand-daughter of the same king also merited the palm of heroic virtue in the same convent.

As for St. Foillan, who, as we have seen, assumed the government of the monastery at Cnobbersburgh after the departure of St. Fursey, he, too, after a few years proceeded to the Continent, and lived for some time in the monastery of Fosses, in the diocese of Liege, which after his martyrdom was to be enriched with his remains. Some of his relics are now preserved in the church of Saint Sepulchre at Abbeville, and some also are venerated at the Sacré-Coeur in Amiens.

The monastery of Fosses, situated between the Sambre and the Meuse, was founded through the munificence of St. Gertrude, the holy abbess of Nivelle in Brabant, and at her request St. Ultan became its first abbot, and soon St. Foillan and several other holy Irishmen enrolled themselves under his guidance. When in the forest of Charbonniere, not far from Nivelle, St. Foillan and three other Irish monks[1] received the crown of martyrdom, St. Ultan saw in vision a dove, whose

[1] Colgan writes that these three martyred companions of St. Foillan were SS. Boese, Columban, and Gobain, who all three had been disciples of St. Fursey. There is a St. Gobain, an Irish martyr, honoured at Mount L'Hermitage, where he is supposed to have been martyred, and where the town which grew up around his sanctuary was called by the saint's name.

snow-white wings were stained with blood, speeding its flight to heaven, and he at once interpreted it as the announcement of his brother's death. Two months later their mangled bodies were discovered, and though St. Gertrude would wish to enshrine them at Nivelle, yet she yielded to the prayers of St. Ultan, and permitted them to be translated to Fosses. A little later St. Gertrude feeling that death approached, sent a messenger to St. Ultan to ask his pious prayers. St. Ultan said to her messenger, " To-day we celebrate the 16th of March ; to-morrow, whilst the Holy Sacrifice will be solemnly offered up, this servant of God will appear before her judge. Say to her to be without fear, for the blessed Bishop Patrick, accompanied by the choirs of angels, will conduct her to her heavenly country."[1] The following day, which was Sunday, the feast of our holy apostle St. Patrick, in the year 659, St. Gertrude received the Viaticum, and whilst Mass was being celebrated rested in peace. The monastery of Fosses long continued to be a favourite resort of Irish pilgrims, and many, too, of the French clergy found a tranquil home within its hallowed walls during the persecution of the wicked Ebroin. St. Ultan's death is placed by Dachery and Le Cointe in the year 686, and he was interred in the church which he had himself erected close to the monastery, and dedicated to St. Agatha. A portion of his relics is still preserved at Peronne.

4. It was one of St. Fursey's Irish companions named Dicuil who first preached the faith among the South-Saxons. They were the oldest of the Teutonic settle-

---

Mabillon, Acta SS. iii. 785.

ments in England, yet they remained the most insignificant of all the Anglo-Saxon kingdoms. They had little more than a strip of the southern coast for their territory, being cut off from all intercourse with the rest of England by the impenetrable Andredeswald, that is, "the wood of the uninhabited district,"[1] a vast sheet of scrub, woodland, and waste, extending for more than a hundred miles from the borders of Kent to the Hampshire downs, and northwards almost to the Thames, whilst on the east an immense tract of marsh separated them from their Kentish neighbours. The people too were the most barbarous of the whole island. When they captured the fortress and town of Anderida, now Pevensey, the last stronghold of the Britons, they slew all that were therein, nor was there one Briton left in their territory. Nevertheless, Dicuil and a community of Irish monks penetrated thither about the year 645, and erected a monastery at Bosham, three miles to the west of Cischester, now Chichester, a Saxon town which took its name from one of Ella's sons. On the semi-barbarous country people they could make little or no impression. "They had a very small monastery," writes Bede, "encompassed with the sea and woods, and in it five or six brethren, who served our Lord in poverty and humility, but none of the country people cared either to follow their course of life or to listen to their preaching."[2] Some of the nobles of the kingdom, however, showed themselves more

---

[1] *Taylor*, "Words and Places," page 244. Eddi, in his Life of Wilfrid, writes of Sussex—" Quae prae rupium multitudine et silvarum densitate, aliis provinciis inexpugnabilis extitit," cap. 40.
[2] *Bede*, iv. 13.

docile to the teaching and religious example of these holy men, and we find that one of the South-Saxons, named Damian, became so remarkable for his virtue that he was made Bishop of Rochester in 656. The king, too, had become a Christian in 661, and though his example was followed by some of his court, yet it was not till the year 681 that the day of redemption finally arose for that benighted kingdom. This was a year of unparalleled scarcity, and St. Wilfrid coming amongst them began to feed their bodies, and thus to gain access to their hearts. The Irish monks, however, were the pioneers of the Gospel, and it was from the little Celtic monastery of Bosham that in after times arose the See of Chichester.

5. We now come to Wessex, the kingdom of the West-Saxons. Its first apostle is known to us only under his Latinized name Birinus. He had presented himself to Pope Honorius in Rome, and promised before him " that he would scatter the seeds of the holy faith in those furthest inland territories of the English, which no teacher had as yet visited." By order of the Pontiff he was consecrated bishop by the Archbishop of Milan, who then resided at Genoa, and setting out for his mission landed in Hampshire, where he found heathenism so dark and intense that he resolved to proceed no further, but to labour to bring its people to the knowledge of God. In the following year, aided by the influence of the Northumbrian King Oswald, he had the consolation of administering baptism to its King Kynegils. It was at Dorchester that the imposing ceremony took place in the presence of Oswald, and tradition marks the site where the venerable abbey church of SS. Peter

and Paul now stands as the place "that witnessed the Christianizing of the dynasty, which grew into the royal line of England."[1]

In the year 650 Agilbert, a native of France, succeeded Birinus in the See of Dorchester, and for at least ten years[2] laboured to consolidate religion throughout the whole territory of the West-Saxons. When St. Columbanus was proceeding to the court of King Theodobert II., he was welcomed at the house of Autharis at Ussy-sur-Marne, and in return for the hospitality which was extended to him, imparted his blessing to that holy household. Agilbert was the son of Autharis,[3] and through desire to visit the country that had given birth to St. Columbanus, he came to Ireland and spent there several years applying himself to sacred studies. "There came into Wessex out of Ireland," writes Bede, "a certain bishop called Agilbert, by birth a Frenchman, but who had then lived a long time in Ireland, for the purpose of reading the Scriptures."[4] We know nothing further of Agilbert's visit to our country. It is probable, however, that he chose the monastery of Bangor for his abode, as it was famed for its Biblical studies, and it was there that his great spiritual father had prepared himself for the apostolate of Gaul. Agilbert was one of the most prominent champions of the Roman usages in the Conference of Whitby, in the year 664. From Whitby he returned

[1] *Bright*, 147.
[2] The Saxon Chronicle places his departure from Wessex in the year 660; others say that he was still bishop of this see at the Conference of Whitby, at which he took part in 664.
[3] *Darras*, "Histoire de l'Eglise," tom. xvi. 73.
[4] *Bede*, iii. 7.

to France, and was appointed Bishop of Paris. He had ordained Wilfrid priest in Northumbria, and now, in the first year of his episcopate in Paris, Wilfrid comes to receive episcopal consecration at his hands. The ceremony was performed at Compiegne, in Neustria, with unusual magnificence. Eleven bishops came to assist Agilbert, and after the consecration, as was the custom in Gaul, they lifted him up in a golden throne and carried him in procession to the altar. How striking it is to find a disciple of the Irish saints imparting the dignity of the priesthood and the episcopal rank to one who, during his eventful episcopate of forty-five years, was destined to exercise a powerful influence in moulding the discipline of the whole Anglo-Saxon Church.

It was during Agilbert's episcopate in Wessex that an Irish monk, named Moeldubh (called by the Saxons Mailduff), came to visit him. He was in erudition a philosopher, as Bede attests, and skilled in all the learning of his age. Attracted by the beauty of the woods around Ingelborne, he obtained leave to erect a cell beneath the walls of its old castle, and there leading a religious life, imparted sacred and profane science to the pupils that flocked to him from all parts. William of Malmesbury relates that he was constant in study, and incessant in prayer. When he read, it seemed to him as if he heard the voice of God addressing him, and that he spoke direct to God when he prayed. He was so abstemious that he scarcely partook of any food. He was never known to go elsewhere except upon occasions of indispensable necessity. So little desirous was he of money, that if any were given him, it immediately passed from his hands to the poor. A constant habit with him was to remain, even during the icy cold of winter, whilst reciting the Psalter, immersed to the shoulders in a stream of water which ran close beside his cell. "He had brought with him all the culture for which Irish scholars were then famous,"[1] and soon a noble monastery grew up around him, which was known as Mailduff's-burgh, and in latter times was called Malmesbury. St. Aldhelm was the most illustrious of Moeldubh's pupils, and, succeeding him as abbot in the year 675, governed the monastery for thirty years, till he was promoted to the see of Sherborne, in the year 705. From Aldhelm's life we learn that he was trained in the knowledge of Latin, Greek, and Hebrew by his Irish masters. He was also skilled in the harp, and an anecdote related by William of Malmesbury shows how he was able to utilize this acquirement for the benefit of his flock. The rude West-Saxons of the district were wont to hasten away from church, as soon as the Holy Sacrifice was offered up, without waiting for the instruction which was given after it. Wherefore Aldhelm took his station on the bridge which led from the little town into the country, and there by his music attracted the passers-by around him, and from the minstrelsy he glided gradually to words of sacred instruction, and he dismissed them after imparting to them some practical lessons of the Christian life. St. Aldhelm, in his writings, more than once speaks with enthusiasm of his Irish masters, and in a letter to Willibrord he does not hesitate to say that countless as are the stars that sparkle in the firmament, yet more numerous were the saints and learned men who at that time adorned the church of Erin.[2]

[1] *Bright*, 259.   [2] *Aldhelm*, epist. in Usher's Sylloge, No. 13.

We have thus briefly sketched the labours of the Irish missionaries in spreading the faith throughout the Anglo-Saxon kingdoms. It was their only aim to diffuse the sacred light of heavenly truth, and to build up the Church of Christ, and if we may select one distinctive feature of their missionary labours we cannot but be struck by their earnest solicitude—a solicitude, too, crowned with complete success—to train up a native clergy for the sacred ministry. They had no thought of perpetuating a succession of their own countrymen, except so long as the interests of religion required it; but having handed on the traditions of faith to fervent priests and religious of the Anglo-Saxon race, they directed their steps to other lands, to bring to other peoples the same glad tidings of redemption. Soon after the close of this Celtic period, the monasteries and schools of England began to decay. They were brought almost to utter ruin by the terrible devastations of the Danes; the first sign of returning life and of the revival of piety and learning among the people was when the Celtic monks began once more to instruct the Saxon youth in Glastonbury.

THE END.

BROWNE AND NOLAN PRINTERS, NASSAU-STREET, DUBLIN.

www.ingramcontent.com/pod-product-compliance
Lightning Source LLC
Chambersburg PA
CBHW031849220426
43663CB00006B/555